SEXUAL SOLUTIONS
An Informative Guide
MICHAEL CASTLEMAN

Simon and Schuster
NEW YORK

Text copyright © 1980 by Michael Castleman
Illustrations copyright © 1980 by David Passalacqua
All rights reserved
including the right of reproduction
in whole or in part in any form
Published by Simon and Schuster
A Division of Gulf & Western Corporation
Simon & Schuster Building
Rockefeller Center
1230 Avenue of the Americas
New York, New York 10020

SIMON AND SCHUSTER and colophon are trademarks of Simon & Schuster
Designed by Jeanne Joudry
Diagrams by Susan Neri
Manufactured in the United States of America
3 4 5 6 7 8 9 10

Library of Congress Cataloging in Publication Data

Castleman, Michael.
Sexual solutions: an informative guide.

Bibliography: p.
Includes index.
1. Sex instruction for men. I. Title.
HQ36.C28   613.9'52   80-16969
ISBN 0-671-24688-7

*Dedicated to
Anne
and to
"The Deke"*

CONTENTS

10 Contents

FOREWORD

Reading this wise, funny, uniquely practical book is like having a low-key chat with a good friend who happens to be a sexuality counselor.

Sexual Solutions: An Informative Guide is much more comprehensive than most sexuality books geared toward men who make love—or want to make love—with women. It covers the whole range of concerns: how to deal with involuntary ejaculation, non-erection and non-ejaculation; what women say they like in a lover; how to recognize a woman's orgasm; how to ask for the lovemaking moves you enjoy and how to negotiate inevitable differences; what to do if your lover gets raped; an up-to-date guide to all the birth control methods, including new information on condoms; and guides to sexual infections, testicular self-examination, and self-care for the male reproductive system.

Michael Castleman is the perfect person to write such a book. He has been a health educator with a special interest in men's health and sexuality since his work in the early 1970s as Coordinator of the Ann Arbor, Michigan, Free People's Clinic. Michael was also the founding Director of the Men's Reproductive Health Clinic in San Francisco, the first public health facility in the country to focus on men's birth control and sexual concerns.

A widely published free-lance writer who left clinical work to concentrate on health journalism, Michael has long argued against the contemporary myth that men and women hold irreconcilable attitudes about lovemaking. In this book, he shows that men's and women's views of fulfilling lovemaking are considerably more similar than different.

Michael and I now work together as editors of *Medical Self-Care* Magazine, and I'm proud that some of the material in this book first appeared as articles in *Medical Self-Care*. Women's health has received a good deal of well-deserved attention in recent years. The equally important field of men's self-care is just beginning to receive the attention it deserves, and Michael is one of the pioneers in this field.

I think the fact that Michael is not a doctor or psychotherapist, but rather a down-to-earth writer and counselor adds a deep yet street-wise personal dimension to this book. He writes not as a remote authority tucked away in an ivory tower, but as an experienced and thoughtful friend. He shares his own experiences dealing with premature ejaculation as easily as he draws from the experiences of the hundreds of men he has counseled. He also understands that making love has its humorous aspects. You'll find no stuffy expert jargon here. This book is written in the language American men really speak. References to the most recent research into sexuality are balanced by a sympathetic understanding of the ways the men's magazines and pornography affect men's love lives.

I think you'll find this book a timely overview of the most useful and practical information about men's sexuality. I recommend it highly.

Tom Ferguson, M.D., Editor, *Medical Self-Care* Magazine

INTRODUCTION:
Any Man Can

This book is written primarily for men, from a man's point of view, about the ways men experience sexual issues, but it is directed to women as well.

The basic message is simple: Men who try to be sexual superstars often find themselves on a one-way trip to many of the sex problems that can turn lovemaking into a nightmare—coming too soon, inability to get it up, keep it hard or ejaculate, no-fun lovemaking, unwanted pregnancies, and unresponsive lovers who are prone to those proverbial late-night headaches. On the other hand, men who drop the idea of sexual domination and learn to appreciate sensuality, men who develop an ability to discuss their sexual tastes specifically, men who listen closely to what women have been saying recently about lovemaking—these men are considerably less likely to fall victim to men's common sex problems. In short, men who take women seriously—both in and out of bed—are more likely than tough-guy studs to become the accomplished lovers most men would like to be.

In no sense does this mean that men should simply take orders from women about sex. As we enter the second decade of modern feminism, most men have been personally affected, at least to some extent, by women's halting progress toward social equality. Some men dislike "women's libbers," while others feel confused and upset by what they see as changing rules in a game they have never felt comfortable playing. Some men support women's liberation when it means going bra-less, but not when it means having a woman for a boss. Others feel guilty about past wrongs, but wonder to what extent their problems with women have actually been their fault. Because of the women's movement, many men who once believed that sex was something men did *to* women have been persuaded—perhaps browbeaten—into thinking that sex is something men should do *for* women. The man who experiences lovemaking as a job whose goal is to "deliver" an earth-shattering orgasm to his lover is as likely to develop the common sex problems of men as the guy who simply wants to get his rocks off. In lovemaking, all-give is no different from all-take.

Mutually satisfying lovemaking involves a great deal more than merely fitting the male plug into the female socket. It means building intimate comfort and working out inevitable differences through repeated discussions during which both lovers make their needs, preferences, and reservations known to one another. It means leaving behind labels like "dominant" and "submissive," "active" and "passive." It means attempting to separate making love from the power relationships that often drive a wedge of mutual distrust and misunderstanding between lovers. This book is for men who feel scarred and confused by what they believe women's liberation has done to their lives, both at work and in bed. But it is also for their lovers because many women do not fully appreciate how men often feel trapped in double-bind situations by recent changes in women's ideas about sexual relationships.

Today there is certainly no shortage of sex manuals. Hundreds of books and magazines offer advice about how to "have sex," but not many deal with "making love." To some, the phrases "having sex" and "making love" might sound synonymous; they both imply sexual intercourse. However, I think there are subtle, yet crucial, distinctions between them that illustrate some of the problems inherent in the so-called Sexual Revolution of the last thirty years. Consider the phrase "having sex." It implies that something happens to you, like having a stomachache or a flat tire. It sounds passive and lifeless. "Making love," on the other hand, is creative, not passive. It suggests an ongoing process, not a static situation. Making love does not happen to you—you make it happen. And making love focuses on the sensual expression of closeness be-

tween two souls, not just the plug-in connection between sex organs. This book is concerned with the everyday problems that interfere with making love, the problems that reduce it simply to having sex, or worse.

The perspectives on lovemaking presented here differ from those of other sex books. First, this book treats lovemaking as relatively simple and straightforward. Second, it suggests that problem-free lovemaking depends equally on an understanding of sex therapy, birth control, and sexual health care, subjects traditionally considered independent of one another. Third, its tone is down-to-earth, not clinical. The background and premises of the book deserve, I believe, a fuller explanation.

Sex Therapy as Common Sense

The information and suggestions presented here have been distilled from the work of leading sex researchers and therapists. That body of knowledge now spans thirty years since the publication of *Sexual Behavior in the Human Male* in 1948 by the Kinsey research team, but many of the concepts central to modern sex therapy were widely known and practiced by ancient cultures 2,000 years ago. Sex therapy involves becoming comfortable with a few basic ideas; from there, it is largely common sense.

The notion that sex therapy is mostly common sense surprises many men, particularly those troubled by persistent sex problems. How could it be so simple, a man asks, when I've had this problem for years and I can't seem to do anything about it? Happily, many sex problems of long duration have relatively simple solutions. Sex therapists share uniformly high rates of success helping both men and women overcome sexual difficulties that have seemed hopelessly permanent for years, even decades.

Many men believe lovemaking is either an automatic reflex, like flipping a light switch, or an incredibly complicated, unfathomable mystery, like jet engine mechanics. The truth lies somewhere in between. Almost anyone can learn to enjoy problem-free lovemaking. The basics of mutually satisfying sex are logical, easy to understand, and not at all mysterious. There are no sex secrets reserved for a chosen few. And you need not drive a Jaguar, splash on Brut, brush with Ultra-Brite or act like James Bond.

Almost anyone can learn the basic physiology, relaxation techniques, and intimate discussion skills involved in problem-free
lovemaking. These skills are not difficult to acquire, but like every
learning experience, dropping old habits—even those you can't
stand—and developing new ones involves concentration, work,
and practice. Learning problem-free lovemaking is a good deal like
learning to dance or play basketball. Imagine yourself trying to do
an intricate dance routine or a turn-around jump shot. It would be
unrealistic to expect yourself to execute a new maneuver with effortless grace on the first or second try, or for that matter, on the
tenth or fifteenth. Mastering any technique—dancing, basketball,
bicycle repair or lovemaking—takes time and practice, but for most
lovers the investment in developing lovemaking skills is worth it
because they can *feel* themselves gaining confidence at each step
along the way. It can be a wonderful experience to abandon old
patterns and become comfortable with new ones you like better.

Frequently, the most challenging aspect of a decision to work on
a sex problem is having the courage to admit that there are some
elements of lovemaking you do not already know. Most men learn
at a tender age that they must never hint to others or even admit to
themselves that they are not all-knowing about sex. It takes courage
for a man to face up to a sex problem. Confronting it can leave him
feeling vulnerable and isolated; many men believe they are the
only one who has ever had such a problem. Worse, a man who is
learning new ways to make love might have to explain some clumsiness to a lover. Learning processes often involve some awkwardness, and most men—most women as well—hate to appear unsure
of themselves in any situation, but especially in bed. In book and
film sex scenes, the lovers never appear awkward or ill at ease.
Given the tremendous pressure many men feel to act confident and
in control of all aspects of lovemaking all the time, it is not surprising that some men would rather live with an annoying sex problem
and make eloquent apologies when necessary than risk looking
clumsy in bed while attempting to resolve the problem.

Finally, increasing your pleasure from lovemaking does not necessarily depend on having a regular or understanding lover. It
helps, certainly, but single men and men in relationships with
women who might not win any prizes for supportiveness in dealing with sex problems can usually learn to become more sexually
fulfilled and fulfilling. There are no tricks. Our bodies were made

for enjoyable lovemaking. All we have to do is sharpen our understanding of them. The rest is common sense.

The Whole Man Concept

Sexual issues are usually segregated into distinct specialty areas:
sex therapy, birth control counseling, and sex-related medicine.
There are advantages to this approach. However, our society tends
toward overspecialization and frequently an appreciation for the
whole person with interdependent concerns gets lost or forgotten.
We need a whole man's book of lovemaking.

Sex therapists, for example, tend to limit their counseling to
strictly sexual concerns. Few discuss the substantial impact of contraception, abortion decisions, or sex-related infections on the
quality of lovemaking. The definitive textbook of sex therapy, *The
New Sex Therapy* (see Bibliography), does not mention birth control or sexually transmitted diseases even once.

Meanwhile, public health physicians who treat literally millions
of sexually transmitted infections each year rarely feel comfortable
offering advice about sex problems or birth control, except perhaps
to mention that wearing a condom prevents the spread of VD. After
the common cold and flu, sexual infections are the most prevalent
illnesses in the country, and a massive, long-standing commitment
of public funds for treatment seems to have had little effect on the
incidence of these infections, particularly among young people. A
more integrated approach to lovemaking might have an impact
where traditionally fragmented sexual health care has not.

Finally, family-planning counselors almost universally confine
themselves to lovers' narrow birth control concerns and rarely
mention lovemaking at all. There are dozens of books, pamphlets,
and flyers that discuss birth control methods, but only rarely do
any point out that oral sex is a 100 percent effective contraceptive
that causes no side effects, costs nothing to use, and does not interfere at all with the sexual spontaneity that many lovers enjoy.

Some might argue that fragmented services allow specialists to
provide the best care and that referrals to other specialists best
meet the needs of those who have concerns in more than one area.
But the best lovemaking involves the whole person, the entire
body. Many lovers with sexual concerns resent being treated as

"erection problems," "vasectomies" or "IUDs" that are shuttled along from station to station on the therapeutic assembly line. Many lovers' sexual, contraceptive, and medical concerns are intimately interconnected. For example, women who take birth control pills have increased susceptibility to vaginal infections. If such infections develop, they are advised that their lovers should wear condoms for a while to prevent "ping-ponging" the infection back and forth between them. But some men lose their erections while fiddling with condoms and resent lovers who tell them their doctors have ordered their partner to use rubbers. The reluctance of a man to use condoms might trigger rebound resentments in the woman, and when lovers resent one another, the lovemaking suffers.

Another example of the interdependence of lovemaking concerns—more and more typical these days—is the woman who would like her lover to share in the responsibility for birth control. Many men might be perfectly willing to do so except for bad memories of condoms, whose proper use is rarely explained to men, or except for fears that participation in contraception might cause sex problems or aggravate those already existing.

Sex problems tend to be uppermost in men's minds and they are given top billing in this book for that reason. Once a man feels confident that he can enjoy lovemaking without worrying about potentially ego-shattering sex problems, he usually becomes more interested in learning about contraception and sexual health.

A Down-to-Earth Perspective

I am not a doctor, psychologist, or certified sex therapist. I am what you might call a "lay" therapist. My perspectives on men's sexual concerns and my experience of helping men overcome sexual difficulties did not result from an advanced academic training program, but from many years of involvement with grass-roots public health facilities that provided counseling and health care to a broad range of men troubled by the same sexual issues that bothered my friends and me: coming too quickly, lack of erection, questions about what turns women on, and concerns about penis size, the Pill, rubbers, and the clap.

I have provided short-term sex, birth control, and medical counseling to more than a thousand men over the last six years. They have ranged in age from fourteen to seventy-five, and economically from destitute to wealthy. They have been black and white, Spanish-speaking and Asian, gay and straight, high school dropouts and PhDs, devoted husbands and believers in the Four Fs: "Find 'em, feel 'em, fuck 'em, forget 'em."

My work as a men's sex counselor began in Michigan in 1973 at the Ann Arbor Free People's Clinic, one of the many free health facilities that blossomed in the 1960s. About two-thirds of our 6,000 patients per year needed birth control methods or treatment of sex-related infections. Part of my job involved promoting the clinic's patient-education library to encourage people to learn more about their bodies so they could take better care of themselves. This library, like so many health education resources, was largely ignored by the patients. The books generally collected dust —except for two small pamphlets that were not only read avidly, but were stolen so quickly we could hardly keep them on the shelves from one night to the next. They were "You Can Last Longer," a brief guide to the Masters and Johnson squeeze technique for developing ejaculatory control, and "When You Don't Make It," a program of relaxation and creative masturbation for men with erection problems (see Bibliography).

At that time, I, too, felt trapped in a seemingly permanent pattern of rapid, involuntary ejaculation and "You Can Last Longer" intrigued me. I researched the subject of ejaculatory control, and with some practice and some help from my girlfriend, now wife, I was astonished how quickly and dramatically my control improved.

I felt a convert's zeal to talk about the simple techniques I'd learned with the men on the clinic staff and with our patients. As an outgrowth of a staff men's group, a few of us developed a small sex counseling program for men, first focused on ejaculatory control problems, then expanded to include erection difficulties. The program proved successful and the word got around. Some men, of course, did not feel comfortable discussing their sexual concerns face to face, but the run on "You Can Last Longer" and "When You Don't Make It" never slowed. Theft of the booklets became so routine, in fact, that budget constraints ultimately forced us to stop displaying them.

After a move to San Francisco in 1975, I continued counseling men with sexual concerns at the Men's Reproductive Health Clinic, an HEW-supported service of the San Francisco Public Health Department. The Men's Clinic was the nation's first contraception clinic for men, and its approach, which combined birth control, genital health care, and sex counseling became a model for other men's programs around the country. The Men's Clinic sex-counseling program drew heavily on the work of the National Sex Forum and the University of California Human Sexuality Program, both of which were pioneering programs in contemporary sex therapy.

Consultants for this book included several sex therapists, doctors, family-planning counselors, nurses, writers in the field, sex educators, psychologists, the editors of *Medical Self-Care* magazine, feminists, a surrogate partner, friends, and many of the men with whom I have worked over the years. But, as I mentioned, I am not a professional sex therapist, nor, frankly, would I like to be one. This book makes no pretense of being a text for sex therapists, though I hope they find it enjoyable. This book is aimed at all the rest of us—the average workaday men—bus drivers, salesmen, builders and lawyers, butchers and bakers—anyone who wants to increase his skills in the natural, pleasurable experience of love-making.

I am a journalist by trade. I have written about health, VD, contraception, and sexuality for many years. Journalists assume that the public is intelligent and emotionally capable of understanding the issues that affect their lives. Unfortunately, many practitioners in the "helping" professions do not share this respect for the public. They often obscure information unnecessarily by couching it in arcane technical terms and by publishing it in out-of-the-way professional journals where it remains, in effect, hidden from all but the most inquisitive and determined members of the public. The intent of this book is to demystify sex therapy and other sexual subjects to allow greater public access to information at present in the hands of a relative few.

The professionalism of most serious sexuality books is certainly understandable in view of the long historical taboo against scientific sex research. It was only after World War II that the Kinsey group first challenged that taboo. And less than fifteen years ago, Masters and Johnson were reportedly so apprehensive that their landmark, *Human Sexual Response*, might be considered kinky (because of its accounts of women engaging in intercourse with camera-equipped dildos) that they couched the book in medical terminology almost unintelligible to the nonbiologist.

Since the mid-1960s when Masters and Johnson first published their research, writers on human sexuality have adopted a more popular tone, but they still tend to present information within a clinical framework. (One welcome exception has been *The Joy of Sex,* the first book about lovemaking to move from the night table to the coffee table.) The clinical approach has advantages as far as scientific credibility and sobriety are concerned, but the drawback is that most people are not inclined to read jargon-filled books.

Men and Women: More Similar Than Different

Men who respect women, who try to treat them as equals—as lovers, coworkers, friends—are likely to be better lovers and develop fewer sex problems than men who regard women as chicks, maids, baby dolls, playthings, pets, punching bags, bitches, pussies, sluts, or cunts.

These sentiments have not universally pleased all the men I have counseled over the years. On occasion, I've been called a "patsy for the women's libbers." On the other hand, I usually become uncomfortable around self-styled "feminist men." I do not consider myself a feminist; I am not sure I understand what the term means, though I support equal pay for equal work and legal abortion, and am appalled at the prevalence of rape, wife-beating, and sexual harassment.

According to conventional wisdom, men and women do not— indeed, *cannot*—understand one another's feelings about lovemaking. "The Battle of the Sexes" is a phrase often used to describe the supposedly irreconcilable differences between us. In fact, men and women are infinitely more similar—biologically, intellectually and emotionally—than they are different. Further, *it is in men's own sexual self-interest to pay attention to women's ideas about lovemaking because the kinds of caresses women say turn them on the most are the same ones that eliminate most men's sex problems.*

This book builds on men's and women's many similarities in the area of lovemaking with the hope of persuading lovers that they *can* understand each other's feelings; they can settle inevitable differences of taste, frequency, timing, and contraceptive practice, among others, when they establish a basis of shared goals and trust.

Lovemaking is often compared to sports in the men's magazines through the use of phrases like "bedroom Olympics." The metaphor is useful if we consider lovemaking as a *team* sport, with men and women on the *same* team. Good teamwork depends on the members understanding of one another's strengths and weaknesses, preferences and idiosyncracies. Team members should complement one another, not compete or take advantage of each other. The same goes for lovemaking.

Men whose approach to making love is "wham, bam, thank you, ma'am" have not discovered that intimacy, trust, and sharing are equally essential to problem-free lovemaking for both men and women.

The bottom line is that men who aspire to be as tough, icy, and domineering as the hero of a John Wayne movie are more likely to wind up rock-hard in the biceps than in the penis.

*"Making love is perfectly natural,
but rarely naturally perfect."*

THEA SNYDER LOWRY

Chapter **1**

OBSTACLES TO PROBLEM-FREE LOVEMAKING

When I was troubled by rapid ejaculation, I could not shake the feeling that my problem might not be limited just to sex. I feared that my lack of self-control in one small part of my body might, like cancer, spread elsewhere until little by little I lost my grip altogether. I tried everything I could think of, including biting my lip and fantasizing traffic accidents, but nothing worked. I was out of control. My sexual apparatus refused to obey my mind and I became afraid that perhaps other parts of my body might do the same. Or worse, perhaps the problem was not in my body, but in my mind.

At the Men's Clinic, the intake form asked: Why are you here tonight? Men with sexual infections or birth control concerns said so, but a surprising proportion of men troubled by sex problems wrote: "I think I'm going crazy."

It may sound unreasonable to leap from a sex problem to a fear of mental illness, but among men, belief in a direct link between sexual prowess and overall mental health seems to be the rule rather than the exception. Many men guage their masculinity by their ability to "do it right." If a man does not function in bed at the level he considers "normal," he may conclude that he is not a whole man—if he ever was one. And if he is not a whole man, what then is he? Many men fear that losing control of their penises is the first step on the road to losing their marbles.

Many men have heads full of ideas that are—figuratively at least —driving them insane. For example, many men are convinced that their penises are too small, too shriveled, or weird-looking to please women. Further, men have heard all their lives that they have "only one thing on their minds" and therefore immediately question their masculinity when presented with a chance to make love that they would prefer to decline. Then, when they are in the mood, many men believe they ought to be able to transform their penises into throbbing ramrods at the drop of a zipper, and consider themselves impotent if they do not get hard in sixty seconds, or thirty or fifteen. Other men become frustrated when their lovemaking does not result in simultaneous orgasm. Some men are upset if a woman becomes too "aggressive." Others resent having to do all the work and complain that their lovers just lie there and never take any initiative. Some men feel that it's wrong to fantasize about anyone other than the woman with whom they are in bed. Others believe they "owe" their lovers at least one orgasm—preferably several—and get upset if their lovers "only" come once or not at all. Many men have difficulty recognizing a woman's orgasm and would like to ask, "Did you come?" but hesitate because they have heard lately that women resent the question.

A head full of ideas like these can lead to a love life full of sex problems.

Penis Size: The Universal Hang-up

For many men, anxieties about penis size are a tremendous obstacle to satisfying lovemaking. The *Playboy* Advisor, the nation's most widely read sex education column for men, receives thousands of letters a year, and according to its long-time writer, Jim Petersen, concerns about penis size consistently rank among the most frequently asked questions: What's normal? How can I make mine larger? Thicker? Better hung? My girlfriend says it's too small. It goes off to one side—what's wrong with it? And a survey of 1,000 men by *Penthouse Forum* * showed that "all respondents, with the exception of the most extraordinarily endowed, expressed doubts about their sexuality based on their penile size."

Men are taught to discuss least what worries them most, to get by on bravado. San Francisco sex therapist Bernie Zilbergeld likes to joke that penises seem to come in only three sizes: large, gigantic, and so big you can barely get them through the door. He also tells the story of a man who asks his girlfriend to marry him. She'd like to, but she vowed long ago to marry a man with a twelve-inch penis. Our hero moans that in that case their relationship is doomed because he wouldn't cut off four inches for anybody!

Sex educators try to reassure men that penis size makes no difference in a man's ability to enjoy or give sexual pleasure. They recite the statistics: The average flaccid penis is three inches long. The average erection measures six inches. All erections are about the same size. The smaller the flaccid penis, the greater the growth to erection. The larger the flaccid penis, the less the growth to erection.

Sex educators also emphasize that most women could not care less about their lover's penis size. Bernie Zilbergeld, in his excellent book *Male Sexuality*, asked a large group of women what they looked for in a lover. The most frequent responses were: tenderness, affection, respect, sensuality, and kindness. *Not one* woman mentioned penis size.

On the other hand, men who read the men's magazines learn month after month how important penis size is in lovemaking. The men who write in to relate their sexual exploits regularly remark how their lovers compliment their endowments. ("When she saw my cock, she almost swooned. 'What a whopper!' ") And many women who write in swear that they appreciate a man who talks softly but who carries a big stick. ("His cock was simply perfect. He was so huge I couldn't get it all in my mouth without choking.") I'm sure many of these communications are fabrications—fantasies that reflect the writers' desires to appear as compelling sexual beings.

In fact, most people prefer to be appreciated for their inner beauty, for who they really are; while general appearance is an important factor in selection of lovers, most women are not all that

* March 1976.

concerned about a man's penis size. They want companions, not just penises; men they can feel close to, not simply silent organs —even big, blood-gorged organs.

Women's real or imagined preoccupation with penis size is similar to many men's fascination with the size of women's breasts, except that men tend to focus more closely on women's breasts than women do on men's penises. Penises are invisible to women most of the time. Only during lovemaking, which often takes place in dark or dim surroundings, is an exposed penis socially acceptable. Women's breasts, on the other hand, are literally out front all the time, and are emphasized by clothing and by the lack of it.

Breast development in teenaged girls is a public event, right there for all the world to see. Women's breasts are a subject of routine conversation throughout men's lives. "Catch the jugs on that one." "What a pair!" "She's a carpenter's dream—flat as a board and never been screwed." Miss America is judged by her measurements and by how well she fills a bathing suit, then, almost incidentally, by her talents. But we never hear anything about Mr. Universe's penis size. Naked breasts are even flashed on television these days, but you never see a shot of the bulge in a man's pants, let alone what's inside them. Women's breasts have become so public lately that they hardly rate a "PG" at the movies anymore. But a naked penis almost certainly means an "X" rating. In the movies, penises are pornographic.

Many women's insecurities about their breasts are compounded by the fashion industry's fickle requirements for the "in" breast. New, "standard" dress forms, from which women's clothing is designed, are created each year; just like cars, dress forms are identified by the year they were built, and the breasts on these forms go through annual model changes. One year, breasts are supposed to look conical and pointy, then round and voluptuous, then flat and unobtrusive, followed by the sculpted "no bra" look, then by a focus on nipple definition. Men may feel anxious about their penis size, but at least the styles don't change.

Men, not women, criticize penises. I will never forget the high school gym teacher who, at the start of a new school year, lined us all up naked beside the supply room to hand out jocks. In addition to the embarrassment of the situation, the locker room was dank and drafty, and everyone's genitals reflexively hugged their bodies for warmth. Naturally, everybody insisted on size large or extra-large, and each new request was greeted with an outburst of joking and snickering down the line. A few guys ahead of me in line was a big football player who stepped to the supply room door. I did not hear his request, but the teacher's reply reverberated around the locker room: *"You don't need a jock, boy, you need a peanut shell and two rubber bands!"* At the high school reunion ten years later, the guys were still laughing about it.

Unfortunately, high school locker rooms have not changed much since then. A high school senior named Anthony was referred to the Men's Clinic by his school psychologist for emotional problems caused by his "immature" or "juvenile genitals." Though quite rare, this condition can arise because of a hormone imbalance or because the mother took the drug diethylstilbestrol (DES) while pregnant. Anthony was very upset. He drove more than 100 miles for counseling. He said he had the smallest penis in his class. How did he know? Because he could *see* it plain as day in the shower after gym—and so could everyone else.

But when Anthony undressed, out flopped an *absolutely normal-sized* penis and scrotum. The counselor quietly informed Anthony that he was normally endowed, but he refused to believe it. His classmates' jeers had convinced him he was too small and no amount of reassurance could shake this conviction.

I encountered similar situations at the Clinic several times. In every case, the "micropenises" turned out to be normal-sized, and in every case, the man involved refused to believe it. Once, we even pulled out a ruler and a medical textbook to show the man he was well within the normal range, even a bit on the large side. He still refused to believe it. He *knew* how big a penis ought to be. He'd seen *Playgirl* and *Hustler.* He'd seen Harry Reams in *Deep Throat,* and he'd seen John Holmes' twelve-inch wang-dangdoodle with his own eyes.

John ("Johnny Wadd") Holmes and his world class member have appeared in 3,000 X-rated films and more than 1,000 pornographic picture books over the last fourteen years. In an interview, Holmes said, "I bet my picture is in more dresser drawers than anyone in the history of this country." Holmes, who off-camera writes children's books under a pseudonym ("Would you let *your* kid read a book by Johnny Wadd?"), continues to be amazed that so many of the fans who write him 600 letters a week believe that he actually *is* the perpetually erect superstud they've seen on the screen. As he puts it, "Seven or eight guys all tied in a knot couldn't do what Johnny Wadd does—nobody could! They think Johnny Wadd walks around having sex twenty-four hours a day. They think he's an animal. But that's *their* image. The real John Holmes is normal. I relax. I have a normal sex life. The real John Holmes is just like anybody else."

Except that between his legs, the real John Holmes has a beautifully hung, twelve-inch penis that makes him the envy of literally millions of men.

Watching John Holmes is enough to give the average man penis envy. Sigmund Freud, the originator of psychoanalysis who developed the theory of penis envy, postulated that women feel deprived of a penis and suffer profound feelings of envy, rage, and inferiority because of this deficiency. According to the theory, an adult woman's ability to enjoy fulfilling lovemaking depends on her ability to reject penis envy and accept what psychoanalysts call women's "submissive role."

These days, the notion of penis envy has been repudiated by many women. They say there is nothing inherently enviable about having a penis. Men do not suffer "breast envy" and women's chests are more visible to young boys than penises are to little girls. More compelling is the fact that attempts to deal with women's sexual problems based on the penis envy theory have not proved particularly successful. Sex therapy, on the other hand, has proved consistently helpful. Many women argue that their envy and resentment of men are the result of men's dominant power position in society, not women's lack of penises.

The concept of penis envy should not be discarded. However, it might make more sense to view it from a different perspective. Women are not the victims of penis envy, men are. Men envy other men whose penises are bigger than theirs. Just sit in an adult theater crowded with men—without a woman in sight—and listen to the quiet sighs as John Holmes' magnificent member rises to erection on the screen. Holmes *is* unbelievably endowed, as are most of the men who appear in X-rated films or in sexually explicit magazines. The sex media select for freak penises just like the men's magazines select for women with large breasts. The men in X-rated media are not selected for acting ability at all—but for their penises and nothing more. When asked about his acting ability, John Holmes shrugged, "It's all between my legs."

Once penises for pornography are selected, they are carefully photographed with the camera aiming up at them from around the man's knees to make them look even larger. Try it yourself: Hold a mirror below your erection so you can look up at it. It will look much larger than it does when you look down at it from above.

When an average man compares his body to those of professional football or basketball players, he feels smaller but not necessarily inferior since he knows that most men are about his own size. He has a basis for comparison. But when a man compares the size of his penis to other men's, he has considerably less basis for comparison. For example, in a locker room, a man looks down at his own penis, but *across* at everyone else's. The subtle difference in perspective makes a man's own penis look smaller than the others he sees lolling around, particularly if he is already persuaded that his own is too small.

Men catch glimpses of one another's penises from time to time, but most heterosexual men rarely, if ever, see other penises up close or erect. The only penises an average heterosexual man ever examines up close are those in the sex media—penises selected to be larger from the start and then magnified to truly awesome proportions with up-from-under photography. In other words, virtually *every* penis the average man examines up close looks a good deal larger than his own. With almost no basis for comparison, he is justified in concluding that he has one of the smallest penises he's ever seen.

The producers of the sex media encourage feelings of penis envy and sexual inferiority in their audience. Men who feel sexually handicapped spend more money on the sex media than men who feel erotically at peace with themselves. The man who feels he is sexually inferior is the guy who prowls the sex shops and peep shows. But there, every penis he sees continues to be bigger and more cooperative than his, and every woman more horny, more "liberated" than the women he knows. And even if he buys all the cameras, stereos, and cars he sees advertised in *Playboy*, he continues to feel cursed with a tool too small for the job.

My own penis is like everyone else's—a little too small. Not that I think size matters, you understand; but still, an extra inch couldn't hurt. . . .

I was leafing through *Hustler* at the magazine stand one day when I came across a full-page advertisement for a Vacuum Enlarger. The ad said: "Some men might still believe that it's not the size of the sword, but the swordsmanship. We won't argue the point, but wouldn't you rather go into battle with a lance than a dagger?"

It sounded ridiculous. In my head I knew that size makes no difference, that the overwhelming majority of men are about the same size, and that no woman I've ever known cared in the least about penis size. On the other hand, I also knew from years of reading men's magazines that a lance is preferable to a dagger. The ad said the device was "scientifically tested, safe and effective." It also promised that the Vacuum Enlarger would "help you obtain an immediate erection, cause the penis to be more sensitive to the touch and increase desire and staying power." Big promises. I suspected that the Vacuum Enlarger was a total shuck, but purely in the interests of scientific research, I dug out the $32.00 and bought one.

Hustler's sex gadget affiliate, Leisure Time Products, sells Vacuum Enlargers which it buys from Saepas Enterprises, Inc., of Houston, Texas. Saepas calls them "Muscle Builders" or "Hyperemiators," from the Greek for "more blood." Saepas Vice President Rick Brumfeld claims to sell about 5,000 a month. No one at either Leisure Time or Saepas knew when, where, or how the device had been "scientifically tested." Brumfeld said it is not regulated by the Food and Drug Administration and added that it has never been tested for medical safety.

My Vacuum Enlarger instruction sheet contained the following disclaimer: "The manufacturer assumes no responsibility for personal injuries. Before using any item on the anatomy, consult your physician. The hyperemiator is sold as an adult novelty item only." A novelty item is a toy. The manufacturer is saying, in effect, do not expect this to work.

The hyperemiator is as simple as it is useless. It consists of a hollow plastic tube with a small vacuum pump at one end. The aspiring organ builder inserts his penis into the open end, then he evacuates the air from the tube with the hand-operated pump. Theoretically, the vacuum created inside the tube draws blood and body fluids into the penis and causes it to swell. In fact, that's nonsense.

A vacuum around the penis might result in some temporary

swelling, but once the penis emerged from the tube, reequalized air pressure would push any excess fluid back out of the penis. In addition, there is absolutely no basis for the claims of accelerated erection, increased sensitivity, desire, or staying power. As Rick Brumfeld said, "Sex is all in the guy's head, anyway." The bottom line is that penis enlargers are a fraud.

They are also potentially dangerous. The instructions warn: "Specks may appear on the organ, but do not be alarmed. They are the same as the hickies you might have put on your girlfriend's neck as kids." Hickies, those purplish splotches on the skin, signal bleeding under the skin surface. The bleeding is caused by sucking. A person giving a hickie sucks on the skin of the recipient and this causes a vacuum. Blood is drawn into the area, but it is more blood than the tiny capillaries there can hold. Some capillaries burst under the pressure and the hemorrhaging from them appears as a discolored splotch on the skin. Hickies are clearly not life-threatening, but it would seem unwise to risk hemorrhage inside the penis because the process of erection depends on blood flow into certain tissues there. You don't want that blood leaking out through exploded capillaries. Vacuum conditions or physical stretching might also injure delicate erectile tissue.

Men who buy penis enlargers can be numbered among the victims of penis envy. Not only do these devices offer no relief from penis envy, they *contribute* to it. The forty-eight-page booklet, "Penis Enlargement Techniques," that comes with an Organ Builder contains very little text. However, there are sixty photographs of "professional models" demonstrating the device. Each model has a typically huge X-rated erection stuffed inside a hyperemiator, another case where all the penises viewed by the average man are substantially larger than his. A man could pump his Organ Builder like crazy, risk hickies of the penis and more serious injury, and never approach the size of the penises in the booklet.

The Saepas hyperemiator is also called "The Muscle Builder." However, the penis is an organ, not a muscle. There is hardly a muscle cell in the entire penis—the muscles that contract during ejaculation lie outside the penis, behind it in the pelvic area (see Appendix I: Sexual Anatomy). The penis cannot be built up like a muscle, just as the liver could not be enlarged by exercises or by using bizarre devices.

But what should a man do if his lover *does* care about penis size and thinks his is too small? Probably the same things a woman should do if her lover complained that her breasts were too small, that is, try to discuss the situation and decide whether, under the circumstances, the relationship can continue in mutual comfort.

Sometimes a woman might lash out about penis size when, in fact, something very different is upsetting her. Anger about a physical trait a lover cannot change is a way to get the last word, to shout the other person down. A woman might feel driven to castigate the endowment of a lover who, for instance, consistently refused to discuss the issues in the relationship that were important to her. It is the ultimate verbal slash at the silent man who believes that showing tenderness, consideration and respect for a woman are signs of weakness.

Each of us has a mental list of requirements for our ideal lover, and not all of them are, or need be, rational. Some men get turned on only by women with a certain kind of figure, or breast size, or height, race, ethnic group—whatever. That's perfectly natural. But if lovers who do not quite measure up to each other's ideals decide to build a relationship despite minor anatomical imperfections, it behooves them not to needle one another about the things they cannot change. If a woman complains about the size of your penis, try to remain calm and get ready to listen. Ask if your size is the real issue or if something else has been bothering her that you might not have realized.

No man can enlarge his penis, but there are a few ways to make the most of what you've got. First, undress where it's warm. Temperature affects the "hang" of the penis and scrotum, particularly the scrotum, the sack that contains the testicles. It hangs outside the body because the best temperature for sperm production is a few degrees cooler than body temperature. The warmer the scrotum, the looser it hangs; the cooler it gets, the closer it hugs the main part of the body for warmth. The penis also reacts to temperature and hangs fuller in a warm environment. A warm shower before lovemaking can make a man look better hung at the same time that it helps him feel relaxed.

Beyond physical warmth, the key to penis size is *relaxation*. When flaccid or erect, penis size depends on the blood volume contained in its internal spongy tissues—the more blood, the larger the penis. Blood circulates throughout the body all the time, but when a person feels relaxed, it tends to collect in the central body which includes the genital area. However, fear, nervousness, or anxiety triggers the body's "fight-or-flight" reflex. This reflex directs blood away from the central body and out to the arms and legs in preparation for self-defense or escape. Anxiety about penis size—or about any of men's other sexual concerns—can set off the fight-or-flight reflex that drains blood from the penis and, in effect, makes it shrink.

Arthur, a doctor in his early thirties, had been involved in a rocky, sexually frustrating marriage for many years. In addition to other concerns, he felt extremely insecure about the size of his penis. Because he was a doctor, Arthur's experience was different from that of most heterosexual men; he had closely examined many penises, and these examinations convinced him that his own was woefully lacking. After the breakup of his marriage, Arthur fell in love with a woman whose tastes in lovemaking satisfied him. For the first time in his life, he was able to relax and enjoy making love. "It may sound silly," he said, "but I swear my penis has gotten bigger."

It did not sound silly at all.

One Thing on Their Minds?

"Men have only one thing on their minds—sex." Most men hear this proverb throughout their lives. Like all generalizations, it contains a germ of truth—at certain times in their lives, most men do think about sex a great deal. Some think of little else. But this maxim can also be taken too seriously. When a man hears time and time again that all men think about sex constantly, in his mind he may transform this half-truth, half-joke into an imperative: Men *are supposed to be* completely preoccupied with sex. Many men feel that they should be eager to make love at any and every conceivable opportunity. They also may believe that there must be something wrong with them if they would rather *not* make love for a while. These beliefs can contribute to sexual anxieties and problems.

Men often feel considerable pressure to "cure" their virginity. At the Men's Clinic, clients were asked to fill out a form that contained several questions about sexuality such as age at first intercourse and any history of sex problems. The form was optional and

many men left all or part of it blank. The question left blank most frequently was age at first intercourse. It was also the question to which the answer was changed most frequently. First a man would write "17," then reconsider and change it to "21." The answer-changers may have suffered a brief lapse of memory, but first intercourse is not the kind of experience most persons forget. More likely, their first impulse was to deny their own experience and fill in the age when men "are supposed to" have had their first intercourse, as early as possible in their teens. The fact is, most men feel terribly embarrassed if they have not "done the deed" by age eighteen, and that embarrassment can last a lifetime.

Herb, a forty-five-year-old merchant seaman, came in for counseling about a lack of erection. He seemed comfortable discussing his sex problem and was eager for any suggestions that might help resolve it. The counselor noticed that Herb had not given his age at first intercourse and asked about it in passing. Herb tensed up and demanded to know what *that* had to do with anything. "Probably nothing," the counselor replied, probing a bit further because the subject apparently bothered Herb. It turned out that Herb's first lovemaking experience took place when he was twenty-three, and in counseling, twenty-two years later, he still felt embarrassed about how "retarded" he had been.

Conventional wisdom tells us that erection problems are more difficult for men to discuss than any other sexual issue. However, as Herb's case illustrates, it is often less threatening for a man to admit that he cannot get it up than it is for him to say he first made love at twenty-three, or twenty-seven, or thirty-four, or never. Losing one's erection is certainly threatening, but men view it, in some sense, as "normal"—they know it happens to many men. But no red-blooded man remains a virgin past age eighteen.

Just as most men are convinced that their penises are too small, they also feel certain that everyone else started fucking long before they did. *Psychology Today* * magazine surveyed several thousand college-aged men and asked what proportion of their peers they thought were virgins. About 1 percent, the respondents replied. Actually, 22 percent of the men who completed the survey said they had not had intercourse. A *Playboy* † survey of college-aged men showed that 26 percent were virgins. And these figures may

* August 1976.
† October 1976.

well be lower than the actual percentage because many men find it impossible to admit to virginity even in an anonymous question-naire.

Despite the fact that it appears to be a widespread fact of life, many men past eighteen (or sixteen, or fourteen . . .) consider virginity to be a problem. In lovemaking, whatever a person *thinks* is a problem becomes one. Probably the most threatening aspect of male virginity past the early twenties is the increasing likelihood that a man's first lover will be more sexually experienced than he. Anxiety about this is certainly understandable, given the tremendous pressure men impose on each other to shed their virginity early, then flaunt their vast experience ever after. Some virgin men fake experience, then feel lost groping around in the dark, under the sheets, looking for the vagina they know must be down there somewhere.

There are rational alternatives to living with this anxiety. A man troubled by his own virginity might try to talk about it with his prospective first lover. Discussing it can often diffuse tensions and promote the kind of trust that contributes to problem-free lovemaking. On the other hand, if a man would rather not mention his situation, it is quite possible that the woman would never know the difference. First experiences with a new lover are not all that different from first experiences, period. Awkwardness and clumsiness are common. It usually takes time for lovers to become comfortable with one another's lovestyles no matter how independently experienced they may be. In addition, sexual quantity has rather little to do with quality. A man who is sensual, affectionate, and understanding, who is not hell-bent to "slide home" before the woman feels fully aroused and lubricated, is likely to be a better lover the first time around, despite inevitable self-doubts, than an insensitive man who has rammed himself into any number of women since he was thirteen.

Many women honestly enjoy guiding a man in the art of lovemaking. Some women find it a welcome relief from men who insist on playing leader in bed. Others simply like to share their experience. Some women might be surprised to learn that a man is a virgin—many women tend to share men's general belief that few men are virgins past age eighteen. A woman might tease a man, either in a good-natured way or nonsupportively. Virgin men rarely see any humor in their situation and sometimes mistake lighthearted joking for abuse. There is often a fine line between the two. If a woman taunts a man about his lack of experience beyond the bounds of supportive humor, he might consider looking for a lover with whom he could feel more comfortable. However, most women say that a man's experience in bed—or lack of it—is much less important than who he is as a person and how he treats her.

The flip side of the imperative to get laid is the pressure a man may feel to make love whenever his lover wants to, regardless of his own level of interest. A man who grows up believing that there should be only one thing on his mind often feels there must be something wrong with him if he would prefer not to make love now and then. Most men do not feel perpetually aroused, and surveys of men's sexual appetites show a slow, steady decline beyond their twenties in both frequency of lovemaking and *desired* frequency. It is often difficult for young men to conceive of turning down an opportunity to make love. Many men work so hard for so long to persuade a woman to say yes, that they cannot believe they themselves would ever want to say no. Most men, however, prefer to say no from time to time.

There are many reasons why a man might turn down a lovemaking invitation. The Superbowl might be on TV. He might be exhausted from a tough day at work. He might feel physically ill (men get headaches too) or emotionally upset about a personal problem or job reversal. A man might not like the woman, or he might want a friendship instead of a love affair. He might be angry at her. He might resent her lack of initiative in bed or her insistence on dictating their style of lovemaking. He might feel he "owes" her sex or that their lovemaking has become boring and routine. There is a myth that women submit to sex as "part of the housework." But it is surprising how many men say they sometimes find lovemaking a duty or chore, and not a pleasure.

It is perfectly normal for a man not to want to make love. But problems may arise if he loses touch with his feelings and says yes when he would rather say no. Men often find it as difficult to say no as women do. A man might think: She'll think I don't love her anymore, or that I'm cheating on her, or that I've got a sex problem, or that I'm still angry that she turned me down last time, or that I'm not a real man. There is no end to the anxiety and conflicts that can be generated by saying no to an invitation to make love when lovers don't give each other the permission to say it.

Some men believe that masculinity demands never doing any-thing halfway, and they find it difficult to distinguish between a desire for friendly affection and an invitation to make love. Some men think they must push themselves to go all the way when perhaps all they (or their lovers) want is a hug, or a few moments of being held or some affectionate kissing. Lovemaking is not an all-or-nothing process. One step does not necessarily lead to an-other. Many women get upset with men who interpret a peck on the cheek or an arm around the waist as an invitation to make love. Expressions of affection need not lead to bed.

The only goal in lovemaking is to share physical closeness and affection with someone whose company you enjoy. You might do this with a hug and kiss or a torrid weekend where you never get out of bed. Five minutes of being held can feel more satisfying than "the old in-out" if what you want is reassurance that your lover cares about you.

Many men learn that it's all right for a man in a conflict situation to lose his temper, but that it is unacceptable for a "real man" to express doubts, especially around a woman's invitation to make love. This flawed logic leads some men to reject a lover's advances by fighting. From a woman's point of view, however, it can feel terribly unnerving to suggest making love to a man and have him pick a fight when it is clear he simply wanted to decline the invi-tation.

Because it is often easier for men to make love when not in the mood than to decline an invitation, a man may be able to fool himself into thinking that he is in the mood when actually he is not. Sometimes a man can fool himself more easily than he can fool his penis. To function at its best, a penis needs relaxed, con-flict-free working conditions. If the working conditions deteriorate, a man's penis may go on strike.

Harry was a thirty-eight-year-old construction worker who had what he called "creeping impotence." He was becoming progres-sively less able to raise an erection. After physical causes were ruled out, the counselor asked Harry about his lovemaking. "No problems," he replied, but further discussion revealed several. His wife did not enjoy making love. They had fought about it early in their marriage and negotiated a "truce" where she let him "do it to her" twice a week. She just lay there, and Harry said it felt like masturbating into her. Harry felt bored and trapped, and so did his penis. Harry said he'd tried to discuss his resentments, but his attempts only seemed to make things worse. He would become angry and incoherent, which made his wife defensive and sullen. The counselor asked Harry how he asked for the moves he wanted in bed. It turned out that he never really asked for anything specifically. He either gave his wife copies of men's magazines and told her to "take a hint," or ordered her to "be sexier." That's like a director telling an actor to "be funnier." It seldom works. Further discussion revealed that Harry had little idea about what turned women on. The counselor discussed some of women's general preferences and recommended that Harry read *For Yourself* (see Bibliography) and try to discuss it with his wife. Their discussion of the book startled them both. Harry learned that his rush to have intercourse did not give his wife enough time to become aroused. His wife was surprised that Harry was still interested in working on their lovemaking so many years after she'd decided he'd given up on her. On a subsequent visit, the counselor asked Harry to compile a list of all the things he wanted his wife to do for him in bed, then rank the list from "least difficult for your wife" to "most difficult." The least difficult group included initiation of kissing, hugging, and snuggling up together while watching TV. The counselor urged Harry to ask his wife to do just one of the least difficult things and to stop blaming her for his erection problem. Harry was surprised that his wife seemed happy to kiss and hug him, and his erection situation began to improve. The counselor warned Harry to be very patient, to continue talking with his wife about the kinds of physical togetherness they enjoyed and not to "up the ante" too quickly. Over several months, Harry began to receive some of the moves he wanted, and he started to give his wife the kind of attentions she liked. Once his penis's working conditions improved, it called off its strike.

The pressures men feel to get laid are often intensified by worries about "performing." The very phrase "sexual performance" conjures up images of a stage, a pair of actors putting on a show, and an audience full of critics including the woman, her friends, and —the most bloodthirsty critic of all—the man himself. Many a man makes love with only part of himself. The rest of him stands apart and watches the "performance," minutely judging its every aspect and comparing it to how the men's magazines say good lovemaking ought to go. Masters and Johnson call this preoccupation with self-observation "spectatoring." It is as though three of you are making love: the two lovers in bed and the man standing outside of himself watching the show.

Performance is a term associated with competitive athletics and with finely tuned machinery, but lovemaking is neither an athletic spectacle nor a grand prix race. You are not in the playoffs, in front of a full house under the hot glare of TV lights. You are under no pressure to be a star or to win a race. In fact, teams that rely on superstars tend to be more erratic than those that rely on teamwork. Lovemaking is a team effort. Unlike sports, however, there is no game to win, no pennant to chase, no coach, front office, or fans to please, no time to beat. There are just the two of you making love with each other. The goal of lovemaking, if there is one, is simply to relax and enjoy being in close touch with your lover.

Instant Erection

Many men believe that their penises should be able to rise to erection on command. In the men's magazines and in pornography, men usually present their lovers with fully formed "throbbing" erections from the moment they remove their clothes. Many, but by no means all, young men can do this without difficulty. For some men, usually guys in their teens and twenties, attaining instant erection is easy and can even be embarrassing. But by their thirties, many men notice that they are not quite as "quick on the draw" as they once were. This is perfectly normal, particularly after a stressful day at work, or a few drinks, or returning home to a broken toaster or problems keeping up with the bills.

Some men allow their penises a warm-up interval, but once they have erections, they expect them to remain rock-hard until ejaculation. This is another unfortunate legacy of the teen years. As men mature, their erections lose none of their potential for pleasure, but they become more sensitive to distraction. If the phone rings, if there is a knock on the door, or if you suddenly remember it's your mother's birthday, your erection may subside somewhat or wilt altogether. An erection might also subside if your lover does something that makes you feel uncomfortable, for example, digging fingernails into your back or tickling you or saying something that distracts you. Erections normally rise and subside during lovemaking. The trick to raising a fallen erection is to relax and ask for some stroking that arouses you. Lost erections tend to stay lost when men get upset, order them to happen again, or berate their lovers for not being sexy enough to keep them hard.

Men who could play full-court basketball all day long in high school usually don't suffer a loss of self-esteem when, at twenty-five or thirty, they would rather play a few half-court games and call it a day. But many men continue to expect their penises to behave like they did years earlier and get angry or anxious if they don't. These feelings can become literally self-deflating. Any emotional upset during lovemaking can trigger the fight-or-flight reflex that sends blood away from the penis toward the limbs, leaving less blood available for erection.

At the Men's Clinic, many men complained of "impotence" when actually they could raise an erection and make love with no problem. Their problem had nothing to do with lack of erection, but rather with the time it took them to raise one. One man said something must be wrong with him if he could not become erect within thirty seconds of getting into bed. The counselor suggested that he might be making unrealistic demands of his penis.

Some women get upset if their lovers' erections subside during lovemaking. Many persons—both men and women—blame themselves if their lover seems less than passionately aroused. If a man's erection subsides the woman may fear that she no longer excites him or that she did something to turn him off. This may be the case, and a man who, for example, dislikes fingernails in the back might gently say so. Frequently, though, erections subside on their own for a while. A man can explain to a concerned lover his penis's sensitivity to minor distractions and reassure her that his ups and downs are normal and not her fault. He might encourage her to fondle his soft penis. Many men enjoy this and many women enjoy stroking a soft penis and feeling it rise slowly to erection.

Most women are also sensitive to distractions during lovemaking and have their own cycles of feeling more and less aroused. Lovers may enjoy sharing the little events that excite or distract them.

"Caveman" Meets "Delivery Boy"

Most men learn that they are supposed to approach women sexually in two opposite ways—as "cavemen" who seize sex from them, and as "delivery boys" who give it to them. Attempts to reconcile these conflicting sets of social instructions often frustrate and confuse men and add to the anxieties that can interfere with enjoyable lovemaking.

The mythical caveman stalks his mate, clubs her senseless, then drags her by the hair to his pallet of animal skins where he "takes" her, a sexual style equivalent to rape. The caveman uses the woman only for his pleasure and gives her nothing in return. The myth is rounded out by the idea that this is what women really want.

Equally damaging is a legacy of the Victorian era a century ago. Back then, doctors and psychologists agreed that women *had no* sexual feelings, and, therefore, men had no responsibility to provide what "everyone knew" women could not appreciate. During Victorian times, the only women who acknowledged their sexuality were prostitutes. Since "ladies" were considered incapable of sexual arousal, whereas men were "ruled by animal lust," the idea that making love involved intimate sharing between two equally arousable lovers made little sense. Men "took" their wives or hired ladies of the evening, and all women—both wives and prostitutes —"submitted" to men. Wives experienced sexual submission as their religious duty; professional women saw it as a business commitment. Domination and submission were built into sexual relationships and sex meant asserting power over women, not making love with them.

Today we understand that men and women are equally capable of appreciating sexual experiences and that lovemaking involves a give-and-take where neither lover simply takes from nor submits to the other. The problem is that antiquated Victorian notions— only a few decades out of fashion—still have a considerable hold on many people's ideas about what is "supposed to happen" in lovemaking. Judging from the popularity of James Bond movies and a good deal of television programming and popular music, many men today still subscribe to the "fuck 'em and forget 'em" approach. And despite the increased practice—if not exactly universal acceptance—of teenaged lovemaking, many young women continue to be told that "good girls don't."

Many women are brought up to believe that they should deny their sexual feelings even if there is a man, or men, with whom they would like to make love. One way to deny responsibility for wanting to make love, while still doing it, is to be coaxed into bed by a man. Then the sex is *his* responsibility. The need some women have to deny their sexual feelings and be cajoled into bed places men in an awkward, contradictory position. If a man respects a woman's initial no when she would like him to continue coaxing, she might feel that he does not find her alluring enough to work at getting her into bed. But if he refuses to take no for an answer when the woman means no, he is at least a pushy son of a bitch, and, at worst, a rapist.

It is difficult for men—and women—to shake the image of man-as-hunter/woman-as-prey because both sexes are still brought up to believe that no might mean yes, and because young men continue to learn that they should get as much as they can and then some. However, the intelligent and sensitive man takes a woman at her word. If a woman says no, a man should assume she means it. He might mention his own desire to make love and his expectation that his interest will continue. The woman can always change her mind. But a man may never be able to change her mind about him if he pushes her to "put out" when she would rather not. Most women are not interested in cavemen. Most women prefer men who take them seriously, men they can trust.

Some men expect women to resist their advances and to get upset; to these men it is all part of the game. Some men ignore resistance until the woman bolts away from them or starts kicking and screaming. Some men ignore a woman's pleas to stop no matter what she does. Sex without consent is rape, and rape is one of the most frequently committed violent crimes in the country. That fact alone is tragic evidence of many men's inability to take women seriously, but even more disturbing is the gray area between consent and force. One survey, for example, asked a large number of women if they had ever been raped. A considerable proportion said they were *not sure*. If women are not clear where persuasion ends and coercion begins, how can men, influenced at least to some extent by the caveman philosophy, know when to stop coaxing? Unfortunately, the answer seems to be that men cannot know for certain.

But one thing *is* certain—coercion usually results in frustrating, unsatisfying sex for men as well as women. Surveys of men's feelings about lovemaking agree that by far the single biggest turn-off for men is an unresponsive lover. Some men may be capable of physically plugging into women who are opposed to the idea, but most men agree that their best sexual experiences involve *equally motivated* lovers, not the man doing it to the woman. The more a woman needs to be prodded into bed, the greater the likelihood

that the man will resent her and feel pressured by the situation—
to say nothing of the woman's potential resentment toward the
man who, from her perspective, may be coercing her. Lovers who
resent one another often have difficulty enjoying problem-free
lovemaking. The message to men is: If you dislike unresponsive
lovers, do not foist yourself on women who are in no mood to
respond.

These days, many men's opinions of their prowess as lovers depend not on how much pleasure they can take from women, but on
how much they can deliver to them. This change in attitude is a
progressive step because it recognizes women's sexual feelings.
Ideally, it might also promote more equally shared lovemaking.
Unfortunately, some men become so wrapped up in giving their
lovers pleasure that they lose touch with their own sexual needs.
Ignoring one's own needs can result in the same frustrations and
sex problems that develop from ignoring a lover's needs.

Men caught up in the "delivery boy" style of lovemaking are
usually warm, sensitive gentlemen who sacrifice their own pleasure in bed for their lover's enjoyment. Delivery boys tend to respect women and abhor the caveman style. Many of these men
have been deeply affected by the women's movement. Some feel
guilty about acting like cavemen in previous relationships and
have vowed to "make it up" to womankind. But in lovemaking,
doing it "for" her causes as many problems as doing it "to" her.

Max, a twenty-six-year-old commercial artist, had, in his words,
"blown" his first marriage. His wife had become involved in a
women's group, and after about a year she decided there was more
to life than being Max's servant. Max blamed himself bitterly for
the breakup and vowed to mend his ways. Now he was involved
with Shelly, whose intelligence and wit he enjoyed. He went out
of his way not to make sexual demands of her. They made love
only when she wanted to, and only the way she wanted. Max
decided that his goal in bed was to give Shelly marvelous orgasms,
which she said he did. The relationship continued for several
months in this way until Max developed the first sex problems he'd
ever had. He found it progressively more difficult to raise an erection, and when his penis did rise, he came almost immediately. In
counseling, he said his problem did not bother him all that much
—he could still masturbate with no problem—but he worried that
he might not be able to please Shelly. The counselor asked Max

what Shelly did to please him. Max seemed surprised at the question. He said he was "past that now," that he never made sexual requests of Shelly as he had with his wife, and that she was not an initiator in bed. Further discussion led Max to concede that he wished Shelly would suck his penis and that he resented "doing all the work" in bed. Max had switched from caveman to delivery boy. His sex problems cleared up shortly after he decided that it was all right to ask Shelly to take a turn providing the kinds of stimulation he enjoyed.

Both the caveman and delivery boy styles of lovemaking grow out of the notion that whatever happens in bed, men are the ones who do it, while women remain essentially passive. But mutually fulfilling lovemaking is always a two-way street. One key to problem-free lovemaking is the idea of "equal time," where both lovers take turns giving and receiving pleasure.

Imaginary Lovers

A noted sex therapist once remarked that good loving depends on "friction and fantasy." Many men have a favorite fantasy—or several—that they use to heighten the pleasure of masturbation. But some men believe that it's wrong to fantasize when making love with a flesh-and-blood woman. One man said he enjoyed fantasizing by himself, but that in bed with his lover, he tried not to. He said he wanted to be right there with her, completely absorbed in her and her alone. Many men pressure themselves to hold their fantasies in check. This pressure, like the others discussed earlier, can interfere with a man's ability to relax and enjoy making love.

People who meditate achieve deep relaxation by allowing their minds total freedom to wander wherever they happen to go. In fantasy, everything is permitted and nothing is wrong. Fantasy is a harmless way to "live out" situations you might prefer not to experience in real life. Fantasies can also add variety to lovemaking and allow lovers to explore their own deepest feelings while sharing the intimacy of lovemaking with each other.

It is fine for a man to imagine that he is making love with someone else or with a whole busload of sexy women. Perhaps S&M fantasies turn you on, or anal sex, or outdoor orgies, blow jobs in the office, pimping—whatever. As long as a man can tell the difference between fantasy images and real-life activities, any fantasy is fine, any time, with anyone.

Fantasies, like dreams, are safety valves for all kinds of constructive—and destructive—desires. Don't try to deny them or rein them in. Let them go where they will. They can help you let yourself go in lovemaking.

Coming Together

Many couples believe that the "best" lovemaking culminates in simultaneous orgasm. It is not clear how or when the quest for simultaneous orgasm began, but it must be a relatively recent addition to lovers' aspirations, for until fairly recently, women were believed to be incapable of orgasm altogether, let alone simultaneous orgasm with their lovers.

The problem with the goal of coming together is that for most lovers things rarely work out that way, and lovers who define the best sex as that which results in simultaneous orgasm are, in most cases, setting themselves up for disappointment. Working toward simultaneous orgasm changes the process of making love from free-form mutual enjoyment into a kind of chore. The pursuit of simultaneous orgasm can distract lovers from the real goal of lovemaking, which is close personal sharing.

Think of lovemaking as a banquet. The only goal of participating in a banquet is to enjoy the feast, to savor each course, appreciate each bite, and enjoy the camaraderie of the other guests. Now imagine that you and your lover are committed to swallowing your last bites of dessert at precisely the same moment. This new goal changes your relationship to the banquet. No longer can you concentrate fully on the meal or the company. Now you become preoccupied with your timing. Are you eating too fast? Why isn't she eating faster? Can you hold off swallowing that final bit until she catches up? And suppose you *do* finish eating at the same moment —does that make the banquet any better? Possibly for some people, but it would make no difference at all to most.

Coming together can be fun on those infrequent occasions when it happens, but ironically, the very act of working toward simultaneous orgasm often prevents it from happening. In general, men tend to lose ejaculatory control when under pressure. The stress involved in trying to delay orgasm until the woman comes can rob a man of pleasure that is his to enjoy, while at the same time, it interferes with his ability to control his ejaculatory timing. Meanwhile, a woman who feels she must try to come quickly tends to feel less relaxed than she would if she were not under pressure to come at the same time as her lover. A woman who pushes herself to come quickly—and not just quickly but at the exact moment her lover ejaculates—denies herself sexual pleasure and may feel so pressured that she might have trouble coming at all.

The idea that the best sex culminates in simultaneous orgasm hinges on another misconception many men have about lovemaking—that the "right way" to do it involves the man's penis stimulating the woman to orgasm through vaginal intercourse. However, every survey of women's sexuality shows that less than half of the women questioned reach orgasm through intercourse with any regularity, and that many women who are able to come during intercourse prefer not to.

The vagina actually has rather little to do with women's orgasms. Fondling the vaginal lips and engaging in vaginal intercourse can be quite pleasurable for women, but the trigger for women's orgasm is the clitoris (CLIT-or-is, not cli-TOR-is; see diagram in Appendix I, page 249), the little penislike organ that sits outside and above the vagina. Most women need direct stimulation of the clitoris—by hand, mouth, vibrator, whatever—to have an orgasm. It is possible for a man or woman to stimulate the clitoris during intercourse, but many women prefer not to come during intercourse, just as many men enjoy ejaculating into their lovers' mouths on occasion, not always into their vaginas.

Both men's and women's climax in orgasm depends on their ability to relax and let go of all the "shoulds" that reduce making love to merely having sex—the feeling that one "should" have a huge penis or breasts, attain erection instantly, start doing it at thirteen, put on an Academy Award-winning performance and wrap it all up with simultaneous orgasm.

There is certainly nothing wrong with coming together if it happens, but the banquet of love can be just as tasty—possibly more so—if you don't judge its overall quality by the timing of the final swallow.

Chapter 2

SENSUALITY: THE KEY TO PROBLEM-FREE LOVEMAKING

For both men and women, the main obstacle to problem-free lovemaking is tension. Tension includes all the anxieties, stresses, self-doubts, performance pressures, anger, and relationship problems lovers take to bed with them.

Some men are surprised to hear that tension interferes with lovemaking. John, a record company administrator, put it this way: "How can tension louse up sex? I thought you're supposed to build up as much tension as possible, then release it through ejaculation."

Yes and no. You want to feel *aroused* and arousal involves some muscle tension. However, you want to avoid tensing up because wholesale tensions interfere with the body's arousal process. When the body feels relaxed, sexual arousal proceeds smoothly and the muscles that need to contract can do so with no problem. However, any worries that result in tense, sore muscles—for example, in the back or neck—can preclude relaxed arousal and contribute to sex problems.

Unfortunately, many men find it difficult, perhaps impossible, to feel relaxed in a culture as fast-paced, ever-changing, and stress-producing as ours. In addition to the pressures that impinge on us from the world outside ourselves—inflation, crime, economic uncertainties, family and lover problems—American men typically fall victim to a particular form of stress, generated from within, that sex therapist Jay Mann calls The Three A's of Manhood: achieve, Achieve, ACHIEVE!

The pursuit of money, fame, and social status which defines "the good life" have turned millions of men into "workaholics." Workaholics rarely unwind from day-to-day tensions; some are convinced they have forgotten how. Even when they appear to be relaxing, part of them is grinding away: selling that product, getting that "A," making that contact, closing that deal—all of which add up to making the bucks. For many men, it feels more "normal" to work than to relax. The stress of overwork may not feel particularly satisfying or healthy, but at least it feels familiar and "natural." After all, a "real man" strives unceasingly for bigger and better achievements.

Deep down, though, most men understand that the stresses in their lives interfere with their ability to make love as well as they would like to. It is no coincidence that men who feel intense pressure from jobs or relationships call these situations "ball busters."

Jody, a twenty-year-old premed student, came in for counseling because his sex life was, in his words, "all fucked up." He said the competition in school made him feel continually tense, irritable, and insecure. There were so many premed students and so few places available in medical schools. Jody felt he was handicapped because he had to work part-time to support himself, which cut into his study time. When he visited the Men's Clinic, he was waiting to hear whether he'd been accepted into any medical school. Jody said he rushed to the mailbox every day and found it impossible to relax "no matter how hard I try." Jody had had a few lovers, but said he never felt at ease around women, either in or out of bed. Now he was involved with a woman he liked, a fellow premed student who understood the problems he faced. Suddenly, however, his erections were wilting on him, and when he was able to maintain one long enough to insert, he ejaculated almost immediately, which upset both Jody and his lover. Jody kept saying his manhood was on the line. Rejection from medical school would emasculate him; meanwhile, his sex problems further aggravated his doubts about his masculinity. Jody seemed so preoccupied with the issue of manhood that the counselor asked, "When did you first feel like a man?'' Jody reflected a while, then replied, "When I first got laid and started worrying about having a career.'' The counselor pointed out that, apart from sex, Jody's sense of manhood seemed to hinge on *worry*, worry about getting into medical school and succeeding as a doctor. The counselor asked if Jody could imagine himself feeling secure in his masculinity. He laughed nervously: "Maybe if I were a rich doctor and didn't have these sex problems. . . .''

Like many if not most men, Jody measured his manhood by the bottom lines of income, job status, and sexual prowess. The irony of such a situation is that as men come under increased job, financial, and sexual pressures, their ability to enjoy problem-free lovemaking decreases.

Many men have trouble relaxing because they are out of practice. Relaxation is a skill like any other. It requires some effort before anyone can feel comfortable with it. Relaxation is different from simply not working. Men who are unemployed often experience not working as *anything* but relaxing.

Most men know how to relax. Like riding a bicycle, it is difficult to forget entirely, but any skill can become rusty when it is not practiced. It would be a mistake to get back into bike riding after several years by signing up for a bicycle race. Better to review the fundamentals first. Men who feel tense and overworked are sometimes in such a hurry to relax when they get the chance, that they hurl themselves into it as they might attack a problem at work, without pausing to take a deep breath and assess what relaxation means. As an introduction to the ways relaxation techniques can resolve sex problems, let's examine the ways overstressed men unwind and answer the question: What's so relaxing about relaxation?

For some men, relaxing means drinking beer and munching potato chips while watching Monday Night Football. For others, it might mean jogging, taking a nap, getting away for the weekend, playing softball, or going to a movie or concert and smoking Colombian.

Relaxing activities have several aspects in common:

—A sense of suspended time. When people relax, they take a "time out" from the "have to's" that define the rest of their lives. They slow the pace a bit, sleep late, and dawdle over the little pleasures they cannot "find time for" Monday through Friday.

—A sense of living for the moment. Relaxing involves a

heightened concentration on the here and now. People tune into their bodies, their feelings, the people they're with. They try to tune out last week's fight with the boss, the up-coming final exam, or the income tax deadline.

—A sense of losing yourself in activities that release tension. At a concert, you feel you're melting into the music; while swimming, a feeling of becoming part of the water. When people unwind, they extend their personal boundaries and touch the larger reality around them. Until their next obligation, they "let themselves go."

—A sense of nonpressure, nondemand. Relaxation means doing what you want, when, how, and with whom you decide to do it. At its most fulfilling, relaxation is self-directed—no one pushes you to "perform." You might play hard, but the motivation comes from within and not, for example, from a coach's threats to drop you from the team if you don't live up to his assessment of your abilities. Running is both satisfyingly strenuous and uncluttered by performance demands other than those that runners set for themselves. People run because it feels good and keeps them in shape. In a marathon race, most people run to finish or to improve their time, not to win. Pressure to win would change the run from a workout to work.

Relaxation may involve competition, but it is less competitive than work. Many people find that watching or playing a close game —volleyball, Monopoly, whatever—can be very relaxing if the competition is friendly as opposed to cutthroat. When relaxing, the emphasis is on having fun, not on "killing" the opposition.

Usually, unpressured situations encourage people to let go and do well. Pressure creates tensions that keep people from letting themselves go.

All these aspects of relaxation are involved in problem-free lovemaking. Making love means taking a time-out from the stresses that define day-to-day living. Lovers consciously slow the pace of their lives, concentrate on each other, and savor the time they have reserved to lose themselves in nondemanding, intimate sharing.

The Whole Body as Erogenous Zone

Sigmund Freud postulated that the body contains three erogenous zones—areas that lead to sexual arousal when stimulated: the mouth, anal area, and genitals. He developed this three-zone con-

cept into an explanation of human sexual maturation. Freud's model has its supporters and detractors, but for men trying to improve their lovemaking skills, its merits are less important than the fact that it emerged from psychoanalytic texts long ago to become part of our culture's general assumptions about sex.

There are two problems with the popularized version of the three-zone theory: It implies that the rest of the body is unarousable and it labels pleasure from other parts of the body as abnormal "fetishes." These are tragic misconceptions. Every square inch of the body can—and should—tingle with arousal during lovemaking.

There are no distinct erogenous zones. This is a key point in resolving sexual difficulties. It cannot be emphasized enough. Likewise, there are no fetishes, only preferences. The whole body is one big erogenous playground. The ways it can experience pleasure are as limitless as the imagination. Problem-free lovemaking for both men and women depends on whole-body arousal. Lovers who become preoccupied with each other's traditional erogenous zones waste vast realms of pleasure potential and risk sex problems. Similarly, lovers who label each other "fetishists" because they derive particular delight from certain kinds of nongenital stimulation foster self-consciousness which interferes with trust and mutual self-abandon in bed. Of course, lovers may have different arousal preferences and these may be compatible or incompatible. Lovers should discuss their preferences to determine if they can enjoy each other's intimate company in mutual comfort. In their discussions, they should try to let go of the narrow three-zone concept. The erogenous zones theory limits the range of arousal seen as normal, while the notion of fetishes reinforces it by labeling whole-body arousal as abnormal.

Mutually fulfilling lovemaking involes *expanding* lovers' conceptions of physical arousal. The traditionally erotic areas certainly deserve thorough appreciation, but to function at their best, the sex organs need support from the rest of the body. Sexual satisfaction depends to a great extent on *sensual* arousal. Sensual arousal is physical excitement of *all the body's nongenital surfaces.* Sensuality involves all five senses—sight, hearing, touch, smell, and taste—and the ways they interact to enhance physical closeness. Sensual arousal includes sex organ arousal but goes beyond it to produce feelings of pleasure over the body's entire surface, from the scalp to the spaces between the toes. The body is capable of incredible pleasure. Why deny yourself any of it?

Sexuality *needs* sensuality. Each complements the other in problem-free lovemaking. An illustration: gasoline makes a car go, but all the gas in the world cannot power an engine that lacks oil. Unless the moving parts are bathed in lubricant, the engine won't work. Similarly, unless the whole body is bathed in sensual arousal, the sex organs may not work. Men who dismiss their sensual needs and focus solely on their penises are on a one-way trip to sexual problems.

Touch: The Language of Lovemaking

The relaxation techniques involved in problem-free lovemaking all heighten sensuality, or to be more precise, "sensual focusing." Sensual focusing is the ability to screen out everyday stresses and concentrate on the input from all the senses. In day-to-day living, sight and sound tend to be the dominant senses. Most people would consider a loss of sight or hearing more traumatic than a loss of any of the three other senses. However, in lovemaking, touch is the primary sense. Making love means *getting in touch* with your lover and *staying in touch.*

Unfortunately, in American society, the sense of touch has lost stature in recent years. In urban/suburban environments, touching can signal violation or attack. As physical distances between people decrease, emotional distances tend to increase. The classic example is the crowded elevator. The passengers distribute themselves so no one touches anyone else.

Touch has been called "the mother of the senses." It is the first sense to develop. A six-week-old human embryo, little more than a jumble of cells an inch across, can react to touch long before any other sensory system has developed. In fact, touch is the *only* sensory input human beings cannot live without. Infants born blind and deaf can develop normally, but those deprived of touching may die.

Men and women are brought up to have different relationships to the sense of touch. Girls are encouraged to savor the touch of shampoo, bubble bath, moisturizers, lingerie, and other clothing. Boys are simply told to wash up and get dressed. Girls are allowed to hug and kiss one another, but boys must limit their touching to back-slapping, elbows to the ribs, roughhousing, and contact sports. Little wonder that many women find men's caresses too rough.

Girls learn that touching another person is all right, but that sexual sharing is discouraged, if not forbidden. Boys learn that touching is sissy unless it leads to getting laid. Is it any wonder that many men feel obliged to go all the way when, perhaps, all they really want is some tender, loving affection?

Sensual touch is a vital ingredient of problem-free sex, but it need not lead to lovemaking. Try to think of touch as an end in itself. Sometimes touching can feel *more intimate* than making love. Many sex therapists have counseled men who developed sex problems to avoid having more one-night affairs than their penises could handle. One sex therapist recommended that a man in this situation incorporate more mutual touching into his lovemaking by starting off with some leisurely massage. The man became uncomfortable: "Massage her? I hardly know her!"

"Loveplay," Not "Foreplay"

A widely held notion about lovemaking is that it is divided into three distinct stages: foreplay, intercourse, and afterglow. The very word "foreplay" suggests that it happens before the "real thing." However, the idea that foreplay precedes actually "doing it" is an indirect cause of many men's sexual difficulties.

There are no such things as foreplay and afterglow. There is only *loveplay*. Loveplay begins with the first caress and continues until the lovers resume their everyday routines. Loveplay includes all the talking, touching, rolling around, playing, resting, and fantasizing that comprise lovemaking. There are no compartments, no separations between this or that aspect of the total experience. Lovers might change the pace or focus of their loveplay several times. They might take turns giving and receiving pleasure. They might move from the sensual to the sexual and back again. The point is that lovemaking is an integrated experience just as the courses of a banquet are all part of one meal.

In sex counseling, some men object to what they call "all that touchy-feely garbage." They say it's just an excuse to put off sex used by women who feel squeamish about "getting it on." Quite the contrary, extended loveplay does not postpone the real thing; it is an *integral part* of the real thing. It expands the definition of lovemaking to include all the sensual delights that arouse the whole body and allow the genitals to work properly.

There is nothing mysterious or difficult about the relaxation techniques that follow. From Indian yoga to Finnish saunas, they have been practiced by many cultures for thousands of years. Some may be familiar to you. Some may seem trivial and unimportant or mechanical. You might be tempted to skip them. Give them a chance. Be patient with them. Don't rush them. Rushing into lovemaking is the path to sexual frustration. Try to savor these simple suggestions. Not only can they be fun, they are crucial to women's sexual responsiveness and to the resolution of men's sex problems.

Try not to view these suggestions as separate from making love. They are all aspects of loveplay, not disconnected "pregame warm-ups" to "get over with" before the "main event." Runners do not complain that warm-up exercises postpone the race. They know that careful, thorough warm-ups help them loosen up and do their best.

"Hold Me"

Before you unzip or unhook anything, try holding one another for a while. Snuggling close can be an enjoyable way to begin the gradual process of unwinding from everyday pressures. At the same time, it can be a first step into the enchantments of sensuality. As preoccupations with the outside world slip into temporary suspension, many men experience a decrease in "static" that prevents them from focusing in on their senses, feelings, and lovers. Holding each other might be compared to wading into water. Little by little, you leave one environment and become comfortable in another.

Try to feel yourself stepping out of your daily routine. Focus on the process of slowing the pace of your life. Concentrate on the moment and on your lover. Think about the places where your body stores tension. Common spots include the neck, shoulders, and back. Wherever your tense places might be, ask for some touching there. Don't ask for a complete rubdown just yet—there's plenty of time for that and more later. Introductory caresses simply identify where you feel knotted up. As your lover's stroking loosens your knots, try to sit or lie quietly and feel the tension dissipate little by little. Breathe deeply. Try to feel the release of tension as you exhale. Guide her hands with simple directions: up, down, left, right, more, yes, there. Your lover undoubtedly has some tension centers also. Take turns identifying these places to one another and applying strokes.

Let your mind wander. Let your thoughts drift and dart wherever they please. Try to loosen the grip of conscious control you exercise over your mind in the workaday world. Fantasize if you feel like it. Remember, your thoughts need not focus exclusively on your lover.

Try not to focus entirely on your penis, but don't force your thoughts away from it either. The genitals are important in lovemaking, but they represent only a small fraction of arousable skin surface. Try to give the rest of your body equal time. During introductory touching you may get an erection, or you may not. Whatever happens with your penis is okay. It's fine not to get an erection and it's equally normal to raise one, then have it subside. Remember, the erection reflex depends on feeling relaxed. Worrying about when an erection "should" rise can give a man an erection problem. Trust your penis. It wants to become erect. It likes to become erect. And it will as soon as it feels safe, trusted, and warmed-up.

Let your lover's genitals warm up, too. Try not to reach into her blouse or pants immediately. Leave her bra and panties alone for a while. Many men home in on the bra and panties right away because of our cultural fascination with women's breasts and genitals. The sexual correspondence in the men's magazines sticks to women's "jugs and pussy" and rarely mentions any other parts of their bodies. However, most women say they prefer other forms of sensual loveplay before any caressing of the breasts or genitals. Women do not dislike breast or genital touch—most say they enjoy it as much as men like their penises fondled—but some women feel "goosed" unless they are given time to warm up to breast and genital caresses. When men go for the breasts right away, a woman might wonder: Who's this guy making love with—me or my boobs? It can be a drag for a woman to want to share her whole body with a lover and have him be interested in only a few small parts of it.

Many men can't wait until the woman puts a hand between their legs, and the women in the men's magazines can't seem to wait either. No doubt some women are "cock crazy," but most are not. Some men reach for the woman's breasts or genitals right away as a signal that they would like their lovers to do the same for them. Meanwhile, women often play the same game, only in reverse. They often wish men would not reach immediately for their breasts, and they keep their hands out of men's pants in the hope that their lovers might take the hint and give them more nongenital loveplay. Try to discuss this aspect of loveplay with your lover. The expectation that a lover will understand telepathic signals is unfair and it can lead to resentments. If you enjoy a hand between your legs right away, by all means ask your lover to treat you to that pleasure. At the same time, you might inquire whether you are reaching for her breasts or genitals before she feels ready for it. Surveys show that women tend to be more whole-body oriented than men. Unless your lover requests otherwise, assume that she prefers considerable full-body sensual touching before any loveplay focused on the breasts or genitals.

Men often experience problems with holding a woman or being held. Some complain that it's a waste of time, an obligation that bores men who have been "creaming in their jeans" all day. Some men feel all right about holding their lovers but become uncomfortable sitting still and being held or caressed. They say that children and pets get cuddled, not grown men.

These reactions are understandable given what men learn about lovemaking as they grow up. Many men learn they must provide some perfunctory touching for the sake of skittish womanhood, but that these slapdash moves are nothing more than a hurdle to jump on the way to getting laid. As teenagers, most men learn about the "Baseball of Balling": first base is a hand on the breast; second base —you get her bra off; third base—you're in her pants; and a home run—you slide on in. In this context, men become persuaded that introductory caresses are simply the first skirmish in the battle to see how far she'll let you go before crying rape. Men rarely learn that the aims of apparently aimless touching are tension release and the development of mutual comfort without which problem-free lovemaking is difficult, if not impossible. Understandably, men who grow up with visions of base running might feel odd "just" touching the woman here and there and not "getting anywhere." Sensual touching does not involve them emotionally; it's just part of the job. This perspective is also seen in the delivery boy approach to lovemaking. Touching becomes one more thing the man does *for* the woman. Try not to view snuggling as something you do for the woman, but *for yourself*. The fact is, you *are* getting somewhere. You and your lover are becoming relaxed. You are helping one another unwind from the stresses that interfere with mutually fulfilling lovemaking.

Many women feel flattered and reassured when nonsexual touching excites their lovers, because it suggests that the man enjoys *them*, not just their nipples and crotch. Conversely, some women feel turned off if they sense that sensual loveplay bores their lovers. Who can let go with a lover who seems detached from sensual explorations? Sensual arousal is contagious; so is nonarousal. Friendly, playful touching is central to most women's sexual responsiveness. It is also essential to the resolution of men's sexual problems. Men troubled by sex problems are often amazed at how quickly their lovemaking improves with the simple addition of ten or fifteen or thirty minutes of free-form caressing. One reason lovemaking often feels more interesting early in relationships is that new lovers tend to engage in more playful touching than established lovers who may feel they are "past all that."

Some men find that sensual touching is easier to give than to receive. In the context of the pressure many men feel to orchestrate their lovemaking, some feel that accepting a woman's touching initiatives symbolically unmans them and, as I have said, reduces them to the level of children or pets. (It is no coincidence that models in the men's magazines are called "pets.") To avoid feeling like a pet, and to shore up their image of sexual leader, some men become perpetual-motion machines, their hands always moving, their moves always in charge, rarely allowing the woman to do anything for them. It may take some getting used to, but a man who welcomes a lover's warm-up initiatives is neither a child nor a pet. He is an emotionally sensitive man. In addition, many women get turned on by a man who can receive sensual touching as well as give it. Acceptance is a sign of trust and most women say they want lovers who trust them. Men who insist on playing sexual leader have not learned what it means to *share*.

Showering

Cleanliness is a mark of respect for yourself and for your lover. Surveys of both men's and women's lovemaking preferences rate lack of personal cleanliness a prime turn-off.

Some lovers enjoy bathing or showering together as part of their initial loveplay. Like holding one another, showering can be a pleasant, sensually arousing way to mark the separation between daily routines and making love. Showering is a whole-body experience not limited to narrow genital focus. It is relaxing, and as mentioned in the section on penis size, it can help a man look better hung. Showering is usually a lights-on activity, and many lovers enjoy seeing each other's bodies before the lights get turned off. Toweling one another can also contribute to whole-body arousal.

Showering also removes the artificial odors—perfumes, colognes, after-shaves, deodorants—advertisers have persuaded us to use to cover our natural aromas. Recent research shows that the subtle aromas of the clean, sensually aroused body, in particular the fragrance of our natural sexual lubricants, play a significant role in overall sexual responsiveness.

On the other hand, it is fine not to shower together. Like every other aspect of making love, there are no "shoulds," only "you might like to's." Talk it over. Experiment. Try to stay loose.

Massage: Let Your Fingers Do the Talking

Massage is a form of intimate conversation without words. In the last decade, after years of quiet neglect in the United States, massage has been enjoying a renaissance. This renewed popularity has had both positive and negative implications. On the plus side, massage is being used not only for sensual arousal, but for healing purposes as well. Acupressure, deep muscle massage, and "the laying on of hands" are becoming increasingly accepted by Western medicine as healing arts. (They have been respected as healing arts in Asia for thousands of years.) On the minus side, however, massage has also been somewhat debased by the proliferation of massage parlors, fronts for prostitution, where a good massage is the only item *not* available.

A comprehensive discussion of massage is beyond the scope of this book. For further reference, see *The Massage Book* listed in the Bibliography. However, this brief overview should introduce those aspects of massage most applicable to sensual focusing and problem-free lovemaking.

The skin is one of our most precious natural resources. It is one of the body's largest organs and the goal of massage is to excite every square inch of it.

Massage works best in the nude, in a warm, cozy place free of interruptions. Indirect lighting or candlelight are also recommended. Practice massage wherever it feels comfortable: on a bed, massage table, air mattress, or deep pile carpet.

Massage authorities recommend use of a massage oil or lotion as a lubricant. Lubricants increase the skin's sensitivity to touch. A demonstration: Dry your lips then run a finger over them lightly and focus on the sensations you feel. Then lick your lips and repeat. Most people find that moist lips feel more sensitive. Mineral oils and body lotions may be purchased at drugstores; however, ordinary vegetable oil is less expensive, often handier, and it works just as well—some say better. If you use a lubricant, it is a good idea to spread a sheet or large towel under you to absorb any excess.

Some lovers decide that wet lubricants feel too messy and prefer to use talcum powder or nothing. Talk it over and decide what feels right for you.

Proper use of the hands is central to massage technique. The hands should be clean, warm, and relaxed. A good way to loosen up the hands is to ask the person about to be massaged to knead your hands a bit before you begin.

Although the hands communicate the massage, they cannot do so by themselves—they need the rest of the body. Like lovemaking, massage is a whole-body activity. Put some weight behind your strokes and apply some pressure. Apply pressure carefully, though. In the beginning, check frequently with the recipient to see if your strokes are too soft, too hard, too choppy or abrasive. After a while, there should be less need to consult.

Vary the speed, pressure, and direction of your strokes. You might use a medium pressure, slow circular stroke on the shoulders, then a heavier pressure, up-and-down stroke along the spine. Mold your hands to fit the body contours they encounter.

Never pinch, gouge, or grab anything in massage. In pornography, the men often grab women's breasts, pinch and bite the nipples. Never do this. Be careful when massaging the traditionally erotic areas of a woman's body. When visiting these areas, a light touch is often the right touch, unless your lover requests otherwise.

Both people should try to let go of conscious control over their breathing. Let your breathing deepen. This aids relaxation and loosens the muscles, which heightens the effects of massage.

Massage strokes can feel ticklish or cause flinching. Ticklishness and flinching are signs that the recipient feels uneasy about being touched in that spot or that way. Ask if the stroke feels too feathery. If so, try pressing a little harder and use more of the whole hand surface to cover the sensitive area. People who flinch at fingertip stroking across the stomach often have less trouble accepting medium palm pressure there. Deep breathing can also reduce uneasiness about being touched in sensitive places.

However, many people have areas of their bodies that always seem to be supersensitive to touch. In that case, leave the area alone, or introduce stroking there gradually, over time, and *only* with the recipient's permission. Don't push it. In films, lovers sometimes tickle and goose one another, then melt into each other's arms moments later. Real life is different. Tickling can be an aggressive act that tightens people because we tend to be ticklish in vulnerable areas; massage should loosen those who receive it, and establish trust. For lovers to relax and trust one another, it is important not to violate each other's sensitive spots.

Massage authorities agree that one of the most sensual areas of the body is the foot. Our feet connect us to the earth; they "ground" us. Tensions in other areas of the body cause compensatory changes in posture. For example, tension in the neck and shoulders can cause us to hunch forward slightly. To maintain our balance, further compensations must be made in the feet. Tension anywhere else in the body results, therefore, in corollary tensions in the feet. The feet house thousands of nerves that are "wired into" a great deal of the body. The theory behind acupuncture teaches that the feet are maps of the body's systems, with areas of the feet corresponding to various organs. From this perspective, a foot massage can be considered a whole-body massage. Try one. A good foot massage can be a truly sublime experience.

How long should a massage last? As long as you both want it to. Lovers new to massage might begin with brief stroking and progress to longer, more complete massages over time. Talk it over and decide what feels right for you.

Some men have the same problem accepting massage that they have accepting a woman's caresses or initiatives in bed. Consider this: Have you ever had a friend who was magnanimous to a fault, always doing favors, but rarely allowing reciprocation? Overly generous friends can be infuriating. A refusal to accept generosity is similar to a refusal to accept criticism. It's a way of saying: I don't need you. But everyone needs feedback and support from others. Sharing and exchange are the basis of friendship. The same goes for lovemaking, which, at its most satisfying, is an extension of friendship into the realm of sensuality.

Chapter 3

HOW TO LAST LONGER

A friend once remarked that doctors and psychologists have an uncanny ability to invent intimidating labels to describe the broad range of human behaviors that are essentially normal. Unfortunately, the labels conventionally used to describe sex problems emerged from this tradition. In addition to being imprecise, they often add to the feelings of helplessness and hopelessness that foster the seeming permanence of so many sexual difficulties.

A man who ejaculates before he or his lover wishes, or before he thinks he "should," is said to suffer from "premature ejaculation." When I was troubled by a lack of ejaculatory control, the label "premature ejaculator" upset me. I thought: If I've got premature ejaculation, I must not be a mature person. If only I were more mature, I might be able to have mature ejaculations. But, I wondered, how long did you have to last before premature ejaculations became mature? And how would I know? Would mature ejaculations feel any different from premature ones? How could I tell? A man who ejaculates before he wants to may be emotionally mature —he simply does not have voluntary control over his ejaculatory timing. He ejaculates involuntarily.

In the sex counseling I do, I have discarded the needlessly threatening, inaccurate label, "premature ejaculation." Instead, I emphasize the idea of voluntary versus involuntary ejaculation. This

71

perspective has several advantages over its predecessor. First, it eliminates any implication that a man's emotional maturity is linked to his ejaculatory timing. Second, it removes the stigma of disease. Many men experience "premature ejaculation" as an illness, like premature senility, something they "have" and are presumably stuck with until science finds a cure. The concept of voluntarism, on the other hand, implies a situation a man can resolve on his own. Finally, the voluntary-involuntary approach implies a *learning process* through which a man can progress from a situation that feels out of control to one that feels under control.

Almost any man can learn to last as long as he would like. Sex therapists enjoy virtually universal success at helping men learn to ejaculate voluntarily. Learning to control ejaculation is like learning to control urination, and most men learn that skill early in life.

In almost every case, coming too soon is not a personal failing, disorder, or disease, but a *habit*. Physical causes are extremely rare; therefore, the situation cannot be "cured" by pills or treatments.

On the other hand, if you have a problem with involuntary ejaculation and have not had a physical checkup in the last twelve months, it would be a good idea to get one, particularly if your problem began recently, after many years of lasting longer. Even in such a situation, the cause is rarely physical, but you might mention your concern about involuntary ejaculation so the physician can look for a possible organic cause. Possible physical causes might be: a nervous system disorder affecting the ejaculatory reflex, a hormonal imbalance, or an infection of the prostate gland which produces most of the seminal fluid.

A word of warning about raising ejaculatory control problems with a family doctor or urologist: Do not expect competent sex counseling from a doctor. They are rarely trained in sex counseling, and, unfortunately, the subject makes many physicians uncomfortable. To make matters worse, contemporary sex therapy concepts have not been incorporated into medical texts, which continue to recommend psychiatric treatment. Referral to a psychiatrist can fuel a man's suspicions that his sex problem is a sign of mental illness. This can aggravate feelings of hopelessness that often cement a habit of involuntary ejaculation. Men who come too soon usually don't need psychiatrists. All they need is a little first aid. But I reiterate that if you suspect a physical problem, by all means have it checked out. A man who is worried about the physical health of his sex organs tends to feel less relaxed than a man who feels healthy, and is therefore more distracted and less likely to be able to learn voluntary ejaculatory control. One of the best things about getting a checkup is that the vast majority of men are pronounced healthy. Hearing that nothing is physically wrong with you is usually a big relief—and it promotes relaxation.

When men become persuaded that a problem is not physical, many decide "it must be all in my head." This conclusion is supported by the subtle pervasiveness of Freudian vocabulary in our daily lives. Most men know rather little about Freudian psychology, but if they have a sex problem, they are familiar enough with the vocabulary to decide they must be neurotic.

Freudian psychoanalytic theory postulates that premature ejaculation (the discarded term seems appropriate here) is indeed a symptom of underlying neurosis. The arguments in support of this view are complex, but for our purpose here, they can be summarized in two core concepts. First, the premature ejaculator suffers an unconscious ambivalence toward women—he loves them and hates them at the same time, but is unaware of this. Second, he is emotionally immature and unable to resolve the conflicts he feels toward women. Therefore, his ambivalence finds expression in premature ejaculation, which frustrates the woman, who presumably has not come by the time he ejaculates, at the same time as it keeps the ambivalence repressed in the man's unconscious.

There are several problems with this perspective on involuntary ejaculation. Many men who ejaculate involuntarily are gentle souls who feel no particular ambivalence toward women. Conversely, some men with good ejaculatory control have ambivalent attitudes toward women. In addition, the Freudian notion that rapid ejaculation necessarily frustrates the woman grows out of the antiquated idea that the "right" way to make love "must" involve the penis stimulating the woman to orgasm during vaginal intercourse. In fact, every recent survey agrees that many women rarely, if ever, have orgasms solely from intercourse no matter how long the man lasts. There are many mutually thrilling ways to make love that do not depend on—or even include—intercourse. Finally, and most compelling, Freudian psychotherapy rarely helps men develop ejaculatory control. On the few occasions it has proven successful, the therapy has taken years. The sex therapy techniques discussed here usually teach men to ejaculate voluntarily in a few months.

If involuntary ejaculation is not caused by physical or emotional problems, how does it develop? It is learned. It emerges from the lovemaking habits many men accumulate throughout their lives. It comes from curbside sex education, and it is alleviated by adopting a more enlightened approach to lovemaking.

Coming too quickly as a problem in lovemaking is a recent invention. A hundred years ago, Western culture assumed that women were incapable of sexual arousal; they were seen merely as the passive receptacles for men's lust. Sex was something Victorian women endured. They did not participate in it or enjoy it. Men felt no need to delay ejaculation for the woman's sake and coming too quickly was not a problem. In fact, Alfred Kinsey speculated as recently as 1948 that rapid ejaculation was a sign of masculine vigor, possibly a genetic trait bred into us by natural selection. Kinsey's research team found that 75 percent of the men interviewed for *Sexual Behavior in the Human Male* ejaculated within two minutes of vaginal insertion. He speculated that rapid ejaculation might have evolved into our genetic makeup because, in our evolutionary ancestors' threatening environment, extended intercourse could leave a man vulnerable to attack and death. The man who came quickly, Kinsey argued, was more likely to father children, and therefore have his genes—including those for rapid ejaculation—passed to succeeding generations. This idea has no supporters today. Authorities agree that ejaculatory control is learned, not inborn and unchangeable, and that almost any man can learn to last as long as he'd like.

However, since Kinsey, sex experts have disagreed over the question: How soon is too soon? Some said "too soon" was ejaculation prior to vaginal insertion. Others said it was one minute after insertion, or three minutes, or longer. Some based their definition on the number of thrusts before coming. And Masters and Johnson defined "too soon" as ejaculation before the woman's orgasm more often than half the time.

Popular sex writers have not helped matters. One calls rapid ejaculation a "major sexual disaster." Another reminds men that it is their "job" to keep pumping away without ejaculating until their lovers climax.

Try to ignore these strange ideas. Not only are they wrong, they subject men to needless anxiety and self-doubt, neither of which help men relax and enjoy problem-free lovemaking.

The habit of involuntary ejaculation usually develops early in a man's sexual life, whether he begins making love at twelve or thirty-nine. It arises with equal frequency in all men, regardless of race, income, education, penis size, masturbation habits—anything. Both circumcised and uncircumcised men share this concern.

First sexual experiences are exciting, but they often feel awkward and confusing as well. They rarely feel as wonderful as they seem to be in books, movies, magazines, and parking-lot discussions. Early lovemaking experiences often generate more tension than passion. Most men feel a responsibility to lead the woman through lovemaking, but it often feels like the blind leading the blind. Either lover—frequently both—may feel nervous, unsure, clumsy, or distracted by other emotions that can detract from the undivided attention necessary for problem-free lovemaking. Many men feel pressured to be two different kinds of lover at the same time—on the one hand, constantly horny and forever on the prowl for a lay; on the other hand, detached and charming, poised and witty, the self-assured Mr. Cool. It's impossible to live up to this double standard, and attempting to do so can cause tensions that contribute to involuntary ejaculation.

It is hard enough for long-time lovers to discuss their sexual tastes. Such discussions can feel impossible to young lovers, inexperienced with sex and with one another, who may be wondering if it was their mouthwash, toothpaste, or blue suede shoes that "gave" them their sex appeal. Then, there are all the fears of getting her pregnant or hassling birth control, catching VD, going to hell, having her parents walk in, losing your erection at the crucial moment, or having her tell you that her Irish setter is more fun in bed than you are.

Few men inexperienced in lovemaking appreciate the importance of vaginal lubrication, nor do they understand how the vagina opens as the woman becomes aroused. It can be mortifying—not to mention erection-wilting—to have trouble locating a woman's vagina in pitch-darkness under the covers before she is aroused enough for her vaginal lips to begin to part. The women in the men's magazines often hold their vaginas open, but few flesh-and-blood women are so obliging.

Early sexual experiences rarely take place in the most relaxed surroundings. Fearful that the police might swoop down on lovers' lane or that she might change her mind about going all the way, many men develop a habit of rushed lovemaking. A man who comes quickly during his first few sexual encounters is likely to continue to do so. A habit develops, and even if rapid ejaculation is not the world's greatest pleasure, many novice lovers are grateful that their penises got hard when they were supposed to, stayed hard, and worked more or less properly. Later, after lovers become more comfortable with basic sexual techniques, they usually prefer to prolong their lovemaking. But by this time, many men find themselves stuck with "wham, bam, thank you, ma'am." Some men become frantic. They try everything they can think of—reciting the baseball standings or imagining getting arrested—but nothing works. A few quick strokes and it just happens. Other men blame it on the woman: I'm not coming too soon; the bitch is frigid. This sentiment does not promote the trust and relaxation necessary for mutually fulfilling lovemaking. The situation begins to feel hopeless. You imagine a depressing lifetime of coming too quickly, filled with lame apologies to frustrated lovers. You wonder if your lovers will tell other women that you're out of control, or if they'll leave you for someone who can last longer. You keep trying, but you feel helpless. Frequently, the feeling that you're trapped in a pattern you cannot control cements the habit of involuntary ejaculation.

The situations that give rise to involuntary ejaculation are hardly surprising. They are as normal as they are tragic. Who among us receives any formal training in the sensual art of making love? No one is allowed to teach himself how to drive a car, build a bridge, or perform an appendectomy. Without training, you might hurt someone. But almost all of us wind up teaching ourselves how to "do it," and often hurt ourselves and our lovers in the process. Most men learn about sex by the time they reach junior high from more "mature" men who may or may not have reached high school. This situation remains basically unchanged today despite the growing number of so-called sex education courses offered in public schools. Unfortunately, sex education has little to do with learning how to make love. School boards limit these courses to truncated discussions of sexual plumbing and warnings about the dire consequences of teen pregnancy, VD, and loss of a good reputation. Teachers promote "responsibility," which means "don't do it." Meanwhile, the vast majority of young people continue to receive their real sex education on the street, on the radio, at the movies and magazine stands. These sources shrink from helping

couples develop problem-free lovestyles, and they rarely offer constructive suggestions for dealing with the normal range of sexual dilemmas.

Some men lose their ejaculatory control later in life, after years of lasting longer. Here again, the cause is rarely physical, but it is well to start with a checkup. There may be nothing wrong with your penis, but you might be ill or recovering from an illness. Feeling run-down can interfere with ejaculatory control, and many men do not allow their bodies enough time to recuperate from illnesses. Jerry, for example, came in for counseling, upset about a sudden loss of ejaculatory control. It turned out that he had just started making love again after a bout with mononucleosis. He still felt washed-out and had the good sense not to play sports immediately, but he saw no reason not to make love and was horrified when it did not work out perfectly.

After possible organic causes have been ruled out, take a look at your erections. Men past thirty often notice that their erections take a bit longer to rise than they used to and may not become quite so hard. This is absolutely normal and does not mean a man is developing an erection problem. Seasoned baseball gloves are not as stiff as new ones, but they work just as well, usually better. However, many men who worry about being "stuck in neutral" ejaculate soon after they raise an erection. They feel they'd better use it before they *lose* it.

Then take a look at the relationship. How do you feel about it? Involuntary ejaculation might occur after a period of sexual abstinence, or the first few times with a new and exciting lover, or with a lover who bores you sexually. Pregnancy or parenthood might also generate enough stress to impair ejaculatory control. Are you preoccupied with outside pressures? Did you get passed over for a promotion or offered an exciting but risky job opportunity? Are you on the rebound from a difficult breakup? Do you like your lover? Not: Do you love her, and not: Do you admire the sculpted look of her breasts and buttocks—but: Is she a friend and confidant? Do you trust her? Do you feel pressured to impress her? Can you relax with her and be your decent, but imperfect, self? Would you rather not make love with her the way(s) you have been doing it? Are you holding back any resentments? Is there any reason you would like to get it over with? Any number of seemingly trivial concerns can contribute to involuntary ejaculation, just as a tiny pebble in a shoe can cause a noticeable limp. If you can identify any factors in your life or relationship that might contribute to coming too soon, try to discuss them with your lover. This may be difficult. Fortunately, you need not solve every problem to regain ejaculatory control. Sometimes just getting things off your chest can alleviate the tensions that cause a sex problem. Even if an issue in a relationship seems trivial, talk it over. Keep in mind that sometimes your penis may react to a relationship problem before your head can face it.

The Do-It-Yourself Techniques

There are two keys to lasting longer: Reduce tensions and become more comfortable with your body's sensual responsiveness. A body under stress for any reason looks for ways to relieve the pressure. If a man bottles up his emotions and denies himself other means of stress reduction, his body may decide that the only way out is to release the stress through ejaculation. Learning to last longer involves transferring stress reduction away from the penis to other parts of the body. In other words, expand sexuality to include sensuality.

The techniques presented here are for men without regular lovers, or men whose steady lovers might not feel comfortable with the couples' programs for learning ejaculatory control. However, men whose lovers are eager to help them learn to last longer should also familiarize themselves with these techniques because they are essential to the couples' programs.

Use these suggestions one at a time or in any combination that feels right for you.

Remember, the trick is to stay relaxed. Learning to last longer is like learning any other skill. It takes patience and practice. Accidents can happen. You may ejaculate before you want to. Don't get angry with yourself; try to maintain a sense of humor. Personal changes rarely happen gracefully. They come in spurts, as it were. Stay loose. Try not to become discouraged if this process takes longer than you think it should. There are no "shoulds." Above all, do not measure your staying power with a stopwatch. The number of seconds or hours you last is absolutely irrelevant. The important thing is the extent to which you feel in control of your ejaculatory timing, whenever you choose to come.

One note of caution: Some men who learn to last longer experience a few episodes of nonerection afterward. About 10 percent of the men Masters and Johnson taught to last longer voiced this complaint. Apparently, these men were so delighted with their new skill that they overdid it a bit and made more demands than their penises could handle. It can be great fun to last as long as you like, whenever you like, but everyone has his limits.

DEEP BREATHING

Breathing is a baby's first independent act of life. It is so fundamental to being alive that most of us take it for granted. Deep breathing is one of the easiest, best ways to release tension from the body. Sleep helps release tensions and a hallmark of sleep is deep breathing. It is also an early sign of sensual arousal. Deep breathing can be one of the most dramatically helpful techniques for lasting longer. Many men are amazed at how rapidly involuntary ejaculation becomes voluntary once they stop stifling their bodies' natural inclination to breathe deeply while making love.

Consciously or not, many men suppress the body's desire to breathe deeply during lovemaking. Deep breathing is a sign of being aroused, but some men work hard at acting cool and detached. Other men don't want to appear too excited for fear that the woman might realize her "power" over them. Some are concerned about bad breath, thanks to the clever advertising of a multimillion dollar industry. Others suppress their breathing in the name of etiquette to avoid appearing too consumed by animal lust.

A man whose body releases tension through deep, uninhibited breathing is much less likely to release it through involuntary ejaculation. Give yourself a chance to breathe. Let yourself go. Don't just breathe with your chest. Try to draw each breath past your lungs, through your abdomen, into your genitals, and down to your toes. Introduce yourself to the ways your body likes to breathe when freed of conscious controls. Breathe with your whole body.

Not only does deep breathing improve men's ejaculatory control, it often enhances lovemaking in general. Signs of sensual arousal tend to be contagious. When one lover trusts the other enough to open up and show signs of being turned on, the other usually becomes more aroused as well. Deep breathing helps many women feel more sensually comfortable with a lover, therefore, more responsive.

FOCUSED AROUSAL

Men who concentrate on "other things" during lovemaking—
the phone bill or a dentist appointment—rarely last longer. In fact,
thinking unpleasant thoughts can increase tensions and actually
hasten ejaculation. It also robs you of sensual pleasure that should
be yours to enjoy.

Instead of tuning out your body, tune into it. The more familiar
a man becomes with his ejaculatory process—and with his own
sensuality—the less mysterious ejaculatory control becomes.

The process of sexual arousal is called the "sexual response
cycle." It describes the body's physical changes during lovemaking. You might think that anything as fundamental to human
experience as sexual response would have been analyzed by scientists long ago, but Masters and Johnson first outlined the four-
stage process as recently as the mid-1960s.

The sexual response cycle is similar for both men and women.
The four phases include: excitement, plateau, orgasm, and resolution. These phases are not distinct and separate from one another.
They flow together and their boundaries are arbitrary. Also, the
phases as described here may not entirely match the changes you
observe in yourself while making love. That's okay. The four
phases are schematic representations, not absolute rules. Each individual's arousal pattern is uniquely his or her own. (The sexual
response cycle in women is discussed in Chapter 6.)

Appendix I might help you to visualize men's sexual response
cycle, which includes:

Excitement: The beginning of arousal. Heart rate increases.
Breathing becomes deeper. Nipples become more sensitive. Chest
and facial tones may become more reddish. Blood flow to the penis
increases and erection begins. The scrotum thickens and starts to
pull up closer to the body. The testicles also absorb blood and grow
larger.

Plateau: Completion of the arousal process. Erection becomes
full, though it may fluctuate or subside. The scrotum hugs the
body. A few drops of clear lubricating fluid may moisten the head
of the penis allowing for easier insertion. As orgasm approaches,
some men's penises subside a bit from full erection.

Orgasm:　A two-step process in men. First, there is a heightening of excitement and a quickening of breathing. This culminates in "the point of no return," when ejaculation feels inevitable, the moment when the prostate gland and seminal vesicles contract and empty seminal fluid into the urethra. Ejaculation follows seconds later as wavelike contractions of the pelvic muscles propel the semen out of the penis. The muscles around the anus also contract.

Resolution:　Heart rate, breathing, and state of mind return to normal. In the vast majority of men, the penis goes soft quickly, the scrotum descends, and some time must pass before the penis is capable of becoming erect again. The older the man, the longer the time from orgasm to the next possible erection. Some men, usually teens or men in their twenties, may be able to raise another erection soon after ejaculation, but the overwhelming majority of men cannot. (In pornography, deft splicing of scenes shot hours or even days apart creates an illusion of immediate reerection.) As men reach middle age, it is by no means uncommon for resolution to take twelve hours, twenty-four, or longer.

Tune into your own unique sexual response cycle. How is it similar to the general case described here? How is it different? Try to appreciate the subtleties of your own sexuality. How do your erections rise? When? What do you feel as the scrotum draws close to your body? How does your penis feel with different kinds of stroking or sucking? Which parts of it are sensitive to what kinds of touch? Which strokes or fantasies stimulate full erection? Which cause your erections to subside? What do you feel during and after orgasm?

When learning to last longer, the plateau phase deserves particular attention. Lasting longer means increasing the time between initial excitement and orgasm, in other words, extending the plateau phase. Spend some time identifying the sensations that lead up to your point of no return. Some men feel a special warmth or twitching throughout the pelvic region. Others feel heightened sensations in the penis. Some can feel their prostate glands and seminal vesicles contract. How do you feel as you approach the point of no return? How long afterward do you ejaculate? And what do your ejaculations feel like?

Ejaculation is a reflex, and some men believe that, like the knee-jerk reflex, all ejaculations feel—or "should" feel—the same. This may be the case for some men, but most experience a range of sensations depending on the situation. Just because a physical process is a reflex does not mean that it is constant and unchangeable. Sneezing is a reflex, but different people sneeze differently, and one person's sneezes may vary considerably. Ejaculations are similar. They can vary from blah to earth-shattering. Their quality depends on many factors: a man's fantasies, level of energy, state of relaxation, his feelings for the woman, the duration of loveplay, and where he comes—in her hand, mouth, vagina, or anus.

Many men are surprised to learn that orgasm and ejaculation are two distinct phenomena. The feelings of pleasure that comprise orgasm may or may not accompany ejaculation, and men need not ejaculate to feel orgasm. Some men experience "dry orgasm" from time to time, while others have "numb come" now and then. The differences between orgasm and ejaculation will be discussed in more detail in Chapter 5. As a man's familiarity with his own unique arousal pattern increases, so does his ability to "fine tune" his lovemaking and practice ejaculatory control.

MASTURBATION

Every man masturbates. There's an old gag that 97 percent admit it and the other three percent are liars. Self-ejaculation is natural, wholesome, and healthy. It is the best way to learn about the subtleties of your own sexual response cycle. It is also crucial to learning voluntary ejaculation.

Ironically, masturbation is often a factor in men's learning to ejaculate quickly and involuntarily. Many young men learn that the ability to ejaculate is a rite of passage from boyhood to manhood and they "beat off," trying their best to come in order to prove they are becoming men. Some participate in "circle jerks," group masturbation sessions, where the first person to ejaculate "wins." This can train men to ejaculate quickly. In addition, any guilt feelings that result from parental or religious injunctions against masturbation can produce enough stress to contribute to involuntary ejaculation.

Some men feel fine about masturbating until they become involved with a steady lover, at which point they might feel that masturbation equals unfaithfulness or becomes a sign that something is wrong with the relationship. After all, some men reason, if she truly satisfied me, I wouldn't have to masturbate. Not true. There is no reason why anyone should give up a long-standing pleasure simply because he hooks up with a steady lover. Masturbation is normal and healthy no matter what your love life might be. It's also a good way to deal with lovers' inevitable differences in desired frequency of lovemaking.

Self-touch is our original sensuality and self-ejaculation is our original sexuality. When learning voluntary ejaculation or any skill, you start with the fundamentals and keep working on them even after the skill has been mastered. After all, even professional athletes at the pinnacle of their profession never stop practicing the fundamentals of their sport. Reviewing the fundamentals of lovemaking is crucial to learning to last longer. It is usually easier to study your sexual response cycle by yourself during masturbation than when you are making love with another person. Most sex therapists recommend self-touch exercises and masturbation three to five times a week for about an hour per session. Continue to explore yourself until you feel intimately familiar with your own sexual responses.

Find a time and place where you can be alone and feel at ease. You might like to shower, meditate, engage in stretching exercises or some other form of relaxation beforehand. Then surround yourself with whatever turns you on: soft lighting, music, men's magazine pictorials—whatever you like.

Undress and begin to explore your body from head to toe. Every square inch deserves equal attention. As in massage, the neck, shoulders, back, hands, and feet are particularly receptive to self-touch. Don't forget about your face. Try not to rush through non-genital self-appreciation. It's not something to get over with. Full-body sensuality is vital to learning ejaculatory control.

Move on to masturbation slowly. Savor the sensations as you stroke your inner thighs, anal area, and scrotum. The scrotum is marvelously sensitive to touch. Scrotal self-touch can also help men appreciate how women experience genital touch. The scrotum develops from the same embryonic cells as the outer vaginal lips in women. Scrotal touch stimulates sensations in men similar to those women feel when the vaginal lips are caressed. (For more on this, see Chapter 6.)

When masturbating to develop ejaculatory control, sex therapists recommend working up to fifteen minutes of self-stroking without ejaculation. This does not mean that fifteen minutes is as long as a man should last, or that he should always last that long. It is an arbitrary length of time. However, a man who can last fifteen minutes can usually last as long as he would like.

As you masturbate, tune into the feelings in and around your penis. Pay particular attention to the sensations leading up to your point of no return. Try mixing slow and fast strokes, more and less pressure, scrotal, shaft, and head stimulation. The head of the penis is the most sensitive area in most men. However, the underside of the head and shaft, the corona, the little ridge at the base of the head, and the frenulum, the ring of indentation just below the corona, are also exquisitely sensitive to touch. Introduce yourself to the sensitive surfaces of your own penis.

When you feel yourself approaching the point of no return, stop stroking your very sensitive areas, but do not stop caressing yourself. Either hold the penis gently or massage other arousing, but less sensitive, parts of your body until the urge to ejaculate subsides.

The first few times, you might misjudge your point of no return and ejaculate before you want to. Don't get upset. This happens to many men as they learn ejaculatory control. Study your mistakes. Try to learn from them. Then wait until your resolution phase is complete and begin again.

Another possibly disconcerting thing might happen when you stop direct penile stroking near the point of no return. Your erection might subside along with the urge to come. This, too, is perfectly normal. Just relax, start stroking your penis again, fantasize and your erection should return. Keep in mind that getting upset about erection loss does not help matters any; it contributes to nonerection.

Start by stroking yourself with a dry hand until you can last fifteen minutes. Then use a lubricated hand until you can last fifteen minutes.

Remember your breathing. Breathe deeply, with your whole body, particularly as you approach the point of no return.

One noteworthy benefit of extended masturbation with deep breathing, fantasy, and sensual focus is that many men notice their orgasms becoming stronger and more enjoyable. Why? Because whole-body arousal results in whole-body orgasms.

After a few weeks of creative masturbation, you may well be able to hold yourself in the plateau phase as long as you like. Congratulations, you're on your way to lasting longer!

If you cannot do it, don't despair, just keep practicing and remember to breathe deeply. If after two months of steady practice, you still ejaculate involuntarily, you might consider individual sex therapy (see Appendix II).

LOVE MOANS AND FACIAL RELEASE

Silence might be golden in some situations, but lovemaking is not one of them. As mentioned earlier, deep breathing is a powerful tool for releasing tensions, and the addition of sound to exhalation introduces another dimension that helps many men last longer.

If you have the privacy and the inclination, try whooping it up! As you vocalize, feel the tension flow out of your body. Some men have difficulty making noise comfortably in bed. Some men like to see themselves as the "strong, silent type." Others would rather not appear too turned on. And, of course, there are times when the walls are thin, when unrestrained celebration is impossible. But given a cozy, private setting, try some love moans. You don't have to scream or groan as loud as the actors in Hollywood lovemaking scenes. Just add a little sound to your deep breathing and see if it helps you last longer.

In addition, try releasing your facial muscles from conscious control as well. Many men wear a "poker face" to bed to appear cool, detached, and in control of themselves. Unfortunately, the body can only control a few things at a time, and men who insist on maintaining a "stiff upper lip" in bed may sacrifice ejaculatory control or stiffness in the penis. See if facial release enhances your lovemaking and helps you last longer. Letting go of facial control can be easier than noise-making because many lovers make love in the dark with their eyes closed, so facial abandon is less public than vocal exuberance. Still, the poker-face habit can be difficult to change. One way to loosen facial muscles is to include some head and facial massage in introductory loveplay.

STOP-START

This technique has been used since ancient times to help men develop voluntary ejaculation. It was introduced into modern sex therapy in 1956 by Dr. James Seamans, then a urologist at Duke University Medical School, who reportedly learned it from a former prostitute turned surrogate-partner sex therapist.

Stop-start is simply an extension of masturbation with focused arousal.

After the penis enters the vagina—or other erotic opening—focus on your level of arousal. When you feel the point of no return approaching, stop moving until the urge to ejaculate subsides. Then start moving again and repeat.

Most men find that that the best way to stop in the vagina is to press in as far as they can. In any other opening, just locate a mutually comfortable spot and suspend pelvic movements. If you are alone, simply hold the erect penis gently as suggested in the masturbation section.

For best results in a couple, both lovers should stop moving. Some like to arrange a "stop" signal, either a verbal request or an unspoken signal, for example, a specific touch or squeeze. On the other hand, men who are trying to learn ejaculatory control on their own might feel uncomfortable involving a lover in the stop-start process. They might not feel enough trust for their lovers to ask for help with the stop-start technique. Do whatever feels most comfortable to you in a given situation. Some men say, "Rest time," or "Hold a moment." Others grasp the woman's hips tightly for a second. As a rule, openness avoids misunderstanding and unanticipated spills. Stopping without letting a lover know why the sudden suspension of movement can cause tensions and contribute to continued involuntary ejaculation.

When you stop, you need not remain absolutely still as long as you suspend movement in the pelvic area. Continue sensual touching of other sensitive parts of the body. Many women like the stop-start technique because of the alternation of sensual focus. Some women complain that as soon as men enter them, they stop touching the rest of their bodies. Stop-start depends on whole-body touch. Some lovemaking positions make whole-body sensuality more available than others, for example, woman-on-top.

WOMAN-ON-TOP

Woman-on-top is simple. The man lies on his back. The woman straddles him, kneeling over his hips, facing his head or feet. This position often results in dramatically improved ejaculatory control.

Why? Because it generates less tension than the traditional man-on-top, or missionary, position. The missionary position is hard work for men. The man must support his weight with his arms and legs to keep from crushing the woman under him. This generates muscle tension in the arms, shoulders, back, and legs. Thrusting during intercourse increases the man's tension level. The fact is, it's harder for most men to ejaculate voluntarily in the missionary position than in any other.

However, when the woman is on top, the man can stay more relaxed. He does not have to support his weight, so this position requires less work. The woman supports her weight by kneeling, which is relatively effortless. Many lovers enjoy the woman-on-top position because it allows the woman more freedom of movement. Many women dislike being pinned under a man during inter-course. Freer movement allows the woman to take a more active, initiating role in lovemaking, and some women say they feel enhanced pleasure in this position. Woman-on-top also leaves both lovers' hands free for whole-body sensual touching. Both lovers' faces, breasts, abdomens, hips, and legs are accessible. Some women like the man to place a hand or fist on his lower abdomen which allows direct clitoral stimulation during intercourse.

The woman-on-top position was a favorite of both the ancient Romans and Chinese because it fatigued the men less than most positions and increased ejaculatory control. It was also popular among Hawaiians, Polynesians, and Africans before missionaries recruited them into Christianity and told them they would go to hell if they made love using any position other than man-on-top.

Unfortunately, until quite recently, many men accepted the idea that it was somehow unmanly for the woman to be on top. Happily, this belief exerts much less influence over men's lovestyles than it did a generation ago. A recent *Playboy* * survey, for example, showed that a substantial proportion of men feel fine about being underneath, and that many men prefer it for the same reasons it was so popular with the ancients.

SIDEWAYS

Here is another position that aids ejaculatory control and provides enhanced stimulation for the woman without fatiguing the man.

* November 1978.

Lying on your sides and either facing each other or "spooning" (the woman's back to the man's front), the woman either holds the man's penis inside her with legs closed—some men enjoy feeling the scrotum between the woman's legs—or she separates her legs and allows them to intertwine with the man's. The couple is then free to hold their upper bodies together or to separate them while holding their pelvises together.

This position, like woman-on-top, leaves the hands free and allows easy access to both lovers' nongenital arousable areas. Also, some men like to brace themselves with one leg and press in deeply.

CIRCULAR OR SIDE-TO-SIDE ROCK 'N' ROLL

The most sensitive, nerve-rich part of the penis is the head. When the penis is pumped in and out of the vagina, the head receives a great deal of stimulation quickly, which distracts some men from focused arousal and may disrupt extension of the plateau phase. In addition, "the old in-out" is not necessarily as pleasurable for women as it is for men. There are some nerve endings for touch in the outer third of the vagina and most women enjoy the sensual closeness of intercourse, but women's sexual feelings are concentrated in the clitoris, outside the vagina and above it. A penis pumping away in the vagina stimulates the clitoris only indirectly by pulling a bit on the inner vaginal lips, but it provides no direct clitoral stimulation.

In addition to sliding the penis in and out of the vagina, try pressing in as far as possible, then using a circular or side-to-side rocking motion. Many men last longer this way because the head of the penis receives less intense stimulation, which aids focused arousal. Many women also enjoy this move because the man's lower abdomen can provide more direct stimulation to the clitoris.

MUSCLE RELAXATION TECHNIQUES

Ejaculation happens when several muscle groups contract in the pelvic and anal areas. Muscles tend to contract more readily when other muscles are tensed in the same general area. Thus, some men's ejaculations can be triggered by muscle tensions in the buttocks or pelvic area.

Some men find they can maintain greater voluntary control if they consciously keep their buttock, anal, and stomach muscles relaxed throughout loveplay. When these muscles tense up, ejaculation may follow quickly in some men.

The woman-on-top position helps maintain pelvic muscle relaxation because the man does not have to support his weight. However, when the man is on top, relaxation of these muscles can also enhance ejaculatory control.

One way to feel your pelvic and anal muscles relax is to attempt to exhale while holding your breath.

Another form of muscle relaxation occurs when a muscle is tensed for a moment, and then relaxed. A demonstration: Make a tight fist for a moment, then unclench it and feel the wave of relaxation spread over your hand. Some men find it helpful to tense the buttock muscles momentarily, then relax them, rather than attempting consciously to keep them relaxed all the time.

Experiment. See what works best for you. Try some muscle relaxation in combination with deep breathing.

KEGEL EXERCISES

Voluntary ejaculation depends not only on pelvic muscle relaxation, but on pelvic muscle *tone*. For thousands of years, yoga masters have known that good muscle tone in the pelvic area improves ejaculatory control and enhances orgasm. Their teachings were introduced into Western medicine in 1952 when Dr. Arnold Kegel (KAY-gill) suggested this exercise to women with certain pelvic muscle problems. The Kegel exercises strengthen the muscle that runs between the legs of both men and women, the pubococcygeus (PEW-boh-cox-ee-GEE-us), or "PC" for short. The PC is the muscle you flex to interrupt urine flow or squeeze out those last few drops. It is also one of several muscles that contract during orgasm in both sexes. As PC muscle tone improves, most people notice more pleasurable orgasm and most men report improved ejaculatory control.

To exercise the PC, flex it for a count of three, then relax it for a count of three and repeat. Alternate with sets of quick flexing and relaxing.

Some men find that flexing the PC during loveplay before the point of no return helps them last longer. See if this works for you.

One beauty of the Kegel exercises is that they can be practiced anywhere—while watching TV, driving, or sitting at a desk.

Do not overdo Kegels at first. Overworking any muscle not used to being exercised can cause soreness, but as the PC grows stronger, any soreness should disappear.

Lovers' Programs for Lasting Longer

The couples' techniques for developing a man's ejaculatory control are direct outgrowths of the do-it-yourself methods. They may be used in combination with the previously described approaches depending on a couple's tastes in lovemaking. Before you begin any of the cooperative programs, however, take some time to discuss this question: Is voluntary ejaculation something you *both really want*? To many men, this question might sound ridiculous. They insist: Of course we both want me to last longer. Coming too soon has been a problem in our relationship for years and lasting longer would fix up everything. When this is the case—and it often is—both lovers are eager for the man to develop voluntary ejaculation, and the couples' programs usually proceed smoothly. But for other couples, voluntary ejaculation might raise as many problems as it solves.

Some men become flabbergasted if their lovers either are not interested in their learning to last longer, or if they say they are, then act as though they resent the programs. If a woman is not as enthusiastic as her lover would like her to be, many men become bewildered or infuriated: How in God's name could she possibly *not* want me to ejaculate voluntarily? As inconceivable as this may sound to a man who comes too soon, from a woman's point of view, such hesitation might feel completely justified.

A sexual relationship is a profound connection between two people. Any change in one lover's sexual abilities or feelings automatically affects the other and the relationship, often in unexpected ways. An illustration: Imagine two lovers who have similar jobs in the same field—he's a nightclub musician and she's a cabaret singer. They support one another emotionally and wish each other every success. Then, suddenly, she becomes an overnight sensation. She cuts a hit record and jumps from bars to concert halls. Meanwhile, he continues to scrape along playing bars. How would the musician feel about his lover's success? Probably ambivalent. It's great when someone close to you achieves a major success, but it would be natural for our musician to feel jealous, left out, or afraid she might drop him for a glamourous pop star. Reactions like these are normal, even if we do not admire them in ourselves.

To return to a couple faced with involuntary ejaculation, the woman might think: If I help him last longer, his self-confidence might increase to the point where he no longer needs me or wants me. He might become unfaithful to me or leave me.

In some relationships, a pattern of martyrdom may have developed where he comes too soon and she sacrifices her pleasure "for him." Her sacrifice might be genuine, or it might meet emotional needs for her that his lasting longer might upset. Some couples develop a kind of "inadequacy bond" where, for example, he might come too soon and she might not come at all with him. If his problem clears up, she may feel the relationship has fallen out of "balance." The point is, *there's more to mutually fulfilling relationships than simply lasting longer.*

A man whose lover is hesitant to help him learn voluntary ejaculation should ask himself: How *would* lasting longer affect me and the relationship? Would it throw us off balance? Would my eye rove? Would I feel tempted to leave her? If the answer to any of these questions is yes—or even maybe—your lover's possible reluctance to participate in a couples' program might simply reflect her desire to preserve the relationship. Try to talk about your emotions around these issues even though the discussion may feel painful. If the answers to all these questions are no, a man might offer to make a trade: If she helps you learn to last longer, you'll help her do something she's wanted to do. In any event, try to reassure the woman that lasting longer will help the relationship, not threaten it.

If a woman remains adamantly opposed to helping a man learn to last longer, he might try some of the do-it-yourself suggestions. But a woman opposed to the idea might interfere with them, consciously or unconsciously. Resentments might easily develop, and hostility toward a lover never helped any man last longer. Quite the contrary, resentments can aggravate involuntary ejaculation. If a woman is unwilling to participate in the programs outlined here, the couple might consider relationship counseling instead of, or in conjunction with, sex therapy.

Other reasonable objections a woman might raise to her lover learning to last longer include:

—Disagreement that he comes too soon. Some women don't care if their lovers come quickly as long as they provide generous clitoral stimulation afterward so they can have orgasms.

—Some women do not particularly enjoy making love and see no reason why it should last all night.

—It might hurt her. Vaginal lubrication can decrease during extended intercourse and cause soreness. Individual women produce different amounts of lubricating fluid, and some become sore more quickly than others. Massage lotions or KY jelly might help resolve this problem.

—Objections to the program's structure. Some women prefer spontaneous, unfettered sex to "cookbook" lovemaking, even for the brief duration of the last-longer programs.

—Fears of being blamed if the program does not work out perfectly. This might happen in relationships where the man blames his lover for his sex problem(s).

—Feeling coerced. No one likes to feel forced into anything, especially in bed. In relationships where the woman feels stifled by the man's insistence on playing leader, she might see a couples' program as simply one more thing he is foisting on her.

—Feeling used. The couples' programs tend to focus on the man and his feelings. A woman might ask—rightfully—what's in it for me?

None of these problems is necessarily serious or insurmountable, though they might prove to be in some relationships. For lovemaking to feel mutually fulfilling, the decisions affecting it should be mutual decisions. Some issues raised above may pose no problem in your relationship, but try discussing them, even if they are ultimately dismissed. Every change in a loving relationship requires adjustment, negotiation and trying to see the other person's point of view.

All the couples' programs begin with introductory sessions of nonpressured sensuality: touching, sensual focusing, bathing, deep breathing, massage—anything that helps you both relax and feel in touch with one another. Don't rush it. Take some time to slow down, to talk about the ups and downs in your lives. Take turns giving and receiving sensual pleasure by guiding each other's hands and mouths over your bodies. Some couples like to share their sexual histories; others feel it is an invasion of privacy. Some enjoy undressing one another or dressing up in sexy clothes. Try inventing some games you and your lover both enjoy.

STOP-START

The stop-start technique is discussed on page 86. The key for couples is to agree on a stop signal that is easy to give and receive. Stop-start lends itself to combination with many of the do-it-yourself approaches: deep breathing, focused arousal, noise-making, woman-on-top, side-to-side rock 'n' roll, and muscle relaxation.

THE EIGHT-STEP METHOD

This is an extension of the masturbation approach discussed on page 86. At each step, allow several sessions. Do not rush from one step to the next—this cannot be stressed enough. Sex therapists recommend at least four sessions per step, with each step extending over a week or two.

After initial sensual explorations, the steps include:

1. The man masturbates with a dry hand until he can last fifteen minutes. He also focuses on his arousal process.

2. He masturbates with a lubricated hand until he can last fifteen minutes.

3. The woman strokes his penis with a dry hand until he can last fifteen minutes. The lovers should also feel free to engage in nongenital sensual touching so that neither one, particularly the woman, feels bored during steps three through eight.

4. She uses a lubricated hand or her mouth until he can last fifteen minutes.

5. The man lies on his back and breathes deeply. She slides his penis into her lubricated vagina or mouth and remains still, simply holding the penis inside her. He moves just enough to maintain his erection for fifteen minutes.

6. Begin as in #5 above, only this time, he remains still and she moves just enough to maintain his erection for fifteen minutes.

7. Begin as in #5 above; he moves more energetically while she stays relatively still until he can last for fifteen minutes.

8. Begin as in #5 above, but both move as they please until he can last fifteen minutes or as long as they like.

Some couples practice all eight steps. Others prefer a more ab-
breviated program. Discover what works best for you. But remember, allow plenty of time to work on the steps you decide to
practice. If one step becomes a stumbling block, increase nongenital loveplay, drop back a step for a while and try not to turn the
practice sessions into demanding experiences.

THE SQUEEZE TECHNIQUE

This is the best-known technique for learning voluntary ejaculation. It is based on stop-start, but a squeeze of the penis replaces
the stops. Dr. William Masters and Ms. Virginia Johnson popularized this technique in the late 1960s, but a similar approach was
used to delay ejaculation in China 1,400 years ago.

After introductory sensuality, the man lies on his back and
breathes deeply. The woman kneels or sits between his legs, or to
one side of him, and slowly massages his body, eventually arriving
at the penis.

During penile stroking, the man signals his lover as he nears his
point of no return. She squeezes his penis as shown in the diagram
on page 96, clasping the frenulum, the area just behind the head,
between her thumb and forefinger. Some couples use one hand,
others prefer two. Some like a gentle squeeze for ten seconds; others prefer a short firm squeeze for five. Some simply squeeze until
the man's erection begins to subside. As the woman squeezes, her
lover's urge to ejaculate should subside.

Once he feels some distance from his point of no return, the
woman stops squeezing and returns to sensual touching. She may
also initiate the squeeze at random.

Most erections get pretty hard, so a good firm squeeze should not
hurt them. If a squeeze does hurt, let your lover know. Help her
adjust her fingers and pressure by telling her specifically what feels
best.

Repeat this process for several squeezes per session and try to
arrange several sessions a week for two or three weeks.

Then begin as before, but after the squeeze, the woman inserts
her lover's semierect penis into her vagina or mouth. She remains
still at first and allows the erection to grow inside her. Then she
starts moving, slowly at first, exploring her lover's ejaculatory control. At his signal, or at random, she withdraws his penis and

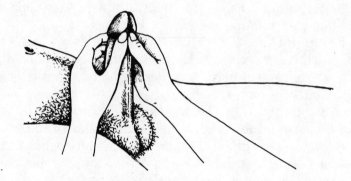

The squeeze may be done with one hand or two.

squeezes. She may squeeze with her hand or she might prefer the Chinese approach of pressing the penis against her pubic area. Masters and Johnson recommend three squeezes per session and four or five sessions a week for a week or two. Do what feels right for you.

Although the squeeze technique is more widely known than other methods for developing ejaculatory control, its popularity among sex therapists has declined in recent years. For many lovers, the squeeze feels more complicated, more difficult, than the stop-start or eight-step methods. Experiment. Use the method that feels best for you.

Ejaculation While Learning to Last Longer

Many sex therapists discourage or forbid couples having orgasms during sessions devoted to developing a man's ejaculatory control. They say preoccupation with orgasm is one reason involuntary ejaculation becomes a habit in the first place. All the techniques for learning voluntary ejaculation emphasize whole-body sensuality where orgasm is not viewed as the one-and-only goal of lovemaking. To return to the banquet metaphor, men who ejaculate involuntarily tend to rush through the feast—often skipping some courses altogether—to get to the dessert. When lovers are learning voluntary control, most sex therapists encourage them to forgo the dessert for a time to learn to savor the rest of the banquet.

Whole-body sensuality *should* be stressed in lovemaking, particularly when learning voluntary ejaculation. Lovers, however, may feel free to come during practice sessions as long as neither pressures the other to "deliver" an orgasm.

A pleasant way to mix practice sessions and lovemaking that includes orgasm is to separate the two to some extent. You might practice a while, then get up and bathe or have a light snack, then make love. Although the focus of voluntary ejaculation training is on the man's sexual response, the woman's needs should not be ignored. An appreciation of the woman's needs is not only integral to problem-free lovemaking, but any resentment on her part about feeling used might interfere with the man's learning process. Lovers should discuss one another's needs and sexual tastes, and adjust their practice sessions accordingly, as long as neither feels pressured to "perform" or to bestow sexual fulfillment on the other on an erotic silver platter.

Other Ways to Last Longer

The following approaches might help some men last longer, but none helps develop voluntary control of ejaculation. They all rely on outside intervention. Men who use these routines, anesthetics, or drugs may become dependent on them for "staying power." This is unnecessary because the key to voluntary ejaculation is to become less dependent on "other things" and more in touch with yourself.

MASTURBATING BEFOREHAND

Men who are able to ejaculate more than once during an evening's lovemaking often notice that they come quickly the first time around, but are able to last longer subsequently. As a result, some men masturbate before joining their lovers in order to last longer with them.

This technique is available primarily to young men, those in their teens and twenties. Review the sexual response cycle on page 81. As a man grows older, his resolution phase grows longer. A small proportion of men can raise second or third erections into middle age, but for the vast majority this ability diminishes as they grow older. In addition, many young men find it difficult, if not impossible, to ejaculate more than once per lovemaking session. Even for those who can ejaculate several times in a few hours, it can at times be inconvenient to masturbate beforehand.

Masturbation is a valuable tool for learning how to last longer, but it is of questionable value as a substitute for voluntary control.

STAY CREAMS AND SPRAYS

These products are sold by the makers of anesthetic antisunburn preparations. The rationale is that rapid ejaculation results from a penis that is too sensitive to the touch. These products numb the head of the penis and reduce its sensitivity, which allegedly delays ejaculation.

There are several drawbacks to using these products. A man with an anesthetized penis robs himself of some pleasure in lovemaking he deserves to enjoy. Some men are allergic to these products and may develop a rash. Men who develop irritations from sunburn preparations should steer clear of stay creams. The stay cream must be applied at least a few minutes before insertion to allow it to take effect. It cannot be applied too long before insertion, however, or its effects may begin to wear off. These time calculations do not promote relaxation; instead, they tend to increase tensions and may contribute to involuntary ejaculation instead of helping a man last longer. Also, any cream not absorbed into the head of the penis might come into contact with the clitoris or outer vaginal lips and numb them. Many women object to the taste of these products and oral ingestion is not recommended, so oral sex must be enjoyed before application.

Finally, stay products are expensive. A half-ounce tube of De-tane® ointment retails for about $3.00 and Stud 100 World Famous Delay Spray costs $6.00 for a half-ounce can. Why spend this kind of money to numb yourself when you can learn to last as long as you'd like for free without sacrificing any feeling?

WEARING A CONDOM, OR SEVERAL

Some men believe that wearing a condom decreases penile sensitivity and reason that one or more rubbers might delay ejaculation. This opinion is open to question. Although many Americans believe that condoms decrease sensitivity, other cultures do not share this view. In Japan, where the Pill and IUD are illegal, 70 percent of Japanese lovers use rubbers, and available information suggests that Japanese men have not complained much about sensitivity loss. Erotic toys have been part of the Japanese lovestyle for centuries, and some Japanese men reportedly feel that condoms *enhance* the pleasure of lovemaking. "French ticklers" are another example of penis covers used to enhance lovemaking.

On the other hand, making love is as much fun as you *think* it is, and many American men have long been persuaded that rubbers are a drag. While they are generally reliable as contraceptives (see Chapter 10), why sacrifice any pleasure, whether real or imagined, in the name of lasting longer? You can learn voluntary ejaculation without relying on condoms.

ALCOHOL

Some lovers enjoy a few drinks before lovemaking to reduce inhibitions and aid relaxation. Some men believe that alcohol helps them last longer. Alcohol is a central nervous system depressant that slows the reflexes. Both ejaculation and erection are reflexes, and while some men report delayed ejaculation as a result of alcohol, *many more* experience erection problems in association with drinking. In addition, alcoholism is one of our most serious national health problems and dependence on this drug for any reason should be discouraged.

MARIJUANA

Considerable controversy surrounds the question of marijuana as an aid to lasting longer. Every sexual claim imaginable has been made for pot: that it helps men last longer, that it hastens ejaculation, and that it has no effect on ejaculatory timing. Some consider it an aphrodisiac; others do not. Whatever its effects, marijuana is not a central nervous system depressant and its use is not associated with episodes of nonerection.

COCAINE

Cocaine is used medically as a topical (skin surface) anesthetic. Rubbed on the head of the penis, it acts as a stay cream. Cocaine shares all the drawbacks of other stay products, but it is astronomically more expensive and, if your lover turns out to be a federal agent, you could wind up practicing masturbation techniques in prison. Detane costs about 20 cents per gram; cocaine costs around $100 per gram, or 500 times as much. Quality is difficult to gauge.

When ingested nasally, cocaine's psychoactive properties stimulate feelings of euphoria, energy, power, and enhanced body awareness. Sigmund Freud, an early cocaine researcher, considered it an aphrodisiac. Some men say a cocaine high helps them last longer. Others say they get so excited on cocaine that it hastens ejaculation. Still others report no effect on ejaculatory control.

Chapter 4

HOW TO DEAL WITH ERECTION PROBLEMS

For many men, "impotence" is the most threatening word in the English language. Unlike traditional swear words that have lost some power to shock as a result of overuse in everyday speech, impotence has lost none of its emotional impact. In friendly bantering, men might call each other "fuckers," but if someone calls a buddy impotent, even as a joke, a real insult may be perceived. Impotence is never a laughing matter for the man who experiences it.

Why? Because for most men, impotence implies considerably more than simply an inability to raise an erection. A man who is impotent often sees himself—and expects to be seen—as a failure as a man. Impotence is experienced as the negation of everything considered traditionally masculine, not only the ability to "perform" sexually, to get it up on command, but the ability to be assertive, to lead and compete, to be—or at least pretend to be—in control. In our culture, where men are taught they must always be self-assured, impotence can shatter a man's confidence and self-respect. It can destroy a sexual relationship, leaving both lovers confused and feeling guilty. The concept of masculine potency, both in and out of bed, is so basic to our way of thinking that it is embedded in our very language: A man "rises to the occasion"; he never "goes soft."

For all the emotion the word impotence can arouse, it is surprising how poorly defined the term is among those who encounter the condition professionally. For example, the latest edition of a respected urology text, *General Urology* (Lange, 1978), defines impotence as: "An inability to gain or maintain erection, premature ejaculation, lack of emission with orgasm, loss of libido, or absence of normal sensation with ejaculation." According to this definition, *every* typical sex problem in men is a form of impotence.

Sex therapists limit their definition of impotence, or "erective dysfunction," to erection problems, which they classify in two, sometimes three, categories. "Primary impotence" describes the man who has never had an erection. "Secondary impotence" means he once had erections but now has none. Then there is "new impotence," nonerection in men who purportedly cannot deal with assertive women.

"Impotence" is a destructive word. The far-reaching emotional reactions it triggers in many men often interfere with the resolution of the immediate problem, a difficulty obtaining or maintaining erection. "Erective dysfunction" is no better. It adds pomposity without increasing clarity. To many men, a "dysfunction" sounds considerably more serious than a "problem." Overly clinical labels suggest diseases. They do not promote the relaxation necessary to rediscover lost or faltering erection. Some erection problems may be complex enough to deserve clinically specialized labels, but most are not.

The intention here is to bring sex therapy closer to the level of first aid, where it usually belongs. This book uses simple terms: "nonerection," and "erection problem" or "difficulty." Simple terms imply straightforward solutions. One of the problems in counseling men with nonerection is that they often believe their "failure" is too frightening to deal with at all. Some men become paralyzed by an erection problem or blame it on their lovers.

The value of sex therapists' nonerection classification system is also open to question. Classification should elucidate. In this case, it often adds to men's confusion. I have counseled men who wondered whether their "secondary impotence" meant that their nonerection was somehow subordinate to other more fundamental psychological problems.

The so-called "new impotence" is particularly misleading. To many people, "new impotence" implies that men with this condition harbor deep-seated hostilities toward assertive women and subconsciously oppose women's progress toward equality. However, I have counseled many men with erection problems who *preferred* self-assured, professionally competent women as both friends and lovers. Their erection problems uniformly triggered anxiety that women would accuse them of subconscious hostility to female equality. The stress caused by the supposed implications of their "new impotence" often cemented a pattern of nonerection that actually had little to do with any inability to deal with strong women.

All erection problems should be investigated the same way: first, by a thorough examination of possible physical causes, and if these are ruled out, by a close look at the man's feelings about himself, his life, his lover(s), and his lovemaking.

The Causation Controversy: Mind Versus Body?

One article of faith among doctors, psychologists, and sex therapists is that the vast majority of erection problems are psychological in origin, not physical. *General Urology*, quoted earlier, asserts: "With few exceptions, the causes of sexual difficulties in the male are psychic." And most books that discuss men's sex problems only mention in passing that now and then an erection problem might be related to a physical condition. Most sexuality authorities use this rule of thumb: 10 percent of erection problems are physical; 90 percent are psychological.

There are two questionable assumptions implicit in this allocation of percentages. First, the either/or approach separates the physical and emotional components of lovemaking when, in fact, they are inseparable and exquisitely interdependent. Second, the 10/90 estimate appears to be based on traditional assumptions not supported by comprehensive research. It implies that the physical and emotional proportions of erection problems are constant and unchanging. In fact, considerable evidence indicates that physical —particularly environmental—factors play an increasing role in these problems. Today men are developing the stress-related illnesses associated with nonerection at younger ages: high blood pressure, ulcers, colitis, heart disease. In addition, an increasing number of drugs have been linked to erection impairment. Finally, men's unprecedented exposure to toxic pollutants, particularly where they work, appears to contribute to an increasing proportion of erection difficulties.

Traditional deemphasis of the potential organic components of nonerection is matched by a tradition of questionable explanations of the condition's emotional causes. Inaccurate, incomplete information frequently compounds the nonerective man's self-doubts and frustrations, contributing to the feelings of helplessness and hopelessness that make so many erection problems seem permanent.

Medical texts continue to cling to antiquated notions about the emotional causes of nonerection. *General Urology* explains: "Most men . . . are certain that the masturbation in which they indulged during adolescence or the gonorrhea they contracted later damaged their sexual organs." In fact, few men nowadays believe that masturbation or VD have much to do with their erection problems, and it's a rare man who stops masturbating after his adolescence. The text then observes that "frigidity of the sexual partner" can also cause erection problems. The blame-the-woman philosophy is never productive. A woman's approach to lovemaking might contribute to a man's nonerection, but sex problems are rarely a lover's "fault." Blaming the woman increases both lovers' tension levels and may preclude the trust and willingness to negotiate so crucial to problem-free lovemaking and to the resolution of erection problems.

Psychoanalytic theory provides the other traditional—and questionable—explanation of the emotional causes of erection problems. Briefly, the theory postulates that nonerection is caused by repressed Oedipal conflicts. This theory asserts that young boys, aged three to five, want to make love with their mothers and kill any rivals for maternal affection, chief among whom are their fathers. But superimposed on these desires is the fear that the fathers are aware of their sons' incestuous, murderous wishes and might punish them by eliminating the ability to have intercourse, i.e., by castration. Over time, prepubescent boys repress both their incestuous fantasies and their fears of castration as they grow to identify with their fathers and reject their mothers as potential lovers. At puberty, the conflict resurfaces, camouflaged as adolescent rebellion. Men who are unsuccessful in repressing the wish to seduce their mothers become nonerective, psychoanalysts say, as a neurotic defense against the ability to have intercourse. To avoid forbidden sexual attractions to their mothers, neurotically impotent men deny themselves erections.

This viewpoint, circa 1905, is open to serious question. It ignores the many organic factors that can contribute to nonerection. It labels nonerective men "neurotic," which often adds to the anxieties that cause many men's erection problems. It locates the cause of the problem in the distant past and ignores the man's immediate sexual situation, usually of considerable importance to the problem. Finally, psychoanalysis as a form of therapy has a comparatively poor track record when compared with other solutions to erection problems. Information about sex therapy success rates is sketchy, but according to Dr. Helen Singer Kaplan, whose book, *The New Sex Therapy*, is considered the definitive text in the field, psychoanalytic treatment resolves about half of erection problems. Dr. Kaplan writes that it is not clear whether the analysis *itself* resolves the problem or whether the man's stress situation changes during the years the analysis process takes. Short-term sex therapy, on the other hand, has a success rate of 80-85 percent, according to Dr. Kaplan.

Physical Factors

This section summarizes for the nonbiologist potential physical components of erection problems. It is important that men understand these factors, for too many doctors dismiss erection complaints with a quick psychiatric referral, without performing an adequate examination. The discussion here may seem detailed. Actually, it's schematic. It concentrates on the more prevalent organic causes of nonerection and omits the array of rare diseases that might also contribute to them.

One important note: Very few of the physical conditions discussed here cause nonerection absolutely. Having a health problem listed here, or taking some of the drugs by no means condemns you to nonerection—far from it. Individual differences are vast, particularly in the area of sexuality. For example, about half of men with diabetes develop erection problems. This means that half do not. Unfortunately, doctors have been known to tell diabetic men that their illness will make them nonerective. The news is traumatic enough to cause many a penis to call it quits then and there. If you have an erection problem, take note of the physical factors that may apply to you. If you do not have an erection problem, feel free to skip ahead.

This discussion ends with some tips on how to visit a doctor for an erection problem: how to decide if your situation warrants a medical examination, and if so, what to take with you, what information to provide, what tests might be necessary, and why.

General Illnesses

Do not expect your penis to stand up if you cannot. Any illness, from flu to cancer, can decrease interest in lovemaking and indirectly impair erection. Decreased sexual interest is the body's way of investing its energy in the immediate task of restoring its health.

Illnesses, particularly chronic illnesses, raise doubts in many men's minds about their masculinity. Men learn that a "real man" can stand up to punishment. A man who contracts a chronic illness may believe that because he couldn't "take it," he is something less than a true man. It's normal to wonder whether an illness might affect one's sexuality. Convalescent men are often eager to test their penises as soon as they begin to feel well again. Frequently, however, they are still not well enough to enjoy problem-free lovemaking. They might have doubts about their sexual prowess to begin with, and if their penises do not jump to attention on their first few tries, they may conclude that their illness has ruined them sexually.

Try not to make unrealistic demands of your penis during a convalescence. Massage and other forms of sensual touch can feel like ends in themselves during a recovery if you let them. Try to refrain from pushing your penis to become erect before you feel fully recovered.

Nonerection might be a symptom of illness. This is especially true in the case of diabetes.

Diabetes is the illness most frequently associated with nonerection. As mentioned earlier, about half of diabetic men suffer erection problems. Diabetes is an inability to synthesize insulin, a protein necessary for the digestion of sugar. It tends to run in families, but is not strictly hereditary. Early symptoms include: thirst, weight loss, frequent urination, and sugar in the urine. Nerve damage may result, and this is thought to be the reason some diabetics develop erection difficulties.

High blood pressure, or hypertension, is another illness, increasingly common, associated with nonerection. It is related to diet, smoking, stress, and family history. Some men believe that because erections depend on increased blood pressure in the penis, the higher their overall blood pressure, the harder their erections. Not true. High blood pressure is a serious health problem, frequently a precursor of stroke and heart attack.

Kidney dialysis, the mechanical purification of blood in people whose kidneys do not work, may cause erection problems. This is thought to result from depletion of the body's zinc content during dialysis. Zinc, an essential trace mineral like iron, is necessary for proper functioning of men's reproductive systems. (See "Prostate Self-Care and 'Vitamin Z' " in Chapter 13.)

Atherosclerosis, the buildup of fatty plaque deposits on artery walls, may also impair erection. In addition to raising blood pressure, the decreased blood volume in plaque-clogged arteries may interfere with the penis's blood supply during erection.

Sickle-cell anemia, a hereditary disease that usually affects black people, results in collapsed, crescent-shaped red blood cells that may clump together and clog blood vessels. Sickle-cell clumps may block blood flow into the penis or cause priapism, painful permanent erection unassociated with sexual arousal and often followed by nonerection.

Heart disease need *not* affect a man's sex life or erective ability. Until recently, doctors often told men with heart disease that lovemaking placed a dangerous strain on the heart. Not surprisingly, many men with heart disease feared for their lives and often developed erection problems. Now doctors understand that lovemaking does not unduly strain the heart and that, in most cases, men with heart disease can make love without problems. (See the excellent book, *Sound Sex and the Aging Heart*, listed in the Bibliography.)

CONGENITAL FACTORS

A man might be born with any of several physical irregularities that might contribute to nonerection. A man who believes that his genitals look abnormal might suffer enough anxiety or depression to cause an erection problem. But it is important to remember the discussion of penis size in Chapter 1; the possibility that any man has "juvenile genitals" is extremely remote.

Other congenital factors might include: hyposadias, in which the urethra opens on the underside of the penis, not dead center on the head; epispadias, in which the urethra opens on top of the penis; cysts of the genital or urinary systems; and chordee, painful erections that bend off to one side.

The hormone DES (diethylstilbestrol) was taken by millions of pregnant women in the late 1940s and 1950s. Sons exposed to DES before birth have abnormally high rates of several genitourinary problems, and may run an increased risk of testicular cancer. Men born during the time when DES was widely prescribed should try to find out if they are DES sons, and if so, they should mention it to any doctor who examines them.

GENITAL DISEASES

Few genital health problems cause nonerection directly. Most cause pain, soreness, or tenderness that may make erection or lovemaking feel uncomfortable or downright excruciating. An erection problem might develop as an indirect result of genital pain.

Advanced gonorrhea can cause painful inflammation of the prostate gland, testicles, or epididymides, the sperm storage tubes adjacent to the testicles. (See the discussions of nonspecific urethritis and gonorrhea in Chapter 12.)

Priapism, a rare disorder of unknown origin involving painful erection unconnected with sexual arousal, is associated with sickle-cell anemia, leukemia, and other cancers, and "Spanish fly," the supposed aphrodisiac discussed in the Drugs section of this chapter, page 112. Erection problems are common after priapism.

Peyronie's disease, also rare, usually affects middle-aged men. It involves fibrous tissue growth in the penis that reduces elasticity and impairs erection. Any of the following painful inflammations might impair erection: inflammation of the prostate gland, epididymis, or the head of the penis. About one-third of men who receive radiation treatments for prostate or genital-area cancers develop erection problems because of damage to the spinal nerves involved in erection.

Central Nervous System Disorders

An erection problem might be an early symptom of a nervous system disorder. The process of erection is controlled by three nerves in the lower spine. Injury to these nerves can destroy the capacity for erection. Other spinal injuries can also result in nonerection, for example, those associated with paraplegia. Advanced syphilis and multiple sclerosis can attack the spine and damage the nerves involved in erection.

Hormone Imbalances

An erection problem might signal an endocrine system disorder. Hormones released into the blood by any of several glands are crucial to normal sexuality and general well-being. Endocrine problems are rare but worth mentioning, for some men believe—usually incorrectly—that a few shots of testosterone, a male sex hormone, will "cure" an erection problem (see page 129).

A shortage of any of the pituitary hormones can cause general sex problems, including nonerection. The pituitary, called the "master gland," exerts significant control over sexuality.

Each of us has both male *and* female sex hormones in his body. Any change in the delicate balance of these hormones can contribute to an erection problem. Too little testosterone, a condition called hypogonadism, or too much female sex hormone, known as Cushing's syndrome, can cause a decline in men's secondary sex characteristics—facial hair, voice depth, etc.—and may also interfere with erection.

Female sex hormones, among them DES, are sometimes prescribed for prostate cancer and may affect erection. Male sex hormones, known as anabolic steroids, are often given to football players to stimulate weight gain. They depress the body's own hormone production and can change the hormone balance. Some football players report breast enlargement and erection impairment while taking anabolic steroids.

Surgery

The removal of the prostate gland, total prostatectomy, usually performed to arrest the spread of prostate cancer, leaves most—but not all—men nonerective because of damage to the lower spinal nerves. Doctors estimate that 90–95 percent of men become nonerective after this operation.

Transurethral resection (TUR) is another prostate operation performed to alleviate problems associated with noncancerous enlargement of the prostate, called benign prostatic hypertrophy. Reportedly, 10–15 percent of men experience erection problems after this operation. (See the discussion of the prostate gland in Chapter 13.) Rectal or lower colon surgery might also damage the nerves involved in erection.

Vasectomy, the male sterilization operation, has no effect on erection. Many men report improved lovemaking after vasectomy because stresses resulting from contraceptive hassles and the fear of unwanted pregnancy have been eliminated. (See the discussion of vasectomy in Chapter 11.)

TRAUMA

Injury of the penis might impair erection. An automobile accident or serious fall could cause internal damage or impair spinal nerve function.

AGING

The belief that men past middle age lose their erective capacity as a normal part of growing older is both widespread and false. Older men generally need more direct penile stimulation over a longer time to produce an erection, but erective capacity remains throughout a man's life. Some older men expect their penises to behave as they did fifty years earlier. If older men have unrealistic expectations of their penises which are not met, the experience of failure may lead to erection problems. Older men should make a point of extending whole-body sensuality during loveplay. The older the man, the greater the need for extensive sensual touching prior to erection.

ENVIRONMENTAL FACTORS

Cigarette advertising associates smoking with virility. However, a growing body of research suggests the opposite, a correlation between smoking and nonerection, lower sperm counts, and depressed testosterone levels. Smoking also interferes with the subtle flavors and aromas of lovemaking, prompting one sexuality authority to remark: Kissing a smoker is like licking an ashtray. People who quit smoking report improved health, increased energy, and greater sensory acuity, all of which contribute to problem-free lovemaking.

Exposure to lead and other toxic heavy metals over time can cause depression and nerve disorders that can contribute to nonerection and many other health problems.

Processed foods tend to be deficient in zinc, the trace mineral increasingly recognized to play a significant role in men's genital health. (See the discussion of zinc in Chapter 13.)

Several pesticides and an increasing number of industrial chemicals have been linked to sterility in men. Some research suggests that long-term exposure to certain pesticides is a cause of erection problems among farm workers. Wash all fruits and vegetables carefully, preferably with soap. Try to avoid exposure to pesticides.

DES was added to an estimated 80 percent of U.S. animal feeds from the 1950s until mid-1979 to fatten livestock. DES residues have been found in meat and poultry samples. The possibility exists that DES residues may accumulate in humans who consume a great deal of meat and may alter their hormone balances.

A recent U.S. government report showed that during 1974–76, 14 percent of meat and poultry sold to consumers contained residues of toxic chemicals, pesticides, hormones, and other contaminants. Pork and beef contained the largest concentrations of these residues. Their health effects are unknown.

Drugs

Use and abuse of many drugs—social, prescription, and illicit —rank as a leading cause of nonerection. The complicated body mechanisms involved in erection are considerably more sensitive to drug effects than most men realize.

Doctors sometimes neglect to inform men that drugs prescribed for anxiety, depression, ulcers, high blood pressure, and other conditions can contribute to erection impairment. Variations on this theme are far too common: A man is given a prescription for a stress-related condition, but the doctor does not mention that the drug is associated with nonerection. Subsequently, the man develops an erection problem that deepens his depression or aggravates his stress situation. His doctor then prescribes more powerful drugs that result in more serious erection problems and increased anxiety.

Never accept a prescription for any drug without insisting that the doctor *and* the pharmacist discuss *all* its effects. If a drug has been linked to sex problems, ask if another can be substituted.

Depressants can impair erection by interfering with the central nervous system. Alcohol is notorious for causing nonerection. In addition to its immediate depressant effects, long-term use decreases the proportion of male sex hormones in the body. Barbiturates such as Seconal, Nembutal, and Tuinal are also associated with erection problems. So are the hypnotics, including Quaalude and Doriden.

Narcotics are well-known causes of nonerection. All the natural opiates—opium, codeine, morphine, and heroin—can cause erection problems. The synthetic narcotics—Demerol, Percodan, Methadone, and Dilaudid—are also associated with nonerection.

Some high blood pressure drugs are associated with erection loss. There are three kinds of antihypertensive drugs: diuretics, which increase urination; vaso-dilators, which enlarge blood vessels; and antiadrenergics, which affect the nervous system. Only the antiadrenergics have a physical basis for association with nonerection, but some men are led to believe that all high blood pressure drugs cause erection loss and they promptly become nonerective while taking diuretics and vaso-dilators. Antiadrenergic drugs, which are also used to treat angina, include: Ismelin, Catapres, and Aldomet, among others. A related drug, Cafergot, used to treat migraine headaches, might also impair erection in some men.

Some drugs prescribed for ulcers, spastic colon, and glaucoma may impair erection if they affect the nerves that control the muscles and blood vessels in the genital area. Some of these include atropine compounds and Pro-Banthine.

Tricyclic antidepressants, such as Elavil and Tofranil, occasionally impair erection. Antipsychotic drugs also may affect erection. They include: Thorazine, Stelazine, Trilafon, Haldol, and Mellaril.

"Spanish fly" a preparation made from the dried, crushed bodies of the beetle Cantharis vesicatoria, long-reputed to be an aphrodisiac, neither increases sexual desire nor helps maintain erection.

Spanish fly irritates the genitourinary tract. It is poisonous and can cause priapism, a painful erection unassociated with sexual arousal, which often ultimately results in nonerection.

This is not a complete list of all drugs that may impair erection. Ask specifically about the sexual effects of any drugs prescribed for you.

How to Visit a Doctor for an Erection Problem

Chances are you do *not* need to visit a doctor if you can produce an erection through masturbation, or by using a particular love-making technique, or if you wake with morning erection now and then. However, your drug use might still be a factor, and increasing difficulty with erection might signal an emerging physical illness. Visit a doctor if you cannot raise an erection at all, if your problem is getting noticeably worse, or if you want to rule out potential organic factors.

If the doctor dismisses your complaint with a flip response, for example: "It's all in your head," or if he or she writes a psychiatric referral without examining you, ask for a referral to a physician who will examine you, or call your local medical society for such a referral. You might also call a sex therapist (see Appendix II). A reputable sex therapist might know a physician in your area who takes the physical aspects of sex problems seriously.

Review the potential organic components of erection problems, then use the following guide to obtain a thorough examination:

(1) Describe the situation in detail. How long have you had the problem? When did it begin? How? Did it develop suddenly or gradually? Has it ever improved? When and under what circumstances? What was happening in your life around the time the problem started? How has it affected your relationship(s)?

(2) Review your medical history. Do you or your family have a history of diabetes, heart disease, high blood pressure, stroke, sickle-cell anemia, prostate problems, or other major illnesses? Did your mother take DES when she was pregnant with you? Are you exposed to any toxic or suspicious substances at work? Have you ever had gonorrhea, syphilis, or other genital health problems? Have you ever had an endocrine system disorder? Do you smoke? Have you ever had a serious back or spinal injury?

(3) Drugs. *Never visit a doctor for an erection problem without taking all your prescription medications with you.* Also, compile a list of all the over-the-counter drugs you use. How much alcohol do you drink? Discuss any illicit drug use, but insist that this information not be written down—medical records are considerably less confidential than we are led to believe. Discuss any combination drug-taking. Combinations often have a multiplier effect on erection impairment—for example, alcohol in combination with narcotics.

(4) Have your blood pressure checked. Elevated blood pressure is increasingly common among young men. High blood pressure is associated with stress, diabetes, arteriosclerosis, and other conditions that can contribute to nonerection.

(5) Obtain a complete physical. The physician should devote particular attention to the genitourinary system. A prostate check is a good idea for any man; it is a must for men over thirty-five.

(6) Depending on the results of the physical, the doctor might want you to have a blood test to check your hormone levels. Inquire about price; these tests can be expensive if you don't have health insurance. Remain skeptical of test results that indicate a testosterone deficiency (see the discussion of testosterone treatments, page 129).

(7) Obtain a hair analysis to check your body levels of zinc and toxic heavy metals. Some doctors might not be familiar with this relatively new diagnostic tool. Hair analysis, however, is earning increasing acceptance as the hazards of heavy metal poisoning become more widely understood. The analysis costs $38 from Mineralab, P.O. Box 5012, Hayward, CA 94540 (415) 783–5622.

Emotional Factors

After potential organic factors have been considered, a non-erective man should take a close look at his lifestyle, his relationship(s), and his ideas about making love. Erection difficulties, like involuntary ejaculation, are usually caused by stress and nonsensual lovemaking overly focused on the "performance" of the penis.

Some men are surprised to learn that nonerection and involuntary ejaculation have similar emotional causes, and wonder why they developed one problem and not the other. The reasons relate to men's individual differences. Similar stress conditions might give different men different sex problems, just as similar stresses might give one man an ulcer and another high blood pressure.

Because the emotional roots of nonerection are similar to those of involuntary ejaculation, the solutions are similar as well. Simple as these suggestions may sound, they have helped many men rediscover lost or faltering erections: Relax, both in and out of bed. Slow down your lovemaking. Deemphasize the role of the penis and try to develop a greater appreciation for whole-body sensuality. Make love only when and how it feels right for you. Discuss any problems with your lover.

Erection Explained

Erection involves the expansion, or dilation, of the arteries that supply blood to the penis. As the arteries expand, more blood flows in than the veins in the penis can carry back out. A blood surplus accumulates and begins to fill the spongy tissues inside the penis. This is the beginning of the erection process. As an erection grows, the veins in the penis become somewhat compressed, further reducing blood outflow, but not stopping it.

A common misconception is the belief that during erection special valves close and hold blood inside the penis as though it were a filled balloon. The veins of the penis contain valves—as do all veins—to prevent backward blood flow; however, these valves play a relatively small role in the erection process. Some men know that a valve in the urethra closes off urine flow during erection and allows for the ejaculation of semen. They incorrectly apply this situation to erection. Actually, blood continues to circulate in and out of the erect penis. In fact, if blood somehow became trapped inside the penis and could not get out, serious health consequences might result, for instance, gangrene.

Recall from the discussion of the fight-or-flight reflex that emotional stress involves redirection of blood away from the central portion of the body, including the penis, out to the extremities. Stress also causes the body to release adrenaline, which heightens energy and constricts blood vessels. Stress interferes with erection in three ways. It reduces the amount of blood available to the penis. It constricts the arteries that must expand for erection to occur. It also depresses the level of testosterone in the blood, which may add to erection difficulties.

The Varieties of Stress

Any number of life situations can cause stress severe enough to impair erection. For example, men from strict religious backgrounds sometimes believe that pre- or extramarital lovemaking will send them to hell or will at least be recorded as a sin in the book of the Great Scorekeeper. Fears of this sort can cause an erection problem.

New-lover anxieties often contribute to erection problems. It is perfectly normal to feel nervous about making love with a new lover, particularly when you are not well acquainted and may not have much basis for trust. These tensions can be aggravated by the pretense that casual sex is cool, when, for many people, lovemaking with strangers is not much fun. Other factors can exacerbate the situation: a few too many drinks, doubts about the relationship, late-night fatigue, and a rushed, nonsensual approach to lovemaking.

Men whose early sexual experiences happened with prostitutes, to whom time is money, may not have developed an appreciation for the leisurely pace the working penis prefers. Prostitutes expect their johns to get hard immediately, take care of business in a few quick strokes, and be on their way before some men even begin to feel aroused. Some prostitutes become impatient with men who are a trifle slow on the draw and ridicule them. This can leave a man upset, confused, and afraid he has an erection problem, which he might indeed develop after a few experiences of this sort.

Contraceptive discontent can also play a role in erection problems. Men who dislike condoms and resent women who insist on them are less relaxed than men who feel comfortable taking part in birth control. Sometimes a man loses his erection while fiddling with the condom. This can be happily resolved if the woman places the rubber on the man (see Chapter 10).

A man who is unable to raise an erection, even though his inability only occurs once, may anticipate having a similar problem the next time. This anticipation can elicit the entire range of stress responses, particularly if he "steels" himself for his next sexual encounter with alcohol or other drugs. A pattern of failure-fear-failure may develop and transform one night's tensions into a regular habit of stress-related nonerection.

A man who feels like a failure in some nonsexual area of life— and who doesn't from time to time?—may take his disappointment in himself to bed with him. Divorce, job loss, car wrecks, injury, illness, business reversals, feelings of growing old, criticism by someone significant, all can contribute to nonerection.

Ironically, success can produce as much stress as failure. Success can be disorienting and unnerving no matter how diligently a man has struggled for it. Erection problems sometimes develop in conjunction with a big job promotion, a sudden increase in responsibilities, or a cross-country move that uproots a man from old friends and familiar surroundings. A lover's career successes can also engender feelings of inferiority and self-doubt that might contribute to an erection problem.

Personal depression ranks as a leading cause of erection difficulties. Depression can cause nonerection and vice versa, raising the possibility of a vicious cycle. Depression and suppressed panic are typical feelings among men with erection problems. Many men find it impossible to seek advice for nonerection because they fear what their condition might "mean." Some withdraw from lovers and lovemaking into a moody private hell. Other men develop a repertoire of apologies to their lovers, with the result that the lovers may think the problem is actually their *own* fault. Some men pick fights just as the mood turns amorous to avoid making love. Others suffer in silence as men have been taught to do. Some tough it out for years, adding layers of hopelessness to whatever caused the original problem. But, as I have emphasized, a stiff upper lip cannot harden a flaccid penis. Depression precludes the stress reduction essential to rediscovering erection.

Relationship problems are another big factor in many erection problems. Some "cavemen" get bored calling all the shots and doing all the "work." They may become frustrated with women who simply submit to them, but are unable to deal with women who are not submissive. Some "delivery boys" acquiesce to lovemaking from a misplaced sense of duty when they would really rather abstain. Many men get upset making love the same old way all the time. In addition, arguments about money, children, marriage, conflicting job schedules, sexual frequency, visits with relatives, or the division of household chores can also take their toll on men's erections.

Below is The Life Events Stress Scale developed by psychiatrist Dr. Thomas H. Holmes and his co-workers at the University of Washington School of Medicine in Seattle. Although each of us reacts to stresses individually, this scale provides a reasonable indication of the emotional costs of normal life events. Studies by Dr. Holmes suggest that an accumulation of 200 points in one year makes a person vulnerable to stress-related illnesses or nondisease conditions such as nonerection.

Life Event	Point Value	Life Event	Point Value
Death of spouse	100	Change in responsibilities at work	29
Divorce	73	Child leaves home	29
Marital separation	65	In-law problems	29
Jail term	63	Big personal success	28
Death in family	63	Wife begins or stops work	26
Serious injury or illness	53	Begin or end school	26
Marriage	50	Change in living conditions	25
Fired from work	47	Change of address	20
Marital reconciliation	45	Change school	20
Retirement	45	Change in leisure habits	19
Illness in family	44	Change in religious observance	19
Pregnancy	40	Change in social life	18
Sex problem	39	Loan less than $10,000	17
New child	39	Change in sleep habits	16
Business reversal	39	Change in number of family functions	15
Change in financial status	38	Change in diet	15
Friend's death	37	Vacation	13
Job change	36	Christmas	12
Increased fighting with spouse	35	Minor legal problems	11
Mortgage	31		
Foreclosure of mortgage or loan	30		

Feel free to expand this list to suit your own life experiences. Assign the point values that feel appropriate to you. Many common life events have not been included in this list. Some you might want to add include: major automobile repairs, getting mugged or burglarized, a rent increase, loss of purchasing power to inflation, rape of a lover, rush-hour commuting, discovery of a lover's unfaithfulness, problems paying bills, or experiences of racial, ethnic, or religious prejudice.

Mark, a thirty-eight-year-old policeman, had just separated from his wife of fifteen years. They considered it a trial separation and were considering both divorce and reconciliation. Mark did not know which he wanted. He visited his two children frequently, supported the family, and occasionally made love with his wife with whom he had never had any sex problems. To save money, Mark moved into his old room at his mother's house. The mother was a devout Catholic; Mark had never been particularly religious. She disapproved of her son's separation, prayed for reconciliation, and refused to discuss the possibility of a divorce. She also berated Mark for dating other women. She refused to allow his dates into her home and castigated her son for "committing adultery" if he stayed out all night. After several casual flings, Mark settled into a relationship with a woman he liked a great deal. They rarely argued, which Mark considered a big relief after years of bickering with his wife. However, this new lover was shy about making love, and after a while, Mark became irritated because he had to "seduce her all over again" every time he wanted sex, in contrast to his wife who had always "given herself" to him when he wanted to make love. Six months into his new relationship, Mark began having erection problems, but only with his girlfriend. Slight at first, the problem grew more troublesome until about half the time he was unable to obtain an erection. Mark continued to have no erection problems whenever he made love with his wife. The counselor asked Mark if anything bothered him about his life at the present time. After initial denials that everything was fine, it turned out that several things were irritating him. Mark was angry with his mother for "sticking her nose in my business and treating me like a kid." He was annoyed that his girlfriend always had to be coaxed into bed. He was spooked that he only had the erection problem with his girlfriend and wondered if that was God's way of punishing him for separating from his wife. The counselor pointed out the enormous changes Mark had gone through in the past year. He was pushing 200 on the Life Events Stress Scale, excluding the considerable stresses of police work. The counselor suggested that Mark consider how he might reduce his stress load. In time, Mark decided to get his own apartment and discuss his "seduction fatigue" with his girlfriend. Two months later, Mark called to say he was living alone and enjoying the peace and quiet. His girlfriend had agreed to trade more initiation of lovemaking for increased nongenital loveplay. The relationship with his wife remained a source of stress. His erection problem, while not completely cleared up, had improved considerably.

New Stresses Create "New" Erection Problems

If a new form of nonerection has appeared as a result of the women's liberation movement, I would suggest that it has little to do with men's alleged inability to accept the social equality of women either in or out of bed. Clearly, some men oppose women's equality and it makes good headlines to say that women's liberation is "hitting men below the belt." However, several recent surveys *—one in *Playboy* †—show that a substantial proportion of men say they *prefer* competent, intelligent, assertive women and credit the women's movement with *improving* the overall quality of their lovemaking. Far from feeling emasculated by women who share the initiative, most men relish it. Men's perennial number one complaint about women as lovers is that they are too passive. The men's magazines, supposed bastions of male chauvinism, publish a steady outpouring of praise for assertive women.

Rather than revealing covert hatred for self-assured women, I would suggest that this "new impotence" is typically the result of a lag in men's adjustment to recent changes in their possible range of lovemaking experiences and to the stress that this lag induces. Today's adult men were raised to expect that they would make the vast majority of moves toward the bedroom. When a man spends a lifetime endeavoring to coax presumably reluctant women into bed, it can be disconcerting to run up against a reversal of the expected roles. Until recently, few men ever had to consider how one might *decline* an invitation to make love. There's the issue of possibly hurting the woman's feelings. In addition, both men and women have been brought up to expect that "normal" men are forever horny and dying to get laid. Many men accept lovemaking offers they would prefer to decline rather than risk appearing "abnormal." There has never been much cultural permission for men to say no, so after a while, their penises begin to say no for them.

Henry was a forty-one-year-old computer designer whose wife

* See *Beyond the Male Myth* in Bibliography.
† November 1978.

died of cancer about a year before his erection problem began. She had been a teacher, and Henry prided himself on the egalitarianism of their relationship. They shared the housework, and he had supported her ambition to become a high school principal. Henry was a charming, physically attractive man, and about six months after his wife's death, some of her friends began suggesting that Henry start dating again. He felt ambivalent, but before she died, his wife insisted that he not mourn her too long. A woman acquaintance asked him out and he accepted. Henry had never been asked out by a woman before and felt flattered to be asked, though he had mixed emotions about "the singles scene." Henry accepted the woman's second invitation to go out and acquiesced to her suggestion that they return to her place to make love. The woman wanted a relationship with Henry; he remained uncertain. After a few months, his erections began to falter. The woman became upset. This had never happened to Henry before and he had no explanation. The woman suggested that in spite of the public egalitarianism of his marriage, perhaps Henry could not deal with strong women. Perhaps he was a "closet male chauvinist." A distraught Henry came in for counseling, feeling shaken that her remark might be true. "Maybe I am a male chauvinist. Maybe I've been fooling myself all these years. Since this thing started, I'm not sure of anything anymore." In counseling, Henry said he had no trouble masturbating and did so frequently, usually fantasizing about his wife. Henry soon realized that both he and his penis wanted more time to mourn his wife's death. He decided to decline all invitations to date until he felt his bereavement had ended.

The steps for dealing with emotionally caused erection problems include: Identify stress factors and try to minimize them. Reestablish intimacy through nondemand sensuality. Be specific about your lovemaking preferences. Masturbate with focused arousal to give your penis some practice with erection in nonpressured situations. Approach vaginal insertion slowly when with a lover.

Identify Stress Factors

In some cases, this might be simple, in others, more difficult. A typical stressful life-style involves an exhausting job, long hours, and the frequent use of alcohol during and after work in conjunction with the normal range of problems at home. If this sounds familiar, try to alter the cycle in some way. Do not attempt any drastic lifestyle revolutions. It is unrealistic—and stress-producing—to transform your entire relationship to the world in one fell swoop. Purification binges, like crash diets, may be popular, but they have limited value when attempting to evolve away from sex problems. Try to change *just one* link in the chain of events you feel contributes to your erection problem. After a while, you might change another, then another, one at a time. On the job, you might delegate just one responsibility or decline to work overtime, if that's allowed. You might stop having beer or wine with lunch or reduce your typical number of cocktails or switch from liquor to beer. You might eliminate alcohol and substitute an after-work nap or swim or jog, some pleasurable reading or talk with a friend or some stretching or meditation. Or you might consider making love at a different time when you feel refreshed instead of tired—in the morning for example.

Of course, it can be difficult to identify—let alone alleviate—sources of stress, particularly if they are embedded deep in a relationship with long histories behind them. Give yourself all the time you need to work on relationship issues. A problem with deep historical roots and many ramifications rarely can be resolved overnight, or even in several weeks or months.

Many men have difficulty discussing their feelings and take refuge behind a general emotional numbness: "I don't feel anything." Few men really feel nothing. Many are afraid strong emotions are irrational—emotions often are. When you think of the role models we've been given—John Wayne, Steve McQueen, Clint Eastwood, John Travolta, *et al.*, it's a wonder we can even *talk*, let alone be honestly emotional. Some men fear that their words will not capture their feelings perfectly—words rarely do. Talking about feelings with a lover can be beautiful or painful. Usually, there are aspects of both.

Try to bear in mind that you need not be the world's most sensitive, articulate, generous man to work out dilemmas in a relationship. Give yourself permission to become a bit petty now and then, if it feels appropriate. The strong silent role model is one of the more damaging barriers to communication in relationships, and evolving beyond that role means voicing both one's positive and negative feelings about a relationship. Often, trivial "little nothings" cause the most knotty problems, because they are simply never mentioned. Developing trust in a lover means that each allows the other to be ridiculous now and then. Try to maintain your sense of humor. Laughter is the universal tension reliever.

Do not expect that simply because you have an erection problem your lover will automatically transform her life, lose twenty pounds, stop pestering you to insulate the roof, and become the sex kitten of your dreams. One mistake some men make is to use their erection problem like a limp sword over their lovers' heads: I won't get hard again until you do this, that, and the other thing. Blackmail is the path to permanent resentments and uncooperative penises. A man's erection problem is never solely his lover's responsibility. Both lovers should try to compromise. Penises only cooperate when lovers do.

Fortunately, relationship difficulties need not be solved as neatly as they are on television for a man to resolve an erection problem. You can't always get what you want. However, problem-free lovemaking does not depend on having an idyllic relationship. What relationship between normal flesh-and-blood people is *ever* without its share of tensions and disagreements?

Try not to let your intellectual ideas about what you "ought to feel" take precedence over your real feelings. Steve's erection problem stemmed from his "commitment" to sexually open relationships. He and his lover slept with other people because they agreed that one person could not satisfy all of another's emotional needs. Perhaps, but deep down Steve wanted a monogamous relationship. He had affairs from a sense of principle, not from any desire, and was afraid he might lose his lover to one of her other men. Meanwhile, he felt reluctant to voice his concerns for fear that his lover might drop him for wanting to renege on their agreement. His erection problem persuaded him to discuss the situation. It turned out that she had some similar doubts, and as an experiment, they decided to suspend secondary relationships for a while. Steve's erection problem quickly cleared up.

Finally, some people get frustrated going over relationship problems again and again without making any progress. Progress in relationships is a lot like progress in learning any skill—sometimes you can get so hung up on your imperfections, you don't realize how much you are actually progressing. It certainly helps to feel you are getting somewhere in a relationship, but simply getting feelings off your chest—once or again and again—has a positive effect on many erection problems.

Reestablish Intimacy

Many men who develop erection problems believe that the penis is their only sexual organ and that all sexual pleasure depends on how well it works. Our penises can sag under the weight of this responsibility. Consider the banquet metaphor—the penis is just one utensil among several at the feast. Use them all: your hands, legs, tongue, breathing—all of you.

Reread the discussion of sensuality in Chapter 2. Try to postpone sexual, that is genital, loveplay for a while and focus on all the nongenital ways you can feel aroused. Your lover probably knows that her fondling of your penis gives you pleasure. What else turns you on? Let her in on an intimate secret or two. She probably has some secrets herself. Try not to demote loveplay into "foreplay." A soothing back rub or foot massage can feel just as important to a man's sexual responsiveness as a quick plunge into a wet vagina.

Many sex therapists recommend that men with erection problems take a vacation from intercourse for a while and concentrate exclusively on sensuality. A temporary ban on intercourse removes any pressure to produce an erection—you don't need one for massage. It allows men the time to get reacquainted with the rest of themselves, time to play any number of sensual games they and their lovers invent.

Be Specific About Your Lovemaking Tastes

This includes everything from saying no when you are not in the mood, to requesting a particular stroke your lover does not provide voluntarily. Try to indulge one another's harmless fantasies. Perhaps one of you is turned on by sexy lingerie. Maybe one of you dreams of making love outdoors. The imagination is one of the sexiest parts of the body.

If your lover does not take as much initiative as you would like her to, don't simply order her to "become sexy." Make specific requests, but remember, she is not obligated to honor them. You may have to negotiate. You may not get exactly what you want, but

you may well get what you need. You might like more or different oral stimulation, or a finger on your anus, or more fondling of your scrotum earlier in the loveplay.

It is perfectly natural to feel shy about making requests you fear your lover might consider weird or kinky. Start with something simple. Move on slowly. Trust takes time to evolve. Remember, there are no "fetishes," only preferences.

In the give and take of lovemaking, you are allowed to lie back and do nothing other than receive pleasure for a while. Take turns giving and receiving, requesting and granting requests.

Rodney, a twenty-seven-year-old bookstore employee, was a bisexual who for years had had satisfying relationships with both men and women. Lately he had developed nonerection, but only with his woman lover of one year. Rodney hoped to father children someday and was afraid his erection problem meant he was becoming irrevocably gay. He was familiar with the psychoanalytic model of the kind of family that allegedly produces gay sons—domineering mother, ineffectual father—which, he said, had been the case in his family. He was convinced he was destined to become gay and that Fate had finally caught up with him. The counselor probed Rodney's lovemaking tastes. It turned out that he really only enjoyed oral sex, an interest shared by his gay lovers but not, apparently, by the woman with whom he was involved. His gay lovers went down on him without being asked, but his girlfriend did not. The counselor suggested that Rodney ask his woman lover for oral stimulation, but he said he just couldn't do it. The counselor said, "Repeat after me: Please—suck—my—penis." At first, Rodney could barely form the words, but by the tenth repetition, he felt more at ease. Rodney was openly skeptical of the counselor's approach. He still considered his nonerection part of a deep psychological problem, but he said he would give direct request a try. A week later, the counselor received an ecstatic note: It worked! Rodney's girlfriend felt shy about providing oral sex without being asked. When he asked, she was happy to oblige and his problem disappeared.

Masturbation

Some sex therapists consider masturbation to be the single most important way to deal with nonerection. Like its importance in the learning of voluntary ejaculation, masturbation is fundamental to restimulating lost or faltering erections.

Do not force yourself to masturbate on a schedule. Do it when the spirit moves you, and only in a comfortable situation that turns you on. Get into yourself.

Vary your experience. Sometimes, masturbate directly to ejaculation. At other times, pause and allow your erection to subside. In masturbation, as in lovemaking with another person, there is no need to have a full erection all the time. It's fine for them to come and go. If an erection subsides during masturbation or lovemaking, there is nothing wrong. Try not to get irritated or anxious. Relax, focus in on your state of arousal and return to the kind of stroking you enjoy. Your erection should return.

Billy, a twenty-two-year-old plumber's apprentice, had considered himself a stud for years. He could make love several times a day, sometimes twice an hour. Several months before he came in for counseling, Billy became involved with Margaret, whom he really liked. He'd had many flings, but Margaret was his first true love. Unfortunately, Margaret did not feel the same way. She liked Billy, but her ardor came nowhere near matching his. She began to pull back from the relationship, not to break up, but to cool things a bit. Billy could not bear "going casual." He clung to her, which made Margaret pull back more. Billy's erections began to falter. He became frantic. After several scenes Billy described as "ugly," Margaret broke up with him. Billy became so depressed he lost the ability to masturbate. "My penis is dead," he lamented. It took several tearful counseling sessions for Billy to begin to let go of Margaret. After his immediate grief subsided, the counselor suggested masturbation, but only when Billy felt good about himself, not when he actively missed Margaret. Slowly his ability to masturbate returned. A few months later, Billy came in for condoms. He was his old self again, still looking for true love, but in the meantime, ready to enjoy "true like."

Approach Vaginal Insertion Slowly by
Successive Approximations

Some men lose their erections at the moment they attempt to insert the penis into an erotic opening. In this case, remember your breathing and try the woman-on-top position to reduce stress on the man. Let the woman take charge of insertion. She should not try to stuff the penis into an opening, but instead, approximate insertion gradually over time while continuing to stroke the penis, scrotum, and other areas with her hands. It is all right to allow several lovemaking sessions before the penis is fully inserted anywhere. If the erection begins to subside when the penis is partially inserted, withdraw and ask for more sensual touching until it returns. Once the man can maintain erection while fully inserted, the couple should gradually introduce pelvic movement while continuing nongenital stroking.

Other Treatments for Nonerection

TESTOSTERONE

Many men would like to believe that their erection problems are caused by a testosterone deficiency. In that case, they reason, a few hormone shots would "cure" them without any real effort or painful reevaluations of their lifestyles, relationships, and approaches to lovemaking.

At one time, testosterone treatments were popular, primarily for lack of sexual desire rather than for treatment of nonerection. They are less popular today, but public fascination with hormone treatments remains high because they are given to football players, who are heroes to many men, and because of the general American faith in "miracle cures."

However, there are serious problems with hormone treatments. A testosterone deficiency may not cause an erection problem— both the deficiency and the problem may be symptoms of something else entirely. Blood levels of testosterone fluctuate partially in response to a man's emotional state. Depression lowers testosterone blood levels. So does alcohol, which many men use when depressed. If a man becomes distraught about nonerection, his emotional state might depress his testosterone level, as opposed to depressed testosterone causing the nonerection. Therefore, it is a good idea to remain skeptical of blood tests that show a testosterone deficiency if you are upset about an erection problem.

Even when a testosterone deficiency appears to be organic, beware of testosterone injections or pills such as Afrodex. Although Afrodex has been credited with some success as therapy for nonerection, it is by no means a panacea. Testosterone treatments suppress the body's natural homone production, and they have a potentially life-threatening side effect—stimulation of prostate cancer.

Male sex hormones have long been known to stimulate prostate cancer, which is why female sex hormones such as DES are used to treat it, to tilt the hormone balance away from the male side. Many urologists believe that testosterone treatments carry too great a cancer risk to be justified for use in men with erection problems. See Chapter 13 for a discussion of prostate self-care.

It would be wise to consider sex therapy before hormone treatments. Many men have rediscovered lost erections through sex therapy after testosterone treatments failed.

LOVE POTIONS

There is no such thing as a secret elixir for dealing with erection problems. Spanish fly is a dangerous poison. Ginseng and other herbal approaches may well improve overall health and indirectly help resolve erection problems, but it is unrealistic to expect them to work erection magic. "Hard-on Pills" or "Passion Capsules" sold by some of the sex gadget companies are cynical frauds that exploit men's distress over nonerection. Some companies even use the word "placebo," which means that any effect is purely psychological.

COCK RINGS

Using a constricting device to obtain or maintain erection makes as much sense as using strangulation to assist in holding your breath. Cock rings are based on the incorrect premise that holding blood inside the penis by mechanical means helps maintain erection. Review the discussion of the erection process earlier in this chapter. Blood circulates in and out of the erect penis, and attempts to stop this circulation can be harmful. Cock rings can reduce outflow and increase back-pressure inside the penis, if they are tight enough. But rather than contribute to erection, cock rings can bruise the delicate tissues inside the penis in which blood collects to cause erection. Cock rings can seriously damage the penis and should be avoided.

IMPLANTS

Two types of implants have been developed to deal with erection problems. Both are inserted into the penis surgically. One is a plastic rod that leaves the penis permanently semierect—hard enough to insert but not so hard that you look like you have "a banana in your pocket," to quote Mae West. The other implant is a more complicated hydraulic device similar to a lift in an auto shop. It involves a set of fitted cylinders implanted inside the penis, a fluid reservoir placed in the lower abdomen, and a pair of control bulbs inserted into the scrotum. Erection is obtained by manually pumping one bulb. Squeezing the other bulb releases the fluid from the cylinders causing the erection to subside. Neither implant affects sexual pleasure or the ability to ejaculate or have an orgasm. Implants can help men with organically caused nonerection. However, they are of questionable value to men whose erection problems have no identifiable physical basis. Surgery always entails some risk, and an operation on the penis can be emotionally traumatic. In addition, these devices do not promote the relaxation and sensuality essential to problem-free lovemaking. Implants should be considered only as a last resort.

One final note: Persistent erection problems may call for individualized assistance. If the suggestions here do not improve your situation within a few months, consult Appendix II for the name of a sex therapist in your area.

Chapter **5**

HOW TO DEAL WITH
NONEJACULATION

An inability to ejaculate—or a problem triggering ejaculation—is the flip side of coming too soon. In both cases, the ejaculation process is not under a man's conscious control. The difference is that a man with involuntary ejaculation comes before he would like to, while a man with an ejaculation difficulty has trouble coming at all.

Ejaculation problems encompass a wide range of related concerns. Some men can only ejaculate under specific, and not necessarily desirable, conditions. Other men produce semen, but it dribbles out instead of spurting. Some men ejaculate without experiencing the pleasure of orgasm, whereas others have orgasm but don't produce semen.

The clinical terms used to describe ejaculation problems leave a great deal to be desired. Sex therapists call these conditions "ejaculatory incompetence" or "ejaculatory retardation"; men with an ejaculation difficulty are called "incompetent" or "retarded" ejaculators. Like the terms used to describe men's other sex problems, these designations do not encourage relaxation or optimism about one's potential for problem-free lovemaking. "Incompetent" and "retarded" are loaded terms. They intimidate many men and aggravate the anxieties that cause so many sex problems.

This book uses the terms "nonejaculation," or "ejaculation problem" or "difficulty." These terms are simple, straightforward and comparatively nonthreatening. They describe only the immediate problem. They do not imply that there is anything inadequate or abnormal about the man.

Traditional Views: From Ancient Fascination to Modern Footnote

Nonejaculation is contemporary man's least discussed sex problem, but ironically it was a central sexual concern to several ancient cultures.

Chinese Taoist physicians of the Han Dynasty (206 BC–AD 219) did not consider infrequent ejaculation a problem. They promoted it as the key to male longevity and sexual fulfillment. The Tao of Loving, part of the *Tao Te Ching*, the bible of the Taoist religion, contends that semen contains a man's "essence of life," and that ejaculating too frequently depletes this vital force and shortens his life. For centuries, Taoist teachers have encouraged their adherents to make love as often as several times a day, while advising ejaculation only occasionally, depending on one's age and health. Young men were instructed to ejaculate every third day, middle-aged men once every few weeks, and elderly men once a month but not at all during illness or winter.

The assertion that semen is the essence of life might strike men educated in the Western medical tradition as strange. Semen certainly helps give life to the next generation, but Western science would dispute the claim that retention of semen promotes longevity.

This belief presumably emerged from observation of increased postejaculatory fatigue as men aged. It might also explain ancient religious taboos against masturbation.

However, the Taoists were actually quite sophisticated about some aspects of ejaculation. For instance, they were aware of the distinction between ejaculation and orgasm. Western medical authorities began to acknowledge this distinction only quite recently as a result of the research conducted by the Kinsey group and by Masters and Johnson. The Taoists encouraged men to have orgasms, but discouraged ejaculation. One reason they frowned on frequent ejaculation was that it left older men too tired to enjoy subsequent orgasms immediately.

Tantric sexuality is another form of lovemaking that involves infrequent ejaculation. Developed in ancient India and still practiced today, Tantric sex is a highly ritualized form of lovemaking that interprets sexuality as a form of interpersonal meditation. One aspect of Tantrism, called Karezza, involves quiet, almost motionless, spiritualized intercourse with orgasm but without ejaculation every time.

Other cultures have also promoted nonejaculatory lovemaking, sometimes known as "coitus reservatus" or "male continence." During the Middle Ages, some Arab societies practiced Imsak, literally "the retaining of semen." A century ago, the Oneida Community, an agrarian/utopian experiment in New York, advocated nonejaculatory lovemaking as a method of contraception.

In their survey of men's sexuality in 1948, the Kinsey group found that only one man in 1,000 said he had problems with ejaculation. And by 1970, Masters and Johnson reported counseling only a handful of men for this concern. Today, despite surveys that show nonejaculation and lack of orgasm to be more prevalent than was previously believed, authorities on human sexuality continue to maintain that these concerns, though not unheard of, are parenthetical to most men's sexuality. Popular sex books and the men's magazines either refer to ejaculation problems in passing or ignore them.

Nonejaculation also holds less fascination for contemporary doctors and psychoanalysts than it did for their ancient counterparts. Physicians and Freudians generally consider it to be a footnote to erection difficulties. Psychoanalytic theory does not pay much attention to sexual physiology and makes no distinction between ejaculation and erection or between ejaculation and orgasm. Doctors are increasingly aware that ejaculation problems may be a side effect of several drugs and surgical procedures, but in general, neither physicians nor psychoanalysts have developed an appreciation for the frequency and variety of ejaculation problems.

Nonejaculation may not be as common as involuntary ejaculation or nonerection, but it is by no means rare. Ejaculation problems trouble many men, particularly older men, and many young men experience them from time to time, frequently the first few times they try to make love. Nonejaculation can be more unnerving than men's other, more widely publicized sex problems because relatively few men understand that this concern even exists. It's scary enough to develop a sex problem you've heard about; it can be mortifying to experience one you never dreamed possible.

The Differences Between Ejaculation and Orgasm

Most men do not distinguish between ejaculation and orgasm. Usually, they happen simultaneously. However, ejaculation and orgasms are distinctly different experiences.

Consider for a moment the range of pleasure in orgasm you have experienced upon ejaculation during wet dreams, masturbation, and lovemaking. Sometimes orgasm feels cataclysmic. At other times, it feels less intense, more localized around the genitals. And at times, ejaculation results in little pleasure or none at all. The fact is, ejaculation does not automatically trigger orgasm. Ejaculation without orgasm has various names, but a simple way to describe it is "numb come."

Orgasm without ejaculation is less widely experienced, but equally possible. For example, it typically results from some prostate operations. When it happens, a man experiences the pleasurable release of orgasm without producing semen. This is called "dry orgasm."

Although ejaculation differs from orgasm, the typical case of nonejaculation involves simultaneous impairment of both responses. Some men can pump away for hours and experience neither one.

Ejaculation and Orgasm Explained

Ejaculation is a two-part reflex generally stimulated by stroking the head of the sexually aroused penis during the plateau phase of the sexual response cycle. The first stage of ejaculation is "emission." The prostate gland and seminal vesicles contract and empty semen into the urethra. Men experience emission as the point of no return after which ejaculation feels inevitable. The second stage is "expulsion," rhythmic, wavelike muscle contractions in the pelvic area that propel the semen down the urethra and out the penis. These muscle contractions are experienced as orgasm.

Ideally, emission and expulsion are coordinated like a one-two

punch, but they may be impaired either selectively or mutually. Emission is controlled by the lumbar nerves, a group of spinal nerves in the lower mid-back. The lumbar nerves are located above the sacral nerves which are involved in both erection and expulsion. Because different nerve groups control the two phases of ejaculation, it is possible to experience one component without the other. Emission without expulsion is numb come—semen dribbles instead of spurting out of the penis and without the emotional release of orgasm. Expulsion without emission is dry orgasm. The pelvic muscles contract, triggering orgasm, but no semen is ejaculated because the phase where the prostate gland and seminal vesicles empty their contents into the urethra is skipped. Men who successfully practice the Tao of Loving or Karreza are able to inhibit the emission phase of ejaculation but stimulate the expulsion-orgasm phase.

Physical Components of Nonejaculation

Like erection problems, ejaculation difficulties may have physical and/or emotional causes. The distinction between the two is fuzzy; it is preserved here for convenience of discussion.

AGING

The older a man grows, the greater the stimulation necessary to produce ejaculation as well as erection. Many men over forty experience a decrease in the urgency to ejaculate, which has prompted some writers on human sexuality to assert that aging "cures" involuntary ejaculation. Older men's ejaculations also tend to feel less forceful than they once did because age decreases pelvic muscle tone. Kegel exercises, which improve pelvic muscle tone, can help older men intensify their orgasms. See the discussion of the Kegel exercises in Chapter 3.

Men who hold the common, mistaken belief that their ability to make love is fated to diminish as they grow older sometimes interpret decreased ejaculatory urgency to mean they are "drying up." Some men give up on their penises if they develop problems with ejaculation, and in turn, their penises give up on them.

Older men need not ejaculate every time they make love. It's fine not to, once you get accustomed to the idea. Lovemaking can feel marvelous without ejaculating every time. This might come as a surprise to men who recall the "blue balls" or "lover's nuts" of their youth. Young men experience some discomfort if sexual arousal is not followed by ejaculation, but the pain, if any, tends to diminish as men reach middle age. Some men may feel considerable discomfort from lover's nuts, but in general the condition might be compared to a stifled sneeze. A tickle in the nose that does not find release in a sneeze might cause momentary discomfort, but breathing quickly returns to normal. Similarly, an older man who does not ejaculate every time he makes love may feel that something is missing at first, but this feeling usually subsides in time, particularly if the focus of the lovemaking is on sensual loveplay. Nonejaculation does not mean that you are inadequate, abnormal, or nearing the end of your sexual rope. Older men who enjoy making love frequently—or whose lovers like to—might prefer not to ejaculate every time because their naturally lengthening refractory periods might leave them unable to raise another erection for up to a few days.

CENTRAL NERVOUS SYSTEM DISORDERS

Spinal injury or disease can cause ejaculation problems, and nonejaculation might be an early symptom of a neurological disorder, though an erection problem would probably appear first.

Multiple sclerosis, advanced syphilis, paraplegia, or diabetes might interfere with ejaculation.

Depending on the part of the spine injured or diseased, a man might experience impairment of emission, expulsion, or both.

GENITAL/PROSTATE PROBLEMS

Urethritis or prostatitis may cause pain on ejaculation severe enough to result in impairment.

Prostate, lower colon, or rectal surgery may damage the sacral nerves that control the expulsion phase of ejaculation. Numb come may result if erection is not impaired as well.

Prostate removal eliminates the gland that produces most of the seminal fluid. Dry orgasm is common afterward.

Some prostate surgery in which the gland is not removed results in "retrograde ejaculation." Emission occurs normally, but expulsion propels the semen backward into the bladder instead of out through the penis. Dry orgasm results. Semen that "backfires" into the bladder is excreted during urination without ill effects. Depending on the urine/semen mix in the bladder, the urine may appear a milky color.

VASECTOMY

Most men notice no difference in their ejaculations after vasectomy. Vasectomy only prevents the sperm from being introduced into its transportation medium, semen. Sperm comprise only about 3 percent of semen by volume. Vasectomy has no effect on the prostate gland or seminal vesicles that produce the rest of seminal fluid, so after vasectomy, the subjective experience of ejaculation remains the same.

If fear of pregnancy is a factor in a man's nonejaculation, vasectomy might help resolve it (see the discussion of vasectomy in Chapter 11).

DRUGS

Many drugs that figure in erection problems also contribute to nonejaculation, particularly those that affect the nervous system. As recommended earlier, be sure to inquire about any sexual side effects of all prescription medications. But bear in mind that taking one or more of the drugs mentioned here in no way condemns you to nonejaculation.

Alcohol, barbiturates (Seconal, Nembutal, Tuinal), narcotics (opium, codeine, morphine, heroin, Demerol, Methadone, Percodan), and hypnotics (Quaalude) may impair ejaculation because of their depressant effects on the central nervous system.

Antiadrenergic high blood pressure drugs can interfere with both the emission and expulsion phases of ejaculation. Guanethidine (brand name Ismelin) is frequently associated with nonejaculation.

Some drugs used to treat ulcers, spastic colon, and glaucoma may impair the expulsion phase of ejaculation and contribute to numb come. Antipsychotic drugs may also impair ejaculation. These include the phenothiazines: Thorazine, Stelazine, Trilafon, and Mellaril; and the butyrophenones, among them Haldol. Mellaril, in particular, is notorious for impairing emission and causing dry orgasm. Antidepressant tricyclics, including Elavil and Tofranil, may also interfere with the expulsion phase of ejaculation and contribute to numb come.

Emotional Components of Nonejaculation

It should come as no surprise by now that stress is the principal emotional ingredient of nonejaculation. Check the Life Events Stress Scale in Chapter 4 to assess your current stress level.

Similar stresses cause different sex problems in different men. However, suppressed anger at a lover or a fundamentalist religious background seem to be factors in a significant proportion of ejaculation problems.

Sometimes a specific traumatic event causes a man's ejaculatory capacity to "freeze up"—for example: being discovered while masturbating, learning about a lover's infidelity, being caught by police in a lovers' lane, or being involved in an unwanted pregnancy.

Any emotions that prevent a man from literally letting himself go during lovemaking can contribute to nonejaculation: fear of disappointing the woman, fear of abandonment, ambivalence toward the woman, or any preoccupation with work, social or family life that prevents him from devoting his undivided attention to making love.

The bottom line is that a man who holds back his emotions may wind up holding back his ejaculations if he does not develop another sex problem first.

Resolving Ejaculation Problems

First, try to analyze the problem. Specifically, what type of nonejaculation is it? A total inability to ejaculate or a difficulty under certain circumstances? Dry orgasm, numb come, or both? How did it begin, suddenly or gradually? Can you link the problem to a specific traumatic event, illness, relationship problem, or drug-use pattern? Has it ever improved? If so, under what circumstances? You may want to have a physical examination. Then, try to discuss the problem with your lover. This is particularly important if you have been faking orgasm.

There is a myth in our culture that only women fake orgasm. They fake it for several reasons: to avoid accusations of unresponsiveness, to bolster the man's ego, or to end a sexual experience they would like to conclude.

Few men—and fewer women—understand that men also fake orgasm and for the same reasons. Nonejaculatory men may fake orgasm to avoid being considered abnormal, since "everyone knows" there's only one thing on a man's mind—getting his rocks off. Some men fake it to reassure their lovers about their sexual attractiveness. Some fake orgasm simply to get sex over with.

Faking orgasm depends on one sex's inability to recognize real orgasm in the other. (It is not difficult to recognize a woman's orgasm. See Chapter 6.) Women can fake it more easily than men because a woman's orgasm is more internal than a man's. Men are expected to ejaculate semen as tangible proof of orgasm, but women produce less physical evidence, despite the men's magazines' exaggerated tales of women inundating men with "gushing love juice." As is the case outside of orgasm, men are expected to "produce"; women are only expected to "feel." After a man ejaculates inside the vagina, a woman experiences "the dribbles," a gradual, sometimes annoying, seepage of semen out of her body. If there is no seepage, a woman might wonder about the honesty of her lover's claims of orgasm. Some nonejaculatory men wear condoms to prevent the "evidence"—really the lack of it—from being left in the woman. Among men who have been persuaded that condoms dull sensitivity, this attempt at a solution can contribute to the problem.

Faking orgasm, no matter who does the faking, sets up negative dynamics in a relationship. The person doing the faking becomes the victim of long-term sexual frustration and may grow to resent his or her lover for not understanding the situation intuitively. Meanwhile, the lover who remains unaware of the problem might have been willing to help resolve it earlier on, but might feel hurt and lied to when he or she finally learns what's been going on. Talk to your lover. Expressing bottled-up emotions is crucial to resolving nonejaculation.

Sometimes a lover might not provide the kind of stimulation you need over a sufficient length of time to stimulate ejaculation. Ask specifically for the stimulation you would like, but remember, she is not obligated to provide it. Negotiate and try to work out a compromise. Use a lubricant to increase skin sensitivity to touch.

You might take a vacation from ejaculation for a while. Temporary elimination of the pressure to ejaculate allows a man to refocus his lovemaking away from the sexual and toward the sensual. Try to let go of the idea that all lovemaking must end with ejaculation.

Remember deep breathing. Try some relaxation exercises: massage, jogging, swimming, yoga, meditation, whatever helps you unwind and appreciate the present.

Fortunately, men whose nonejaculation has no overriding physical basis, rarely wind up absolutely unable to ejaculate. (If you cannot ejaculate at all, consult Appendix II for a referral to individual assistance.) In most cases, restoration of problem-free ejaculation involves building on whatever ejaculatory ability you have. For example, a man might be able to ejaculate by masturbation under specific conditions, but unable to ejaculate inside his lover. He might begin by working on increasing the number of ways he can masturbate to ejaculation. He might vary strokes, fantasies, speed, or lubricants. He might try a vibrator or other sexual aid. During masturbation he should focus on his arousal pattern, paying particular attention to the kinds of stimulation that trigger ejaculation. Then, he might generalize further by masturbating with the assistance of his lover, after which she might masturbate him by herself. Over time he may be able to ejaculate closer and closer to her erotic openings, then while touching her, and, finally, inside her.

Many men experience nonejaculation now and then as the stresses in their lives change. If you develop an ejaculation problem, try not to panic. Consider the possible causes of the problem, then relax, breathe deeply, and concentrate on whole-body sensual loveplay. Ask for the kinds of touch that turn you on. In time, your ability to ejaculate should return.

Don, a thirty-one-year-old roofer, had been having trouble ejaculating for a few months. He could still come, but only after a great deal of manual and oral stimulation by his lover of several years with whom he enjoyed a basically good relationship. There seemed to be no physical or drug-related components of his problem. At first, the situation had not bothered Don. He had been troubled by involuntary ejaculation and initially welcomed his ejaculation problem as a relief from coming too soon. But lately, it had begun to feel like too much of a good thing. His lover was beginning to wonder whether he still found her sexually attractive. Don said he still found her alluring, but his problem caused him some doubts as well. The counselor asked about any recent changes in the relationship. It turned out that Don's lover, Maureen, had recently become a real estate saleswoman and had to be "on call" almost all the time. He worked days; she was working more and more nights and weekends showing property; and they were spending less time together than ever. Don felt neglected. He said the only time they spent together was during lovemaking. As he talked, Don began to realize that withholding ejaculation was one way of increasing the amount of time Maureen devoted to him and his needs. The counselor suggested that they discuss the situation with a view toward structuring some nonsexual time together into their lives. Don was pessimistic about Maureen's willingness to take any time off from work; she was very ambitious. He felt angry that she devoted so much more time to her job than she did to him. A few weeks later, Don called to say they had arrived at a workable compromise. She would not show homes two mornings a week, and he would work Saturdays, as she did, so they could have two mornings a week off together. Don said he was still adjusting to this new schedule, but that his problem had already improved.

Harold was a forty-seven-year-old businessman who enjoyed making love with his wife of many years. He had "no real sex problem to speak of," but now and then he had trouble ejaculating. Whenever it happened, he would ask his wife to massage his anus with a finger, which stimulated him to orgasm. He said this was becoming necessary more frequently lately and he wondered if something might be wrong with him. After a physical checkup ruled out other possibilities, the counselor assured Harold that as he grew older, he would probably need more stimulation over a longer time to stimulate both erection and orgasm. The counselor advised Harold not to become concerned if he needed anal finger massage more often in the future.

Chapter 6

WHAT TURNS WOMEN
ON—AND OFF

"Women! I don't understand them. I can't please them. What am I doing wrong? What do they want from a guy, anyway?"

What today's women say they want from men is simple and elegant. *Women say they want the very things that prevent men's sex problems and promote mutually enjoyable lovemaking.* They say they want intimacy, trust, relaxation, sensual touching, and a leisurely pace that builds to orgasm for both lovers. Women say they want the kind of lovemaking that makes most men feel their best in bed.

A note of caution at the outset: This chapter is by no means the definitive analysis of what every woman wants from every man each time they make love. Such a comprehensive description would be equally impossible for either men's or women's sexual tastes. The possibilities for mutually satisfying lovemaking are as limitless as the imagination—and isn't that marvelous?

The observations and suggestions presented here are generalizations distilled from interviews with many women, from the insights of leading women sex therapists, and from several recent surveys of women's lovemaking preferences. They are flexible precepts that couples should interpret for themselves. No doubt, the

144

discussion here may not emphasize some aspects of women's sexual tastes important to the woman or women you love. That underlines the need for ongoing discussions among lovers.

This chapter is designed to provide men with a basic understanding of what contemporary women say turns them on—and off—in bed. It should clear up some of the fundamental misconceptions many men have about their lovers' sexuality. The hope is that this presentation will promote wide-ranging intimate conversations that might lead almost anywhere.

Men and Women Want Similar Traits in Lovers

If asked how women's feelings toward lovers compare with their own, many men would reply without hesitation that men's and women's attitudes are worlds apart. This is hardly surprising since our culture focuses considerable attention on the so-called Battle of the Sexes, that ever-raging conflict that stresses not only the vast no-"man's" land between men's and women's views of each other, but also implies that it cannot be crossed. On one side of the sexual trenches, men learn that unless there is something peculiar about them, women never want to "do it" as much as men do. Women are "naturally" moody, irritable, difficult, and complicated. They are so generally prudish that men must wine and dine them (emphasis on the wine), then cajole them into bed where they exhibit all the sexual enthusiasm of mummies. If only women realized, as men do, that what they really need is a good fuck. . . . Meanwhile, behind their own emotional fortifications, women learn that men are vulgar, loud-mouthed, sexually insatiable beasts generally inclined toward rape, who, in the words of novelist Tom Robbins, do not know the difference between a clitoris and a carburetor.

Like most human hostilities, the Battle of the Sexes is based on perceived differences that are more imaginary than real. The fact is, men and women share remarkable *similarities* in their tastes in lovers and lovemaking. Their patterns of sexual arousal are similar, their sex problems share identical causes and solutions, and their orgasms are, when described subjectively, indistinguishable.

Two recent surveys asked large numbers of men and women which personal attributes were most important to them in a lover. Bernie Zilbergeld collected women's descriptions in his book,

Male Sexuality, and Anthony Pietropinto and Jacqueline Simenauer compiled men's opinions in *Beyond the Male Myth.* Sample
desired attributes from both surveys are listed below. Can you
identify which responses came from the men and which came from
the women?

I	II
Mature	Fun
Honest	Intelligent
Kind	Sensitive
Aware—physically, emotionally, intellectually	Supportive
	A listener
Cares	Tender
Really listens	Enjoys our bodies
Good body	Playful
Outgoing	Sensual
Intelligent	Tells me what feels good sexually
Needs me	Tolerates imperfections
Good sense of humor	Caring
Friendly	Communicative
Affectionate	Willing to experiment
Dresses well	Encouraging
Warm	

Notice how similar the lists are. List I came from the men; list II
from the women. But they are basically interchangeable.

Among the hundreds of women who responded to Zilbergeld's
questionnaire, *not* one mentioned penis size or staying power as a
factor in choosing a lover. The small number who said they found
men's sex problems annoying were generally less turned off by the
problems themselves than by the men's tendency to withdraw into
reclusive silence because of their sex problems. The John Wayne
syndrome rides again.

Women say they want companions, not cocks; friends, not fuckers; men, not supermen. They want lovers with whom they can
laugh and cry, work and play, give and receive support. In bed,
they want sensuality with their sexuality.

In the words of one respondent: "Time spent in bed is only a
small part of total time together. The sexiest part of the body is the
mind." Who do you think wrote that—a man or a woman?

How Women Become Turned On

Men's and women's sex organs not only look different, but most people are brought up to believe that they also feel and respond differently. For some men, fondling a woman's genitals feels as strange as jumping behind the wheel of a tractor trailer truck with fifteen forward gears.

Actually, men's and women's sexual equipment has a good deal in common. Our various parts might have different proportions and arrangements, but they are simple variations on the same elegant design.

Human sex organs take shape in the fetus before birth; the genitals of both sexes are identical for most of the nine months of prenatal development. Only during the final two months of development do they begin to differentiate into recognizable genders. The embryonic cells that become the penis in men become the clitoris in women. Their wiring into the nervous system is similar. The cells that become the scrotum in men become the outer vaginal lips in women and their wiring pattern is also similar. Sometimes, even doctors cannot tell the difference between newborn boys and girls. Baby girls are occasionally mistaken for boys because the infant clitoris and vaginal lips can look deceptively similar to the infant penis and scrotum. These shared embryonic roots have a useful application to lovemaking. As mentioned earlier, a man who wonders how a woman feels when he caresses her vaginal lips or clitoris can get a pretty good idea by focusing on the sensations he feels when his scrotum or penis is fondled. Touching breasts, nipples, pubic hair, buttocks—indeed, every part of the body—stimulates virtually identical sensations in both men and women. We are not that different from one another.

Recall men's sexual response cycle described in Chapter 3. During sexual arousal, women experience similar physical changes:

Excitement: In men, blood flow into the pelvic area increases and erection begins. In women, extra blood also flows into the pelvic area, and, specifically, into the outer vaginal lips. The lips gradually enlarge as excitement builds. As the lips fill with blood, they begin to part, though the amount of parting varies from one woman

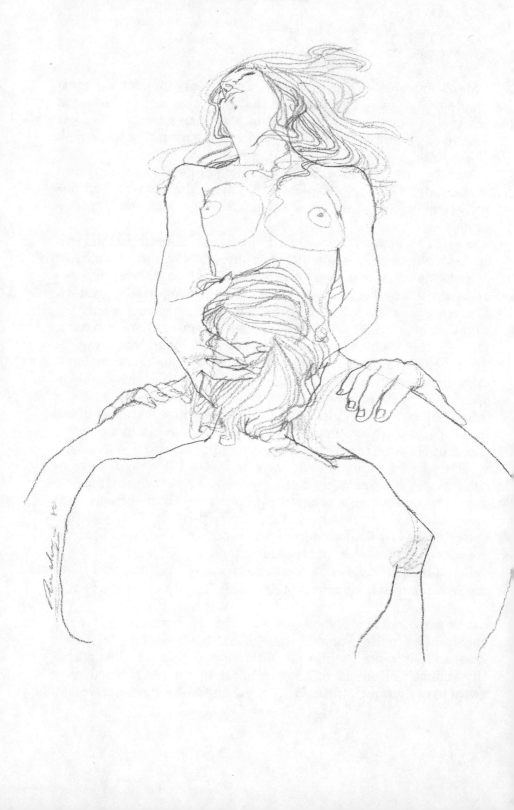

to another. Blood also flows into the inner vaginal walls. This surplus blood increases fluid pressure there to the point where some fluid seeps into the vagina itself. This is vaginal lubrication.

Many men call the vagina a "hole" or "cunt," from the ancient German for hollow space. Actually, the vagina bears little resemblance to a hole. It is more like a flower bud that unfolds into a blossom when it senses that conditions are favorable. In fact, beneath the outer vaginal lips, the vagina looks remarkably like a flower, like a half-open rose. Vaginal roses are clearly visible in most *Hustler* pictorials where the models "show pink." They obligingly pull their outer lips apart to reveal their inner floral arrangements. (Pulling the outer lips apart feels about as comfortable as having your mouth clamped open for oral surgery. However, *Hustler* "beaver shots" provide a view most men rarely glimpse if they make love in dim surroundings under the covers.)

One of the few—and most crucial—differences between the two sexes' arousal processes is that a woman's excitement phase takes longer than a man's. How much longer? It varies, but in general, men should assume it takes *considerably* longer, even if the women is the initiator of the loveplay. A standard theme in women's criticisms of men's usual lovestyle is that men do not allow women sufficient warm-up time. Sex counselors, not to mention most women, advise men: slow down, then slow down even more.

Some men have full erections by the time they unzip their pants, but most women's intimate blossoms unfold rather slowly, particularly if they feel ambivalent about making love. One reason some women prefer older men as lovers is that their erections take longer to rise than do younger men's, resulting in a closer match with women's pace of arousal.

Some men believe that the moment their fingers feel the woman's vaginal lubrication, she is ready for intercourse. For the vast majority of women, nothing could be further from the truth. Vaginal lubrication is among the first, repeat *first,* signs of women's arousal. The presence of vaginal lubrication signals only that the woman is gradually beginning to get interested in the idea of further sensual explorations. Sometimes, of course, a woman might become lubricated during an erotic film or daydream or at the sight of a man who excites her. The men's magazines regularly publish letters from women whose panties become soaking wet at the wink of an eligible eye: "Just being near Bill made my vagina swollen and wet. . . ." The small proportion of women who are quick to lubricate might prefer a bit less sensual loveplay than those who start out dry. However, that is by no means clear. They may want as much sensuality, or more, just as a man who has a full erection when he undresses may prefer leisurely lovemaking to a headlong sprint around the erotic bases. Instant lubrication in women is definitely a minority experience. Lubrication is an individual difference among women, like eye color. Wet does not necessarily mean ready. Most women need considerable time and sensual—as opposed to sexual—touching to become fully lubricated. The time women need to become lubricated is an important reason why playful touch, massage, and other forms of sensual loveplay are so crucial to their sexual responsiveness.

Chief among the factors that can inhibit vaginal lubrication and women's overall sexual responsiveness is our familiar nemesis, stress. The same anxieties that cause nonerection in men also interfere with lubrication in women—and for the same reason. Recall that stress triggers the fight-or-flight reflex that constricts blood vessels and redirects blood away from the genitals out to the extremities. A woman whose uncertainties about lovemaking cause significant stress winds up with less blood available to her vaginal lips and walls than a woman who feels relaxed—hence less vaginal lubrication. Pestering a woman about why she takes so long to self-lubricate has the same effect on her vagina that berating a man for nonerection has on his penis.

Contraceptives might also interfere with vaginal lubrication. Some women report that birth control pills interfere with their ability to become lubricated. And any birth control method—or lack of one—that distracts a woman from devoting undivided attention to making love might do the same. Tampons can also absorb some vaginal lubrication.

During the excitement phase, some—but by no means all—women's nipples become firm and erect and possibly darker in color. In men's magazine correspondence, visible nipple erection is the rule: "I must have gazed at her breasts too intently because suddenly her nipples began to grow." Boing! In reality, however, nipple erection is about as common in women as it is in men. Sometimes nipples become erect; sometimes they don't. At times, they become erect, then subside. And sometimes, they become erect in nonsexual situations, for example, when cold. Check out the pictorials in the men's magazines. Some of the presumably aroused models have erect nipples, but others do not.

As the excitement phase progresses in men, the scrotum pulls up closer to the body and the testicles become elevated. A similar process occurs in women. The uterus, which usually occupies the back portion of the vagina, tips up and forward. A man who inserts his penis deeply before the woman has become aroused may jam into the cervix, the mouth of the uterus, before it has tipped forward out of the way. The cervix itself is relatively insensitive to touch; however, the impact of the penis against the cervix can jostle the uterus. If the uterus is prodded in this way, the ligaments that hold it in place can pull and annoy the woman, which can be distracting.

Plateau: In men, the plateau phase is marked by full erection. In women, the outer vaginal lips become fully engorged with blood and the clitoris becomes extremely sensitive to touch.

The clitoris, or "love button," is the woman's version of the head of the penis. It is the site of greatest nerve concentration and sexual pleasure. Clitorises of different women look and respond differently. In some women, the clitoris becomes noticeably erect and peeks out from under the clitoral hood formed by the joining of the inner vaginal lips, the woman's version of a foreskin. In other women, the clitoris may not protrude beyond the clitoral hood. Sometimes, it peeks out for a while, then subsides, rather like some penises that subside a bit from full erection prior to ejaculation.

Men should treat the clitoris gently, *very gently.* It contains as many nerve endings as the head of the penis, but because it is so much smaller, millimeter for millimeter, it is more sensitive. A minimal tweek to the head of the penis that does not hurt a man might hurt a woman whose clitoris is touched the same way. Do not squeeze, poke, pinch, bite, or grind down on this petite but magnificent organ. Too much direct pressure can be painful and distracting. Unless the woman requests otherwise, it is not a good idea to fondle the clitoris until the woman is well lubricated. Dry fingers digging for an unlubricated clitoris can feel like taking sandpaper to the head of the penis. Initially, a man might stimulate the clitoris by tenderly kneading the outer vaginal lips where they cover it. Once the outer vagina becomes lubricated, a man can "fingerpaint" some lubricating fluid up around the clitoris. Remember, do this lovingly—swashbucklers make good characters in pirate movies, but lousy lovers. Many women enjoy other sensual lubricants in addition to their own, for example, cocoa butter or a man's saliva. Talk it over. Experiment. Even after the clitoris has become lubricated, some women prefer indirect clitoral touching to any direct bearing down on the clitoris itself. Close but slightly oblique stimulation can be applied by finger, tongue, or vibrator on either side and on the clitoral hood. Ask what kinds of clitoral stimulation your lover likes at different stages of arousal.

How to Recognize a Woman's Orgasm

Orgasm: Women's orgasms are a mystery to many men. Some men don't care if their lovers reach orgasm—that's their problem, they say. However, most men care deeply about their lovers' fulfillment, but a man may have difficulty deciding if the woman he is with has climaxed. Some men simply assume their lovers have orgasms because the women, for a variety of reasons, never say anything to suggest otherwise. Some men would be delighted to continue clitoral stimulation after their own orgasms, but do not feel comfortable asking the woman, "Did you come?" Asking that question can be difficult. It is an admission that the man is not entirely in control of the lovemaking, a difficult admission for some men. A man might blame himself for a woman's lack of orgasm, or, if it turned out that she had climaxed, he might feel embarrassed that he had missed The Big Event. As if these problems were not intimidating enough, lately women have been saying that they resent the question: "Did you come?" This leaves many men feeling they're damned if they do and damned if they don't.

Take heart; the situation is far from hopeless. The fact is, women's orgasms are *identical* to men's, except that they do not result in ejaculation. (As discussed earlier, some men's orgasms do not include ejaculation either.) In both men and women, orgasm involves a series of quick, rhythmic, wavelike muscle contractions throughout the pelvic region that last for a total of a few seconds. The same muscles contract in both sexes, notably the pubococcygeus, the PC, that was discussed in the section on Kegel exercises.

Men's and women's orgasms appear to feel so similar that in one study, where descriptions of orgasm were edited so the writer's sex could not be determined, a group of men and women *could not distinguish* women's descriptions of orgasm from men's.

The chief reason so many men have difficulty recognizing women's orgasms is that *relatively few women ever reach orgasm solely from intercourse.* Men who equate lovemaking with vaginal intercourse may never have experienced a woman having an orgasm. Most women need direct clitoral stimulation in order to climax. Several recent surveys have asked women how they reach orgasm. Depending on the survey quoted, only one-third to one-half of women have orgasms during intercourse. A majority rarely, if ever, comes during intercourse. In fact, *a substantial proportion of perfectly normal women never reach orgasm during intercourse no matter how long it lasts.* In addition, many women who can climax during intercourse sometimes prefer not to; they say they often prefer to come from direct clitoral stimulation because those orgasms feel different, often more intense.

Intercourse may be the key to procreation, but from the perspective of women's sexual fulfillment, it leaves a good deal to be desired. Vaginal intercourse provides some stimulation to the outer vaginal lips and the inner vagina. However, only the outer third of the vagina has nerve endings sensitive to touch. The walls of the inner vagina are relatively insensitive, which allows them to stretch during childbirth without causing the woman additional pain.

Most women find that intercourse provides little stimulation to the clitoris which sits far enough above the vagina to receive only glancing stimulation from an in-out penile movement. It receives more from the side-to-side or circular movements mentioned in Chapter 3, but these moves may still provide only minimal stimulation.

This is not to suggest that intercourse is no fun for women. Quite the contrary. Many women enjoy it a great deal as a form of sensual touching and as a way to provide pleasure for their lovers, just as many men thoroughly enjoy oral-clitoral kisses.

Even after they accept the fact that most women do not climax during intercourse, some men wonder why their particular lover is not among those who can. Recall that intercourse provides the greatest stimulation to the outer vaginal lips, the part of a woman's anatomy analagous to the scrotum. How many men would come if their lovers confined stimulation to a quick rubbing of the scrotum by a tubular object with little or no penile touch? Probably not many. A third? Half? It's hard to say. Similarly, like women who can reach orgasm during intercourse but sometimes prefer not to, many men who could ejaculate solely from scrotal massage might also prefer direct stroking of the penis occasionally or most of the time. Would there be anything wrong with a man who needed direct penile stimulation to come? Of course not. Which brings us back to the fine points of recognizing women's orgasms.

The women's orgasms most familiar to men are those in books, magazines, and films, what might be termed "media orgasms." Media orgasms are wild and dramatic. The woman pants and moans in a rising crescendo of excitement. She frequently urges her lover on: "Faster, oh, harder, ooooh, faster, more, more." Then, just to make sure we all know what's about to happen, she announces: "I'm cominnng!" Finally, she arches her back, throws her hips about uncontrollably, and breathes a long delicious sigh as she subsides into afterglow. Media orgasms are hard to miss.

Few women's orgasms have the intensity of media orgasms. However, even less cataclysmic orgasms can be recognized without much difficulty. Simply look for the signs you experience in yourself: a quickening of excitement, genital-area muscle contractions, and some involuntary hip movements that lead to a release of breath and tension as the orgasm subsides. Orgasmic muscle contractions can be felt by a finger placed at the mouth of the vagina, on the anus, or on the flap of skin between the two. Some women do thrash around during orgasm, but others do not. Both men's and women's reactions to orgasm vary, depending on mood, level of energy or fatigue, amount and kind of loveplay, outside life concerns, and the level of mutual trust. You and your lover might like to discuss the subtleties of your orgasms.

Some men enjoy continued stimulation throughout orgasm; others find it distracting and prefer light stroking or none after orgasm begins. Women have the same range of possible preferences. Many lovers' preferences change over time, which is fine. Lovers might like to keep each other updated on their stimulation preferences during orgasm.

Suppose that a man has climaxed during intercourse but is not sure that his lover has. This happens frequently—a man in the throes of orgasm cannot be expected to remain completely in touch with his lover's state of arousal. In general, a man should assume that his lover does not come during intercourse. He should assume she needs direct clitoral caresses. He might stimulate her clitoris by hand, tongue, vibrator, or whatever she enjoys, but he still might doubt his ability to recognize her orgasm. Men in high-trust relationships might ask their lovers to tell them when they reach orgasm—assuming that they do. However, this is easier said than done.

Many men ask their lovers, "Did you come?" out of genuine concern for their satisfaction. However, some women resent this question. Why? Imagine your own feelings if a woman climaxed courtesy of your oral-clitoral stimulation then asked *you:* "Did you come?" Many men would resent the question: "How can you even *ask* if I've come? I've been stimulating you. You haven't touched me where it counts!" Women feel the same way. Asking a woman if she has climaxed during intercourse is a sign that the man knows little about what turns women on. In addition, the way the question is worded puts women on the spot. Admitting "no orgasm" can be difficult because some men indignantly assume that any woman who does not climax with "a great lay" like them must be unresponsive and hung up.

Rather than asking: "Did you come?" a man might say something that lets the woman know he understands that few women reach orgasm during intercourse; for example, "What can I do for you now?" or "Your turn. What more would you like?" This approach allows the woman to remain relaxed and focused on her own arousal—in short, more ready to have an orgasm.

Faking It

Recall the discussion in the previous chapter of the reasons why lovers sometimes fake orgasm. The problem for a man whose lover does so is that the opportunity to learn what really turns her on is replaced by an ongoing deception. Many men get more upset about being lied to than about their shortcomings in the technique department. Women are not the only ones sensitive to "kiss and tell" issues. A man whose lover has been faking it may feel mortified at the thought that she has informed all her friends what a lousy lover he is. A man might also feel angry that his lover did not trust him enough to tell him the truth about her situation.

On the other hand, a woman needs only one or two experiences of being slapped around, given the brush-off, or being called a "frigid bitch" to get the message that she must fake orgasm to avoid abuse.

A man who is unsure if a lover has orgasms with him should raise the subject *very delicately*. But first, he should review his own sexual expectations of her and try to recall any bad manners he may have displayed in the past. Rather than demanding: "Do you come with me?" a man might begin a discussion of his lover's orgasms—or lack of them with him—by asking her what kinds of caresses she enjoys, when, and for how long. Then he might inquire whether any of his moves detract from her enjoyment of their lovemaking. Many women, frustrated with men who assume they know what pleases women, are delighted to discuss their arousal preferences as soon as men drop the know-it-all facade and *ask*.

It takes courage to drop the pretense of all-knowingness—a good deal more courage than it takes to continue living a Joe Stud fantasy. However, a sincere willingness to work on lovemaking usually deepens a couple's mutual trust. It can also expose some raw nerves. A woman may feel skeptical of the man's sincerity, particularly if he has abused her in the past, or if she has been faking orgasm for a long time. Some women avail themselves of the opportunity to lash out at a man for a whole catalogue of insensitivities. That would be unfortunate, but you can't learn boxing without taking a few on the chin. Many women who fake orgasm have considerable anger stored up about it. However, most women get past their anger and welcome a chance to suggest ways their lovers can give them more pleasure.

Couples engaged in this process should try to remain patient with one another. It's a rare woman who can let go all at once of resentments that have built up while faking orgasm over a long time. By the same token, it's a rare man who can let go of "the *Playboy* philosophy" overnight and really act on all his lover's suggestions about her needs. Moving a relationship away from the sore point of faked orgasm requires more than just a one-shot discussion. It is a gradual, lurching process, a mutual unfolding bound to hit some snags. Those who succeed, persevere.

Don't Expect Multiple Orgasms

Resolution: One of the more controversial results of Kinsey's survey of women's sexuality in the early 1950s was the finding that some women were capable of more than one orgasm at a time. Instead of moving from orgasm to the final resolution phase of the sexual response cycle, women who have multiple orgasms return to the plateau phase where they remain highly aroused and can be stimulated to orgasm again almost immediately. However, the vast majority of women, like men, are capable of only one orgasm at a time.

Unfortunately, some men believe that a woman is somehow less than responsive if she has "only" one orgasm during loveplay. Women discussed in the men's magazines seem to have multiple orgasms routinely: "After her first orgasm, I continued to stroke her crotch. She bucked again and again until she collapsed, weak from exertion." And a man who measures his own lovemaking talents by the number of orgasms he "gives" his lover may want the woman to keep coming over and over again, not for her sake, but for his.

A man who expects his lover to have more than one orgasm at a time is being as realistic as a woman who insists that her lover raise another erection one minute after he ejaculates. After all, a woman might say, if you really loved me, if I really turned you on, you'd be able to get hard again right away like all those guys in the men's magazines. . . .

Some women capable of multiple orgasms may like them every time they make love. Others prefer to stop at one. In some women, the clitoris becomes extremely sensitive to touch after orgasm, and it may feel uncomfortable to experience more stimulation before this extra sensitivity subsides.

What proportion of women experience multiple orgasms? No one knows for certain, but clearly, it's a minority. A man who pressures a lover, however subtly, to "just see if you might be" multiply orgasmic may introduce enough tension into the relationship to reduce the pleasure for both of them.

A tragic irony of contemporary discussions of lovemaking is the amount of attention devoted to multiple orgasm, when women's much more typical experience is an inability to have even *one* orgasm with a man, let alone several in a row.

No Such Thing as "Frigidity"

A woman who cannot reach orgasm during lovemaking with a man has traditionally been labeled "frigid." Like the loaded term "impotent," frigid implies a good deal more than simply a problem with orgasm. A woman termed frigid is usually seen—and may see herself—as cold, cruel, bitchy, man-hating, hung up, averse to lovemaking, possibly lesbian, and generally lacking in human kindness.

Frigidity also conjures up an image of psychological imbalance. Traditionally, orgasmic difficulties in women are associated with the labels "neurotic" and "repressed," a result of psychoanalytic theory which postulates that these problems are rooted either in penis envy or in unresolved Electra conflicts, the woman's version of the Oedipal complex in men.

Psychoanalytic theory postulates that little girls want to make love with their fathers and eliminate their mothers. As they grow up, sexually healthy women reject their fathers as potential lovers and identify with their mothers. However, if they harbor unconscious desires for their fathers, then sexual responsiveness with any man might rekindle their incestuous wishes. In order to defend against these taboo desires, "frigid" women allegedly deny their sexuality entirely and become incapable of orgasm.

The penis envy theory is similar. Freudians postulate that little girls feel deprived of a penis, and that healthy sexual adjustment depends on their ability to cope successfully with feelings of rage, envy, and inferiority resulting from his alleged deprivation. Sexually well-adjusted women are said to reject their desire for a penis by rejecting the clitoris, the female penis, in favor of the vagina as the seat of their sexual pleasure. Hence, "immature" clitoral orgasms give way to "mature" vaginal orgasms. Women who allegedly become "arrested" in clitoral eroticism, who cannot accept a submissive role in relation to men, become not only frigid, but aggressive, driven, competitive, and castrating.

It is not difficult to understand why so many contemporary women—and men—blame popularized psychoanalytic theory for their sex problems. The Electra theory of frigidity, like its counterpart explanation of nonerection, locates the problem in the remote past, ignores the present context, and may trigger feelings of depression and helplessness, the very emotions that cause most sexual problems.

The penis envy notion is flatly inaccurate, to put it kindly. Scientists have demonstrated that there is no such thing as "vaginal orgasm." All women's orgasms are a function of clitoral stimulation. Like men's orgasms, they involve muscle contractions throughout the pelvic region. Women's orgasms have little, if anything, to do with the vagina or with acceptance of a passive social/ sexual role. Not surprisingly, psychoanalysis has a poor track record for resolving women's problems with orgasm. Sex therapy, on the other hand, has an excellent record of helping women discover their orgasmic potential.

Another aspect of the "frigidity" issue is the tendency among some men to call women frigid as a way of blaming them for any problems *they* might be having with lovemaking. If she doesn't want to make love as often as he does, she's frigid. If she doesn't come during intercourse, she's frigid. If her sexual tastes are less adventurous than his, she's frigid.

Blaming the woman for a sex problem in a relationship is never constructive. It aggravates mutual resentments and precludes negotiation and compromise. It causes considerable stress and we know what that means.

On the other hand, sometimes the man gets blamed for a woman's sex problem. An old saying goes: "There's no such thing as a frigid woman; there are only inadequate men." Blaming the man is no different from blaming the woman. Don't berate—negotiate.

Except for medical texts that still cling to the word and its grotesque implications, the term frigid is passing out of general use more quickly than the traditionally intimidating labels for men's sex problems. Women who have orgasmic difficulties are now called "preorgasmic." Like the term "nonerective," preorgasmic focuses only on the sex problem, not on any supposed shortcomings in the rest of the woman. It does not trigger the anxieties and self-doubts set off by the term frigid. Preorgasmic correctly implies that any woman can have an orgasm, but that some have not quite gotten there yet. It implies a learning process. Almost any woman can learn to become orgasmic, just as any man can learn to last longer. In fact, the learning processes are basically the same. They

involve relaxation, focused arousal, extended sensuality, masturbation, and intimate conversations about pleasurable preferences.

How Men Can Help Preorgasmic Lovers

A man can help a lover with a sex problem the same way a
woman can help a lover in a similar situation. He should let the
woman know that his affection for her is independent of her sex
problem—if that's true. He should make time to listen to her feelings about the problem and try to support her in any way she feels
appropriate. He should try to cultivate a willingness to discuss
differences in their sexual tastes and negotiate compromises. He
can reassure her that her situation is not at all hopeless and that
most women become orgasmic after relatively brief sex therapy.

A man should not take a lover's sex problem so personally that
he decides it must be all his fault. On the other hand, there may be
some aspects of his lovemaking style that contribute to his lover's
sexual difficulty. In that case, a man might try experimenting with
any loveplay alterations his lover suggests.

When helping a lover with a sex problem, bear in mind that men
do not "give" orgasms to women any more than women "give"
them to men. Each of us is responsible for our own sexual satisfaction. Each of us brings orgasm out from within ourselves. Lovers
can help or hinder the process, but no one can do it "for" anyone
else.

One crucial aspect of helping a preorgasmic lover is to refrain
from insisting that she seek sex therapy. Feel free to present options and discuss what you consider their advantages and disadvantages, but do not badger her. Do not make her decisions for her.
Women and men should make their own decisions about their own
sex problems.

How would a man feel if his lover said, "You know, Jim, you
really ought to do something about that limp dick. It frustrates you.
It frustrates me. Why don't you go get some sex therapy?"

"And why don't you *shove it?*" a typical man might reply. Many
men would feel outraged at the presumptuousness of such a suggestion: "Who is *she* to tell me about *my* sex problem? I have to
live with it more than she does. Does she imagine I haven't thought
about it?" In addition, though, most men would grow more upset
about the problem: "If she's this insistent, I must be in terrible

shape. Maybe she's really giving me an ultimatum—either deal with the problem or I'll leave you."

Men sometimes feel they "own" their lovers' sexuality. A corollary follows, that they own their lovers' sex problems as well. However, a sex problem is an intimately personal concern, and it is vital that the person with the problem be the one to decide whether and how to deal with it. There is an old belief among farmers that a hatching chick must break its own shell. If anyone else breaks it —no matter how kindly motivated—the chick may die.

Why might a woman hesitate to deal with a sex problem? For the same reasons many men choose sexual frustration over efforts toward resolution. She might feel embarrassed admitting that she does, indeed, have a problem. She may fear that her problem is incurable and prefer not to confront that possibility. She might see sex therapy as overly self-indulgent or too expensive.

There are also a few reasons men generally do not consider, including the possibility of a personal history of incest, rape, or both. Although this book does not look favorably on the Freudian blame-it-on-your-childhood approach to sex problems, clearly, deep sexual trauma at any age can result in long-term sex problems and reluctance to consider sex therapy for fear of dredging up painful memories a woman—or anyone—would rather forget.

Most men know next to nothing about child sexual abuse, and little wonder. Research into incest has only quite recently begun. Estimates of incidence vary widely, from ½ of 1 percent to 15 percent of girls. However, there is general agreement that sexual abuse of young girls happens at or before puberty. It is generally confined within the nuclear family—the typical molester is the girl's father, step-father, uncle, other relative, or family friend. A woman's realization later in life that she was sexually exploited by a man or men she was brought up to love and trust might result in difficulty in trusting any man.

Men should definitely not jump to the conclusion that a lover's reluctance to seek out sex therapy is based on a history of sexual victimization. However, because so few men even admit the possibility, keeping it in mind might encourage a man to be extra-patient and gentle with a lover's sex problem.

Women with sex problems need exactly what men with sex problems need: affection and support, a lover who is willing to listen, willing to help, and willing to adjust the lovemaking to foster a sensual, nonpressured atmosphere.

Women's Chief Complaint About Men as Lovers

Too little whole-body loveplay. Too much narrow genital focus. Sex educators have an adage: Women make love in order to touch; men touch in order to make love.

Women's most pervasive criticism of men's standard lovestyle is that men are so preoccupied with their penises and the mechanics of intercourse that they ignore what really turns women on— total-body sensuality. Most women prefer to explore the entire playground. They say too many men stick to one small corner.

To paraphrase one woman who discussed her sexual tastes in *The Hite Report*, lovemaking is at least 75 percent sensuality and at most 25 percent sexuality. Unfortunately, many men reverse the proportions and place their emphasis on sexuality. This can lead to sex problems for both lovers.

There appears to be nothing innate in the difference in preferences in lovestyle between men and women. The differences develop because men and women are brought up to seek different kinds of fulfillment from relationships. Men certainly receive cultural approval for falling in love and developing lasting relationships, but a competing cultural message tells men—particularly younger men—to "get laid." Little wonder that many men believe a relationship is simply the means to intercourse. Women, on the other hand, tend to experience intercourse as the means to a different end, that of a lasting relationship.

Men's chief complaint about women in bed is that they are not responsive enough. The main reason for this aloofness is that the "wham, bam" lovestyle precludes the leisurely pace and sensual caresses necessary for most women to begin to become aroused.

Unhurried whole-body loveplay is the solution to both men's and women's chief complaints about the other's lovestyle. Sensuality gives men the aroused, responsive lovers they want, at the same time that it gives women the whole-body sharing they want. In addition, as time spent in sensual loveplay increases, a man's likelihood of developing sex problems decreases. And women are more likely to feel comfortable enough to reach orgasm. Extended loveplay means more time to become adventurous and experimental, with less likelihood of slipping into a boring routine. A relaxed

pace also makes it easier to discuss birth control or other possibly stressful issues. Touchy subjects feel less threatening when lovers are in touch.

As mentioned in the discussion of sensuality, one way to explore how much nongenital loveplay your lover enjoys before she feels genitally aroused is to refrain from touching her breasts or pubic area until she asks you to. This gives the woman a chance to enjoy as much caressing as she would like without feeling pressured to "get it on." It allows men to learn how much sensual loveplay their lovers like. It gives both lovers practice in intimate discussions and it's a chance to try some different moves.

Many men's preoccupation with "the old in-out" traps them in a no-win situation—they develop sex problems and their lovers become frustrated. Extended sensuality, on the other hand, is the key to no-lose lovemaking. Men become the lovers they would like to be and women become the lovers men would like them to be.

Other Issues

Deep Thrust: Many men enjoy penetrating women's erotic openings as deeply as possible. Some believe this signifies women's total acceptance of them. Others see it as a measure of their mastery over the woman. A regular theme in men's magazine cartoons is the situation where a man jams his penis so far into the vagina, it comes out the woman's mouth. Deep penetration certainly has its devotées among women, but many women find it less than optimally pleasurable.

The most erotically sensitive parts of the mouth, vagina, and anus are the openings themselves where most of the nerves sensitive to touch are located. The deeper you push, the less touch-sensitive the tissue. This is true for both men and women. Consider how it feels when a lover runs her tongue around your lips. The lips are extremely sensitive to touch and most men find this quite arousing. Now, how does it feel if she pushes her tongue down your throat? Some men enjoy this; others find it uncomfortable. The vagina is the opening best suited to deep penetration—assuming that it is fully lubricated and that insertion proceeds gradually —but deep penetration of the mouth or anus makes many women turn off. In pornography, the penises regularly plunge "deep throat" and far into the actresses' anuses which suggests that women in general enjoy these moves. Some do, but many do not. It's best to ask a woman how she feels about deep thrusting. As a general rule, though, women tend to prefer caresses of the openings themselves or their near-inner areas.

Oral Loveplay and Menstruation.   Some men feel reluctant to go down on women who are menstruating for fear of tasting menstrual flow or being exposed to unpleasant odors. However, a tongue that visits the clitoris need not come in contact with menstrual flow because the clitoris sits outside and above the vagina. Menstruation may change a woman's vaginal aroma somewhat, but many men enjoy oral-clitoral loveplay regardless of their lovers' periods. Tampons or diaphragms minimize menstrual seepage and odor because they collect the flow at the cervix toward the rear of the vagina. There may be more seepage and odor if napkins or other menstrual products are used.

Despite cynical efforts by manufacturers of "feminine hygiene sprays" and douches to convince us that the vagina smells foul, many men thoroughly enjoy the vagina's natural aroma throughout the menstrual cycle. Most men do not find vagina aroma any more unpleasant than women find the aroma of the aroused penis. Both of these natural perfumes resemble a slightly salty "clean sweat" smell. Many lovers find these aromas attractive and arousing. Recent research suggests that these aromas play a subtly important role in sexual arousal. However, some men balk at giving the gift of oral stimulation during a woman's period because "it's too funky down there." A man may feel this way, but it's important not to make the woman feel self-conscious about it. That would interfere with her ability to relax.

Anal Finger Etiquette.   If a woman enjoys being touched around, upon, or inside her anus, be sure to keep track of which fingers do the touching. Do not use the same fingers to caress the vagina or clitoris. Bacteria necessary for proper digestion and general good health live in the digestive tract, and some of these friendly organisms populate the anal area. If they get into the vagina, however, they can cause annoying infections which may turn the woman off not only to lovemaking, but to the man who was less than careful with his hands.

The Hymen.   There is a pervasive myth that a woman's first inter-course is painful because of the hymen, the thin membrane that surrounds the entrance to the inner vagina. Many men are con-fused about the hymen. It is a thin flexible skin that surrounds the vaginal opening like the lips surround the mouth. Only very rarely does the hymen actually cover the vagina. If it did, virgin women could not menstruate. The men's magazines often describe inter-course with virgins as "piercing her armor" or "popping her cherry." In fact, the hymen is rarely "torn asunder." It is stretched like the outer skin of the penis during erection. Depending on how much hymen a woman has, any part of the membrane eliminated during first intercourse is sloughed off much the way calloused skin is rubbed off the hand. Because the hymen does not ordinarily prevent entry into the vagina, a virgin woman need not bleed or experience pain if the man follows a few simple suggestions simi-lar to those recommended throughout this book:

—Take your time.

—If you know that the woman is a virgin, by all means mention your intention to be extremely gentle and leisurely. Some women have been taught to expect that first intercourse will be painful, which can easily become a self-fulfilling prophecy. A man might ask the woman to tell him if she feels any discomfort.

—Make sure the vagina is fully lubricated before you insert any-thing. You might consider additional lubricants. Like all living tissue, a moist hymen is more pliable than a dry one. A moist hymen can stretch. A dry one is apt to tear and cause pain.

—Insert a finger first, then two.

—Insert the penis very slowly. If insertion hurts the woman, withdraw and concentrate on sensuality for a while.

Painful Intercourse.   Lack of lubrication is the leading cause of painful intercourse. Many men would never dream of driving a car that was low on oil, yet they pay little attention to vaginal lubrica-tion, which is absolutely essential to "smooth-running" lovemak-ing.

Some women experience pain during "doggie" position inter-course, also known as rear entry. This position, which many lovers enjoy, can place pressure on the front of the vagina or on the woman's urethra and may feel uncomfortable. However, many women enjoy this position because it leaves the man's hands free for clitoral and sensual loveplay. If you enjoy this position, be careful about depth of insertion and try not to thrust too furiously. Other individual idiosyncrasies in lovestyle might also cause discomfort. Try to discuss mutual preferences with your lover.

Several infections can result in painful intercourse for women (see Chapter 12).

It can be difficult to tell a lover that a particular move hurts. For a woman, it can lead to accusations of unresponsiveness. If either lover feels uncomfortable, both lovers suffer because pain introduces stress—and possibly sex problems—into the relationship. During initial loveplay, particularly with a new lover, a man might encourage the woman to let him know if any loveplay causes her discomfort. He might also let her know if she hurts him. Clearing the air at the outset usually results in more mutually satisfying lovemaking.

Other Fears.   Any fear that causes men anxiety during lovemaking can do the same for women. Some women feel self-conscious about various parts of their bodies. Others fear pregnancy, personal rejection or the "choice" of submitting to painful moves or facing charges of being hung up.

A man whose lover likes to make love more often than he does might accuse her of nymphomania. Women react to this label like men react to being called sex fiends. It is perfectly all right to decline a sexual invitation graciously, but it is insensitive and stress-producing to engage in name-calling.

Many women fear their lovers might "kiss and tell." No one enjoys being an object of gossip, particularly when the subject is as personal as lovemaking. Some men feel considerable pressure from friends to tell "how far they got" or "how good she was." These questions can be difficult to deflect. However, before a man answers them, he might consider how he would feel if at that very moment the woman in question were broadcasting the details of his intimate talents—or lack thereof—to a group of her friends.

In the end, women turn on to the moves that make men look and feel their best in bed: gentle, imaginative, unhurried playfulness, reciprocal give-and-take, and an appreciation for the whole woman, not just her genitals, breasts and buttocks.

Chapter 7

IF THE WOMAN YOU LOVE GETS RAPED

In James Dickey's book, *Deliverance*, four friends take a canoe trip down a whitewater river in a remote corner of Georgia. Two of them, Bobby and the narrator, get waylaid at gunpoint by a pair of backwoodsmen who force Bobby to strip naked and lie face down over a fallen log. While one of the assailants presses his shotgun to Bobby's ear, the other rapes him anally.

The narrator, tied to a tree, describes the scene:

> A scream hit me. It was a sound of pain and outrage. . . . I had never [imagined] such brutality and carelessness of touch, or such disregard for another person's body. . . . The man worked steadily on Bobby, every now and then getting a better grip on the ground with his knees. At last, he raised his face . . . and quivered silently while the man with the gun looked on with an odd mixture of sympathy and approval. The man . . . drew out. Bobby let go of the log and fell to his side, both arms over his face.

The assailants turn to rape the narrator when one of the friends, Lewis, shoots the rapist in the back with an arrow. He falls over dead and his partner flees into the woods.

168

Lewis stands over the dead man and says he figured it was the only thing to do. The narrator agrees completely but wonders what they should do with the body. Drew, the fourth member of the group, suggests that they turn it over to police downriver. But Lewis warns against being "so all-fired boy scoutish." If they report the incident, they would surely face a murder charge for shooting a man in the back, and they would be judged by a jury of mountain folk sympathetic to the dead man. Lewis insists that they bury the body.

They ask Bobby's opinion.

> He was sitting on the same log he was forced to lean over. He got up, 20 years older, and walked over to the dead man. Then, in an explosion so sudden that it was like something bursting through from another world, he kicked the body in the face again and again.

Bobby votes with Lewis. " 'Do you think I want this to get around?' "

The men conceal the corpse and vow silence about the attack, but it haunts them the rest of their lives. Bobby's life is shattered. He quits his job, fails at a new business, and finally moves to Hawaii. The narrator, who refuses to discuss the canoe trip with his wife, is gripped ever after by a "special fear" every time he hears a strange voice on the telephone, every time unfamiliar headlights pull into his dead-end street.

> And so it ended, except in my mind. Everything I remembered became a possession to me, a personal private possession as nothing in my life ever had.

Few men would argue with the group's actions. But imagine that they reported the incident and were treated as women rape victims usually are. Criminal justice officials with traditional attitudes about rape might reach some different conclusions from the narrator's account:

—The complainant invited the alleged attack. Those men had no business venturing into the woods to begin with.

—The complainant's fashionable camping outfit provoked the alleged assailant who interpreted an open shirt and rolled-up trouser legs as an invitation to lovemaking. After all, mountain men will be mountain men.

—The complainant consented to anal intercourse because he did not struggle sufficiently against it. The complainant appears to have been sexually attracted to the gentleman with whom he made love because the two spoke prior to the alleged assault. The complainant did not scream nor did he attempt to dissuade his lover prior to the intercourse—and silence implies consent. Even with a shotgun held to the head, true rape is so horrible to contemplate that a reasonably prudent person would resist it no matter what the risk. Finally, although the complainant did scream during the lovemaking, sex is frequently painful for the submissive partner, therefore mere screaming cannot be considered indicative of resistance or lack of consent.

—The complainant should be booked for participation in sodomy, a heinous perversion, and a felony.

—The deceased was falsely accused. After all, the group of murderers, who outnumbered their victims four to two, had to concoct some justification for shooting a man in the back.

If this interpretation sounds ridiculous, imagine how it sounds to the *hundreds of thousands* of women sexually assaulted each year. If a woman lives through a sexual assault—and many do not —she is faced with an agonizing choice at a time when she is least capable of making reasoned decisions. She can decide not to report the attack and risk being raped again by the same man or men, perhaps accompanied by other friends. Or she can report the assault and face figurative "rerape" by the criminal justice system whose officers typically force her to endure accusations that she invited or consented to the attack, that she did not struggle "enough," that she made a false accusation (itself a serious crime), and the ultimate insult, that she's simply another whore who didn't get paid.

These days, legal reform efforts are underway and they appear to be doing some good. More women police officers are being assigned to interview victims. Some police departments train officers in the humane treatment of sexual assault victims. And some courts have placed limitations on the extent to which a victim may be interrogated about her sexual history at a rape trial. Despite these reforms, most women remain extremely skeptical of the benefits of reporting rape. *The accepted estimate continues to be that only one victim in ten reports sexual assault.*

Sexual assault inevitably precipitates a deep, long-term sexual crisis in a relationship. Few men give much thought to the agony of sexual assault until it hits home, and if it does, they are usually unprepared to deal with it. Many relationships break up in the aftermath of rape. Some men truly want to be supportive but cannot figure out how. Others arm themselves and set off to kill the rapist. Some men believe that rape is impossible without consent and jump to cruel conclusions. Others castigate themselves for not taking better care of their lovers. Few men realize the depth of guilt and shame victims typically feel or the time it can take to recover sufficiently to be able to make love again.

Men's naiveté about rape is hardly surprising. Apart from lurid news accounts, sexual assault has become an acceptable subject for serious discussion only in the last decade, since the start of the contemporary women's movement. Most information about sexual assault has been gathered by women for dissemination to other women generally through the woman-oriented media. The bulk of this material has been written by rape counselors whose work with brutalized victims has shown them the handicraft of men at their predatory worst.

As a result, men have been largely excluded from meaningful participation in victims' recoveries. For a man, the rape of a lover is a wrenching personal—and sexual—trauma. His reactions to the attack can play a pivotal role in his lover's recovery and in the future of their relationship. Based on interviews with rape counselors, this chapter gives men a chance to be supportive and suggests how best to react if this terrible violation touches your lover, your life.

"Sexual Assault," Not "Rape"

The term "rape" presents the same problem as "impotence" and "frigidity" because of its connotations. To most men, "rape" means coerced sexual intercourse. The word tends to gloss over the violence, beating, and degradation most victims find considerably more unnerving than the mere fact of uninvited intercourse, which unfortunately is a regular event in many women's lives. Men tend to view "rape" solely as a sexual crime, when actually, intercourse may have nothing to do with it. As we have seen, men under stress develop sex problems, so it should come as no surprise that many rapists, who tend to be consumed with fear and loathing, suffer severe sex problems that often leave them incapable of raising an erection. In interviews, convicted rapists freely admit that the sexual component of rape is secondary to the desire to humiliate the victim, to dominate her (or him), to violate the victim's personal integrity as a means toward enhancing the rapist's own power fantasies. Sexual assault may be a crime of lust, but it's a lust for power, not necessarily for intercourse.

For this reason, sexual trauma counselors uniformly prefer the term "sexual assault" to "rape." "Rape" focuses too much attention—particularly men's attention—on the dimension of intercourse, while "sexual assault" emphasizes the brutalization fundamental to this crime.

Sexual assault is similar to mugging except that the woman's dignity is stolen instead of, or in addition to, her money. Any man who has ever been beaten up and robbed on the street can appreciate some of what women go through during and after sexual assault. The typical mugging victim feels an overriding fear of being killed during the attack, followed by the realization of extreme vulnerability, the feeling that there is no safety anywhere, and that one's ability to control one's own life is a cruel illusion. Now suppose that instead of simply intimidating a man with a pistol, knife, or tire iron, imagine that the mugger ripped the man's pants off and shoved his weapon—or his penis—up the man's anus. Would that be a sex crime? Possibly, but most men would focus on the degradation. Sex might be part of it, but men who become victims of sexual assault, like women victims, experience the "sex" much less than the "assault."

"Did You Hear About the Midnight Rambler?"

Most authorities agree that sexual assault is the nation's number two violent crime, second only to wife beating. In 1973, the FBI documented 51,000 cases. If that figure represents the standard 10 percent estimate, then 510,000 sexual assaults were committed that year, one every minute of every day, 24 hours a day for the entire year.

The vast majority of sexual assailants get away with their crimes. During one recent year, New York City prosecutors obtained 18 rape convictions among 1,000 men arrested on the charge whose arrests were based on 2,500 victim reports. In other words, men accused of sexual assault in New York City during that year were convicted in less than 1 percent of reported cases.

Why are so few sexual assailants convicted? At least part of the answer has to do with continuing widespread belief in a number of myths about sexual assault:

Nice Girls Don't Get Raped.   This is the myth that women invite rape if they dress provocatively, venture into neighborhoods where they "don't belong" or arouse men by cock-teasing. It fails to explain how nuns, seven-year-old girls and eighty-year-old grandmothers wind up sexually multilated in their own beds. Women have every right to dress comfortably—in sleeveless tops, bra-less, in halters, shorts, whatever—without fear that a man will take it as an "invitation." Most men who go shirtless in warm weather would feel outraged if anyone considered their bare chests an invitation to drag them into the bushes. Women have every right to move about freely in society. The fear of sexual assault, in effect, imprisons many women in their homes. The notion that nice girls don't get raped makes as much sense as saying that frugal men don't get robbed.

You Can't Thread a Moving Needle.   This myth declares that rape is impossible because the victim must cooperate with the attacker for him to be able to insert his penis into the opening of his choice. It has as much merit as saying that mugging is impossible because the victim must consent to the transfer of funds for the thief to be able to remove his wallet. Clearly, sexual assault victims have no choice but to submit, which is why this crime is so degrading. What would have happened to Bobby in *Deliverance* had he played the moving needle? He would have had his head blown off. Death threats are the rule during sexual assault, and afterward most victims say their chief fear was a terror of being killed. People usually become remarkably cooperative in the face of death threats while stripped naked at the hands of brutal attackers who generally appear to be quite capable of murder. Many assaults are "gang bangs" which lend credence to the death threats and make it even easier for the attackers to pin down the victim. Finally, "threading the needle," that is, penetration, is not necessary for the victim to feel severely traumatized.

They Fantasize About It. They Must Want It.　The difference between the fantasy and reality of sexual assault is that in fantasy, the woman retains total control over all events, whereas in reality, she has absolutely none. A man might fantasize about rescuing a beautiful woman from a burning high rise without the slightest wish to be caught in a fire on the thirty-fifth floor.

Nancy Friday, who collected women's sexual fantasies for *My Secret Garden* and *Forbidden Flowers*, develops the theory that rape fantasies occur largely to women from sexually repressed backgrounds. Women brought up to believe that sex is evil have as much interest in lovemaking as anyone else, but they have been taught that they are not supposed to want it. Rape fantasies allow them to dream about sex without feeling responsible for it—the responsibility belongs to the fantasy-rapist. Friday observes that rape fantasies are more common among older women than younger, and concludes that younger women brought up in a more sexually permissive atmosphere feel less conflict about sex and more comfortable owning up to their sexual desires.

Women have not been the only ones brought up in sexually repressive surroundings. Many men have similar backgrounds, and for Friday's theory to be persuasive, men should also have fantasies of sexual violation. This is precisely what Carol Tavris found in a survey for *Psychology Today.** Half the respondents of *both sexes* said they occasionally fantasized being ravished by the opposite sex. However, less than 10 percent said they had rape fantasies often.

Who ever enjoys being forced to do anything against their will? Some women may fantasize about rape but they don't want it to happen to them any more than men do.

False Accusations.　"Rape is an accusation easily made and hard to prove," wrote Lord Chief Justice Matthew Hale, an esteemed seventeenth-century English jurist. But how easy *is* it to make a false accusation of sexual assault? About as easy as accusing someone of a $50 mugging at gunpoint. A person bent on avenging some personal wrong could easily make a false accusation of mugging. The "victim" would not have to show any injury, only emotional distress which is easy to fake. The "mugger" would not have to be arrested with the money or the gun for the crime to have

* January 1977.

taken place. In fact, it would be *easier* to make a false accusation of mugging than sexual assault. In a mugging, no one is interested in the state of the victim's clothing or genitals, or the victim's relationship to the mugger. But if it's so easy to make false accusations of mugging, why don't more people make them? Because any criminal accusation, whether true or false, invites intensive police interrogation, life disruption, and unwelcome publicity, not to mention the possibility of criminal indictment if the charge proves false. An accusation of sexual assault inevitably results in victim humiliation no matter how kindly the criminal justice system might treat her. How many men would report a *true* case of anal rape, let alone a false accusation?

Yet, law enforcement officials say more false accusations are made in sexual assault cases than in any other crime. Susan Brownmiller writes that in 1973, New York City police judged 15 percent of rape accusations false, seven times the rate for other violent crimes. Then, police*women* replaced policemen as rape victim interviewers. The false report rate immediately fell to 2 percent, identical to the false report rate for other violent crimes. It would appear that either policewomen fall for lies or policemen have difficulty believing the truth. In her landmark study of rape, *Against Our Will*, Brownmiller writes: "Women believe other women. Men do not."

You Have to Force Them Anyway.   Many men do have to coax women into bed, and women as well as men may be brought up to believe that no might mean yes. However, a reasonable person can distinguish between coaxing and coercion. There is a quality of playfulness in coaxing that becomes ruthlessness in coercion. Some men have trouble differentiating lovemaking from sexual assault because they have been persuaded that intercourse is "normally" painful for women. But pain causes sex problems. A woman who wants to make love should feel no pain during loveplay. What about women who are into sado-masochism? According to a 1972 survey sponsored by the Playboy Foundation, only 3 percent of women say they are fond of sado-masochism. Mutually agreed-upon S&M encounters are as theatrical as they are sexual. They tend to be carefully worked out beforehand so no one gets hurt, and the limits are clearly understood by both participants. Spontaneous expressions of pain during loveplay mean "stop!"

Why Don't They Just Lie Back and Enjoy It?   Try suggesting that one to Bobby in *Deliverance.*

She Invited Me to Her Place.   An invitation to a person's home does not imply a license to smash the furniture. An invitation to a woman's home is not an invitation into her vagina. Similarly, a woman who accepts a man's invitation to dinner, a movie, a sauna, a drive in the country, or a visit to his place may or may not want to make love. Some men feel women "owe" them a lay if they underwrite dates. Most women would rather share the expenses early in the evening than get that kind of "bill" later.

What to Do—And What Not to Do

A woman brutalized by sexual assault needs the same kind of help, support, and comforting a man in a similar situation would need. Above all, a woman needs two things: *To be listened to* and to *decide for herself* how to deal with the assault.

Imagine that you're jogging in a park when suddenly five punks jump you, beat you, and force you to suck some of them off while the rest violate you anally. They leave you battered and semiconscious. Somehow you manage to drag yourself to a friend's house nearby. You're in shock. You can't believe the attack took place. You can't quite believe you survived it. Do you need your friend to lecture you on the foolishness of jogging alone in the park? Hardly. You'll probably spend a good long time kicking yourself for not escaping the attack. Do you need your friend to accuse you of having invited the assault? Certainly not. If anything, you might wonder how anyone who knew you well could even *ask* such a question. Do you need your friend to berate himself for not being along to protect you? As if he could have. No, you'd probably want him to attend to *you*, and not get sidetracked by his own imagined shortcomings. Do you need him to load his shotgun and bound out the door swearing vengeance? No, you've just finished dealing with a gang of violence-crazed lunatics—who needs another one? Do you need him to grab you and rush you off to a police station and demand that the police take pictures of your anus? Clearly not.

Men can best support sexually assaulted lovers by keeping their heads and following a few suggestions:

—Listen to the woman. Really listen. It's normal for a sexual assault victim to cry, scream, sob, rant, and rave. That's her right. It's also her right to withdraw and be silent, if she chooses.

—She should make *every* decision in response to the assault. She was the person attacked. The important thing is for her to regain a sense of control over her life after being stripped of that control by her attacker(s). Many men pride themselves on "taking charge" in emergencies; taking charge is what society expects men to do. However, this is one case where men should hold themselves in check. This can be difficult, particularly for men who are used to making the important decisions in a relationship, but it's vital. Rather than ordering her: "Lie down while I call the police," ask her what she wants to do and what she wants you to do. Offer options, suggest alternatives, help her weigh pros and cons, but all the decisions should be hers. The *only* time a man should make a decision for a sexual assault victim is if she appears too seriously injured to take care of herself; for example, if she is bleeding from the head or vagina, losing consciousness, has broken bones, or cannot remember her name. Otherwise, she should make the decisions.

—Support the woman for surviving. Most victims' chief fear during an attack is a fear of being killed. In this context, *anything a woman does to survive an assault is the right thing to do.* Many victims torment themselves for being stupid: "I shouldn't have gone there alone at night." "I'm such an idiot for agreeing to change his dollar bill." "How could I be so dumb to fall for that stalled car routine?" The catalogue of possible "should haves" is endless, and victims tend to be quite hard on themselves. The important thing is that whatever happened, whatever the victim did or did not do, she survived. She was resourceful enough to escape with her life from a potentially life-threatening situation. Later, a few weeks or months afterward, a man might help his lover figure out what she'd do differently in a similar situation, but in the immediate aftermath, the victim does not need to hear what she should have done. She needs to be reassured that she did the right thing because she survived.

—Continue to listen. Then listen some more. There is a natural tendency when comforting the victim of any personal tragedy to try to turn attention away from the terrible event: "It's over now. Try to put it behind you. You've got your whole life in front of you.

Don't dwell on it." Nevertheless, many victims need to keep talking about the attack over and over again in order to come to terms
with it. Let the victim decide how long to dwell on the assault—it
might take quite a while before she feels ready to turn her attention
elsewhere. Encouraging trauma victims to relive their tragedies is
central to crisis intervention. Encourage the victim to discuss the
assault in any way that feels appropriate to her. Try not to dismiss
any feeling as unimportant no matter how trivial it may seem. As
in relationship disputes, admitting the thoughts that seem silly
often has a significant cathartic effect: "As he ripped my blouse off,
I thought, dammit, I just sewed those new buttons on. . . ." Try not
to accuse a lover of being overly obsessive, self-pitying, or repeti-
tive. Most victims would gladly forget about the sexual assault if
they could.

—Don't become the injured party. Don't start raving and ranting
about "the animal that did this," or swear revenge or whatever.
Your anger at the assailant will be misplaced because he's not
there. Only your lover is there and she doesn't need you to be crazy
or angry. If you act crazy, your actions may be read as being angry
at your *lover*, which is the last thing in the world she needs. *She*
was assaulted. Listen to *her*.

The Stages of Recovery

People recover from severe trauma in a three-stage process: initial shock, resumption of routines, then integration of the experience into their lives. These stages are not distinct from one another
—each evolves slowly into the next. In addition, they do not evoke
uniform reactions—people recover from trauma individually.

Initial shock can involve disorientation, numbness, temporary
memory loss, or physical symptoms. Some people become hyster-
ical; others become eerily subdued.

Men familiar with rape victim assistance programs often believe
that specific immediate reactions are called for: gathering any
physical evidence, calling a rape hot line, then immediately whisk-
ing the victim off to an emergency room for a medical examination,
VD and pregnancy tests. None of these is absolutely necessary. *The
woman should decide for herself how she would like to proceed*,
assuming, of course, that she's in a condition to do so.

If a victim chooses to report the assault to the police, the sooner she reports, the better—at least from a law enforcement point of view. If she would like to report, but later, that's all right, though it may hamper efforts to prosecute the rapist. A woman may decide not to report. This is also her prerogative.

Some communities have rape-crisis counseling services and/or telephone hot lines. A victim may or may not want to talk with a victim assistance counselor. That, too, should be her decision.

Some victims want medical examinations right away, particularly if a beating has resulted in injury. Others prefer to bathe, rest, call a friend, and postpone any checkup until they feel emotionally equipped to deal with it. VD and pregnancy tests can wait.

So can the morning-after pill—up to seventy-two hours. Some women insist on taking the morning-after pill immediately because they feel repelled by the thought of pregnancy by a rapist. However, the morning-after pill is a hazardous drug, and it's often a good idea to postpone a decision on it until the woman has calmed down a bit from the initial terror of the assault. For one thing, the victim may not be fertile. She might calculate where she is in her menstrual cycle (see "Fertility Awareness" in Chapter 11). Even if she is fertile, scientists estimate that the chance of becoming pregnant from a single unprotected intercourse is no greater than 30 percent. The morning-after pill contains DES, the synthetic estrogen shown to cause cancer in the daughters of women who took it while pregnant. DES daughters should not take the morning-after pill. Ten pills must be taken over five days and may cause side effects which resemble those of the birth control pill (see "The Pill" in Chapter 11). Typical side effects include: nausea, vomiting, headaches, and menstrual irregularities. Half the women who use the morning-after pill have late periods; this delay mimics pregnancy. Life-threatening side effects are also possible. If any warning signs associated with the serious side effects of the pill develop, see a doctor immediately. Some sexual assault victims prefer the ordeal of abortion if they become pregnant to the ordeal of the morning-after pill when they might not be.

Within a week or two after the assault, most victims begin to resume their normal lives. This can be a painful process because many women feel certain their lives can never return to normal. Some adopt a what's-the-point-of-anything attitude. A supportive lover can try to provide some perspective on this understandable reaction. A woman's life may never be the same as it was before the assault, but it can return to some semblance of normalcy if she works at making that happen.

Lovers should continue to encourage victims to discuss their feelings about the assault and urge them to take any steps that feel appropriate. Some women want the kind of short-term counseling provided by many rape-crisis centers. Others want longer term therapy. Some opt for self-defense classes. Others want to spend more time with family or by themselves. Lovers should try not to lobby for one approach over another. They should continue to "be there" and suggest options for action even if it means having the same discussion over and over again.

Some victims remain disoriented for quite a while. Headaches, nightmares, insomnia, paranoia, and depression are common and sometimes take years to subside. Some victims quit their jobs. Others move, start carrying purse-sized tear gas canisters, or get Doberman pinschers. Some women become terrified of doing anything alone. Others insist on going out alone to prove to themselves that they can.

As the months pass, victims slowly begin to integrate the sexual assault into their lives. The process is similar to the way people come to terms with any personal tragedy. A widow can feel sharp stabs of grief years after her husband's death, and many sexual assault victims, like the men in *Deliverance*, feel the aftereffects for the rest of their lives.

I Failed Her

Men who understand that women do not invite sexual assault often blame themselves for "failing" to protect their lovers from it. These feelings are normal, as are shame, rage, and overprotectiveness after the fact. One emotion that can be particularly upsetting to those men who have more sexual energy than their lovers is a fear that the assault will leave her even less interested in making love than she used to be. That thought often triggers a burst of guilt: "Here she's been beaten and raped and all I care about is getting laid." A man may not feel proud of this emotion, but it is as understandable as the feelings of relief that accompany bereavement when a loved one finally dies after a long lingering illness.

While men should focus a good deal of energy on helping their lovers deal with the assault, they should not ignore their own needs for support and comforting in the aftermath of a lover's rape. Just as sexual assault victims need someone to listen to their pain, their lovers need good listeners as well—preferably not the victim, who already has enough to deal with. A man might turn to a friend, family member, or professional counselor. Most lovers of sexually assaulted women have deep feelings of outrage, shame, and guilt to work out. These emotions can be hard to exorcise alone. Men who internalize them often wind up with stress-related health problems: ulcers, high blood pressure, sex problems. Let yourself get help dealing with *your own* reactions to the assault. Men who take care of their own emotional needs tend to provide better support to their lovers.

Making Love Again After Sexual Assault

For many men, the most difficult aspect of helping a lover recover from sexual assault is the issue of making love again. She may not want to for quite a while, and when she feels ready, the continuing stress of the assault might detract from the lovemaking or cause sex problems. Like all other decisions in response to sexual assault, the decision to make love again should be left to the woman, as difficult as that may be for many men.

Women's sexual reactions to rape vary considerably. Some want to make love again right away to reassure themselves that their lovers still love them, do not blame them, and do not consider them "soiled." Other women cannot make love again for a long time. One woman may want to be held and sensually caressed immediately, but may need time before she feels comfortable being sexual again. Another might get angry with her lover and remind him of the times he may have crossed the line from coaxing to coercion.

Men should reassure their lovers that they still find them sexually attractive, still love them, and still want to make love. Men should also abide by their lovers' decisions how and when to resume lovemaking. Some men have a long and painful wait. It can be trying for a man to allow his lover to define their sexual relationship, particularly if he has made most of those decisions in the past or if he fears that her reluctance is based on his own history of less-than-gentle loveplay.

Sexual assault counselors say women assaulted in their own beds have the most difficult time readjusting to making love. Attacks in the intimacy of a woman's own bed result in tremendous feelings of personal violation and increased likelihood of sexual reluctance and sex problems afterward. Some women take two or three years to feel relaxed enough to reach orgasm again after sexual assault in their own beds. Men may also experience sexual difficulties, particularly if forced to watch or participate in the assault.

A victim may want to engage in sensual loveplay, particularly massage, as a therapeutic tension release long before she feels ready to resume lovemaking. It can be difficult for a man to stop at the sensual without becoming sexual. We have seen, however, that an ability to appreciate sensuality apart from sexuality is a crucial ingredient of problem-free lovemaking. It becomes paramount when helping a lover readjust to physical intimacy after sexual assault. The myth that women invite rape by dressing "provocatively" is a result of men's assumption that sensuality automatically leads to sexuality. Some men's inability to distinguish between sensuality and sexuality leads them to become sexually assaultive. A man supporting a lover's recovery from sexual assault should cultivate the sensual while holding off on the sexual until the woman feels ready for it.

At the conclusion of *Deliverance*, the narrator returns home to his wife. He's an emotional wreck. His side is cut open. He's just witnessed the rape of one friend and the drowning of another. He's terrified that the police will arrest him for murder. He can't sleep.

He dozes fitfully. Whenever an odd noise startles him back to consciousness, his wife comforts him: " 'I'm right here with you.' "

That's where a lover belongs.

Chapter **8**

HARDCORE/SOFTCORE: LEADING CAUSES OF MEN'S SEX PROBLEMS

Producers of sex films, magazines, and books have long maintained that hardcore pornography and softcore men's magazines deserve First Amendment protection as a form of free speech because they provide sex education to men who desperately need it. Critics agree that these media are educational. However, they argue that they teach men how to be sexually assaultive toward women.

The debate crystallizes around X-rated "adult entertainment." Pornographers say hardcore media inspire masturbation, not sexual assault. They evoke the image of the dirty old man who quietly masturbates into his trenchcoat at the Beaver Theater, and they are quick to refer to the men's magazines as "one-handed" publications. Pornographers insist that their explicit films and picture books not only are harmless, but that they serve the public interest as psychological "safety valves" for potentially assaultive men, whose use of pornography allows them to vent their sexual frustrations without resorting to rape. They cite research conducted under the auspices of the President's Commission on Obscenity and Pornography which suggests that the average convicted rapist was exposed to *less* pornography prior to conviction than the average man on the street.

Opponents of pornography, on the other hand, say that films depicting wholesale cruelty to dogs or horses would be forced out of theaters by public outcry, yet films that show women bound and beaten are lauded as free speech. They say the spankings and "discipline" increasingly incorporated into X-rated cinema persuade men that women enjoy violence and humiliation with their sex. Opponents of pornography also cite research collected by the President's Commission which suggests that exposure to pornography increases men's sexual aggressiveness toward women and plays a role in triggering the attacks that lead to sex offenders' imprisonment.

Pornographers dismiss their detractors as "antisexual puritans." Some critics reply that they support film portrayals of lovemaking, but object to representations of women as penis-fixated holes just aching—and sometimes literally dying—to be plugged.

The Boom in Sex Media

While the impact of hard- and softcore pornography on the incidence of sexual assault remains controversial, no one disputes that its tremendous volume has made it a major source of men's sex education, for millions of men, the *only* source:

—The sex media have become a $4 *billion* a year industry, according to a 1978 report in *Forbes,* the business magazine.

—The 10 leading men's magazines, rated "R-and-a-half," gross $500 million a year, an enormous sum, but less than 15 percent of pornography's total income.

—X-rated media gross $3.5 billion a year, excluding the burgeoning market in pirated materials.

—The nation's 780 adult theaters admit 2.5 million customers a week and gross more than $1 million a day.

—Exhibiting movies that cost only 25 cents, some of the nation's 1,400 peep-show parlors gross $10,000 a day.

—Up to half of the 400,000 prerecorded video casettes sold in 1978 were X-rated, according to the *New York Times.* "Deep Throat," "The Devil in Miss Jones" and "The Story of O" have been on the list of the 10 top-selling video casettes ever since the list was established.

Sex media have become increasingly visible and respectable in recent years, from *Playboy* interviews with Presidential candidates to bound-and-battered-woman billboards advertising record albums. A growing number of sexuality authorities are incorporating hardcore pornography into their sex education work. One pioneering and highly reputable national sex education organization uses X-rated media to wean people away from their apprehensions about discussing sex openly. And some sex therapists recommend pornographic films as an introduction to the scope of contemporary sexuality for couples who complain of being locked into boring sexual ruts.

Although the pervasiveness of sex media provides some justification for its incorporation into sex education programs, the problem with hard- and softcore materials as educational tools is that *they depict a lovestyle that causes sex problems.* Sex media have a great deal to do with the genitals, but almost nothing to do with mutually fulfilling lovemaking. They confine their interest to "fucking and sucking," a preoccupation which is a major turn off to women and a leading cause of men's sex problems. Using pornography in sex education makes as much sense as using films of bloody highway accidents as driver training. Most pornography perpetuates the very myths this book is trying to dispel.

Hardcore Pornography: Touch Me Not

X-rated media concentrate on "hardcore action," pumping the penis in and out of any or all of the "girl's" erotic openings. Virtually all physical contact revolves around the genitals, most of it around the penis. Token sensuality is confined to quick stripping, perfunctory swipes at the woman's breasts, and perhaps a few finger pokes or tongue flicks around her clitoris. Then the fucking and sucking begin. They go on and on in a variety of gymnastic positions until the man ejaculates, at which point the "action" ends along with the film.

From a perspective of problem-free lovemaking, the most glaring sex education error in pornography is the absence of leisurely, whole-body sensuality. Hardcore media fixate on the sexual and exclude anything the least bit playful. Except for generally brief and never tender attention to women's breasts, the focus is almost entirely genital, which reinforces many men's view that lovemak-

ing *is* all genital. As we have seen, however, problem-free lovemaking depends on a mix of the sensual and sexual, with the emphasis on whole-body loveplay, not narrow genital focus. Frequently, in order to present the most explicit crotch shots of intercourse, the only parts of the actors that touch one another are their genitals. Pornography never includes any kissing, hand-holding, caressing, massage, reciprocal undressing, tenderness, or discussion of lovemaking preferences. It is the logical conclusion of the "wham, bam, thank you, ma'am" lovestyle.

There is certainly nothing wrong with true-to-life film portrayals of genital loveplay, just as there is nothing wrong with enjoying dessert after a good meal. The problem with pornography—like the problem with eating too much dessert—is one of proportion. In order for men to enjoy extended genital loveplay, their penises and the rest of their bodies need considerable sensual warm-up, best accomplished by relaxed, nongenital loveplay. The same goes for women—only more so. Imagine a film that purported to teach good nutrition but focused entirely on people stuffing their mouths with strawberry shortcake. If the producers of such a film responded to criticism like pornographers do, they would accuse critical dieticians of being "antifood." The real issue, however, would not turn on being "pro-" or "antifood," but rather on the proportions of the various foods that belong in a balanced diet. There would be nothing wrong with nutrition films that included strawberry shortcake as long as they did justice to the variety of foods essential to good health.

Hard on Relationships

Unlike most lovers, the actors in pornography appear perpetually aroused. The women are always eager to get down or go down. And the men boast not only enormous penises that inspire penis envy in the average man, but instant ever-hard erections as well. These traits have been a standard feature of pornography since the "blue movies" of the 1920s. Many men have spent their entire lives absorbing the notions that big dicks, instant erection, and continuous arousal are the rules in sex. As we have seen, these phenomena are the exceptions.

A man who expects himself to measure up to the speed of arousal or penis size in pornography usually concludes that he must be a woefully inadequate lover. The stress engendered by this "failure" can contribute to sex problems.

Similarly, men who expect their lovers to become sexually aroused at a moment's notice, show a tragic misunderstanding of what we have seen actually turns women on. The myths inherent in the pornographic lovestyle can make normal human beings seem abnormal.

It is not uncommon for a man to come home from an after-work "cocktail" of a few peep-show loops and foist himself on his wife, plow directly into her vagina before she feels at all aroused, and then come immediately. Afterward, he may spend the rest of the evening kicking himself for coming too soon, which he decides must be the reason why his wife is so prudish, temperamental, and irritable all the time. The pornographic lovestyle not only ruins lovemaking, but also relationships.

All Work, No Play

One of the more stilted aspects of X-rated films is their general silence. As we have seen, problem-free lovemaking depends in part on tension release, and whooping it up is an excellent way to do this, while at the same time, letting your lover know what a good time you're having, an emotion that tends to be contagious. However, pornographers do not appreciate the erotic quality of sound in lovemaking. Eight millimeter peep-show loops contain no sound at all, and higher class 16 millimeter films generally limit speaking parts to the women, whose stock lines include: "What a magnificent cock!" and "Fuck me, oh, fuck me harder," punctuated with moans and grunts near the border between pleasure and pain.

The men are almost always silent, and always in control. Any emotional response might suggest a lack of control, so the men never show emotion. They never smile, never breathe deeply, never sigh, and rarely speak except to bark orders: "Strip, suck, spread." They usually look bored or grim. If sex were not assumed to be enjoyable for men, the audience would be hard-pressed to find a scene in any X-rated film where the men appeared to be enjoying themselves.

The men look sullen because pornography treats sex as *work*. It's no fun, just another job, with all the fascination of assembling tail lights for GM except that the screws fill different holes. The view that lovemaking is no more than the daily grind with a hard-on is another ingredient in many men's sex problems and many women's lack of interest.

Only the Men Have Orgasms

X-rated media usually depict a good deal of female hip thrashing, but as a rule, only the men have orgasms. The hardcore action labors along until the man ejaculates—almost always outside the woman so there can be no mistake.

Pornographers say they film "come shots" on—instead of inside —the actresses to capture the hardcore action most explicitly. However, in the context of men's difficulties in recognizing women's orgasms, perhaps pornographers fear that if they filmed internal ejaculations, the audience might miss the men's orgasms.

The women in pornography appear to derive considerable joy from being ejaculated upon, and many X-rated films end with a satisfied smile on a woman's semen-spattered face. The actresses are rarely stimulated to orgasm by clitoral caressing, even in "lesbian" films. On the rare occasion when a woman does seem to reach orgasm—always preceded by the announcement: "I'm coming!"—it usually happens as a direct result of intercourse, which as we have seen, is a minority experience among women and an impossibility for many.

Given what women have been saying recently about the kind of lovemaking they enjoy, their increasingly strenuous objections to pornography become less difficult to understand. The sex in pornography recognizes neither their preference for sensuality nor their need for clitoral appreciation.

Boring

Two marvelous aspects of problem-free lovemaking are its limitless variety and lifelong fascination. Pornography, on the other hand, tends to become boring after a short time. Psychological studies show that men become more aroused than women from visual stimulation. But it's a rare man who can elicit more than a twitch from his penis after a few hours of watching pornography.

In contrast to the tedium of X-rated media, focus on a nonpornographic film you found particularly arousing. What made it erotic? Probably some combination of the ingredients of problem-free lovemaking discussed throughout this book: mutual trust and relaxation, leisurely undressing while kissing and snuggling, and whole-body sensuality. In fact, many highly erotic R-rated films show no genital sexuality at all.

In a fascinating study of media-induced arousal discussed in the report of the President's Commission, a group of men was asked to rank erotic photographs from most to least arousing. Sensual caressing with the participants partially clothed ranked *more arousing* than all of the following: explicit oral-genital stimulation of both men and women, female masturbation, a trio of two women and a man engaged in oral sex and intercourse, and all forms of sado-masochism. In film terms, R-rated lovemaking was more erotic than X-rated material.

Softcore Men's Magazines: The Television of Sex

Men's magazines aim at the largely single eighteen to thirty-four-year-old audience, though *Playboy,* a quarter-century mature, includes more married readers in their thirties and forties. Hardcore pornography largely attracts married men thirty to fifty, according to the President's Commission. It sticks to X-rated action because its married patrons are less interested in the seduction exploits that pass for "foreplay" in the men's magazines. In recent years, some timid sensuality has been added to *Penthouse* and *Oui* "sexploits," but progress toward whole-body loveplay has moved only a few yards on a scale of miles.

Although the men's magazines are far less explicit (and less popular) than pornography, the underlying assumptions are similar: Women are assumed to be sexually eager and available to men, and the bigger the penis, the better the intercourse, which is allegedly what turns women on. In recent years, the men's magazines have become more appreciative of the clitoris and women's sexuality in general, but the emphasis is still too genital, the orgasms still disproportionately simultaneous and multiple.

We read little in the men's magazines about massage, contraception, women's lovemaking preferences, relationship problems, sex problems, differences in lovemaking tastes, or suggestions for working them out. We never read *anything* about sexual assault—not, in my opinion, because the publishers condone it or encourage it, but because it would inject a jarring note of reality into the daydream world the men's magazines create.

Like the sex in pornography, sex in the men's magazines is mostly genital, mostly penis-centered and it gets boring after a while. Little wonder that month after month the *Playboy* Advisor reanswers questions about penis size and involuntary ejaculation. The lovestyles depicted in pornography and in the men's magazines take different steps down the same path—the path to sex problems.

The men's magazines are to lovemaking what television is to real life. Both contain enough reality to seduce the audience into suspending its disbelief. Both are colorful, action-packed, engaging, and entertaining—nice packages for their advertising. But they sidestep the important issues in their audience's lives. Neither is really *useful*. Neither television nor the men's magazines face life's inevitable problems head-on—like a man.

Chapter 9

SHARING BIRTH CONTROL ENHANCES LOVEMAKING

Why should a man be involved with birth control? Since it is the woman who gets pregnant, shouldn't she deal with contraception? And what could birth control have to do with the quality of lovemaking?

The answer to this last question is—more than you might imagine. The risk of unwanted pregnancy can introduce considerable stress into a relationship. A man who takes an active interest in birth control decisions is more likely to be trusted by his lover. Their relationship is less likely to be burdened by the resentments women often feel for men who put the entire contraceptive burden on them. Lovers who cultivate the ability to discuss birth control are more likely to be able to discuss other intimate issues. Some women say the Pill turns them off to lovemaking, and many women have similar complaints about other methods.

Contraception is the couple's responsibility, not just the woman's. Although one lover might actually use the method, both can be equally involved in deciding which one to use, just as a couple might decide together which car to buy though one of them does most of the driving. There is a tendency to assign "the job" of birth control to the sex associated with the method in use, but most methods work better and with less hassle when both lovers are involved. Several methods lend themselves to shared use: condoms, foam, diaphragm, nonintercourse lovemaking, and the scientifically accurate form of rhythm called fertility awareness. The Pill and the IUD cannot be shared directly, but men can take an active interest in them—particularly in their side effects—just as women can take an active interest in their lovers' sex problems.

Many men have difficulty understanding how infuriated women may become with lovers who are interested only in seduction, not contraceptive responsibility. But the trauma of unwanted pregnancy does not just fall on women. Men have never been the only ones to get carried away without considering birth control. In the not-too-distant past, men could be forced to marry women who accidentally got pregnant. Sometimes it was no accident. Imagine that a woman who liked you more than you liked her assured you she was protected, then two months later, her father and a few beefy brothers—all armed—showed up at your door to escort you down to City Hall to take out a marriage license. How would you feel about your prospective wife? Could you trust her? Relax with her? Respond sexually to her? And how would you feel about the child? Would you like to embark on fatherhood with a gun at your head?

Birth control can be a hassle, no doubt about it. It can be a difficult subject to raise, particularly with a new lover, but it's easier to discuss than sex problems or the moves you like in bed. Discussing birth control can be *excellent practice* for talking about other intimate issues that feel more personal. A problem might arise if you and your lover have different contraceptive preferences. Birth control decisions require as much patience and give-and-take as any other aspect of lovemaking. Fortunately, there are several highly effective methods to choose from. Lovers can match the methods to their own tastes and needs.

As we have seen, most of men's sex problems stem from the "wham bam" approach to lovemaking. Problem-free lovemaking, on the other hand, is less hurried, less focused on the genitals, and more sensually playful. Sensual loveplay leaves plenty of time to mention birth control. Taking some time to discuss contraception need not interfere with the excitement or spontaneity of making

love any more than slowing down for a left turn detracts from the pleasure of driving. Taking care of business before you get down to pleasure often enhances lovemaking by reducing stress and building trust.

Most women express a strong preference for men who are as eager to get involved in birth control decisions as they are to get into bed. Problem-free lovemaking means nobody gets screwed.

Heard the Latest? Changing Fashions in Birth Control

Contraceptive options have expanded considerably over the last twenty years. The number of methods has increased and our understanding of them continues to evolve as research reflects more experience with them.

If you find the subject of contraception confusing, you are by no means alone. Conflicting claims for the various methods have perplexed doctors and birth control counselors as well as the general public. For example, when birth control pills were first introduced, health professionals (mostly men) and the news media (mostly men) embraced them enthusiastically. Except for a few critics whose reputations suffered, everyone believed the Pill manufacturers' promotional claims that birth control pills were a technological breakthrough, the answer to every woman's contraceptive needs. Only years later did doctors and the public become aware of the Pill's potentially life-threatening risks. The intrauterine device (IUD) was also introduced with great fanfare, followed years later by warnings about its possibly serious risks.

Meanwhile, once the Pill and IUD were declared official miracles, the traditional birth control methods—condom, foam, diaphragm, and rhythm—were dismissed as obsolete and ineffective, despite the fact that millions of lovers had been using them successfully for generations.

Today we understand that the Pill and IUD fall short of being technological miracles. Because their side effects have become the focus of so much publicity, they are no longer as fashionable as they once were. Use of the Pill declined in this country 25 percent from 1976–1979. (However, Pill use has increased dramatically in the Third World where its risks have not become widely known.) Meanwhile, the more traditional methods are enjoying a revival in popularity in the United States because they are quite effective and easy to share with no risk of serious side effects.

No doubt, the experts will continue to refine their views about the various methods as new information becomes available. One thing, however, remains certain: each method has advantages and disadvantages, costs and benefits. These vary from couple to couple depending on individual priorities, tastes, and personal histories. There is no single "best" method of contraception for everyone—and there never will be. In addition, no single method is always "best" for any couple. Most lovers change methods several times during their lives as their needs change. Couples should weigh for themselves each method's costs and benefits. This cost-benefit analysis should be reviewed and updated regularly. The best method for your relationship is the one—or combination of several—you feel most comfortable using consistently. Rhythm used carefully all the time works better than Pills left in the dresser drawer. The best method for you is the one you and your lover decide fits best into your lifestyle and lovestyle.

Effectiveness: Your Mileage May Differ

Which methods of birth control are most effective in preventing pregnancy? Many people would reply: the Pill and IUD. However, the combination of condoms and foam can be as effective as the Pill, and many birth control authorities now consider the diaphragm more effective than the IUD.

Comparative effectiveness is one of the more confusing aspects of birth control decision-making. Statistics can be fudged to make misleading claims and should always be viewed with some skepticism. In addition, there are important differences between "theoretical effectiveness" and "use effectiveness." Theoretical effectiveness figures assume that the method is used properly all the time. Use effectiveness figures involve estimates of the actual experience of couples who use the method regularly, including those who may not use it consistently or perfectly. Effectiveness depends as much on the couple as it does on the method. Contraceptives do not work just *for* you, but *with* you.

Contraceptive effectiveness statistics are similar to EPA gas mileage estimates. Just as "your mileage may differ," your experience with a particular method may not agree with what the statistics predict.

Effectiveness rates are based on "100 couple-years." Each couple-year represents one couple using the method for one year. If a method is rated 95 percent effective, that means 5 pregnancies would be expected among 100 couples who use the method for 1 year, or among 25 couples who use it for 4 years. It does *not* mean that you personally should expect 5 pregnancies every 100 times you make love.

Bear in mind that effectiveness statistics are averages with a built-in margin of error of 1 or 2 percent. A method considered 95 percent effective is actually effective somewhere in the range of 93–97 percent.

Chapter 10

A CONSUMER'S GUIDE
TO THE CONDOM
COMEBACK

How did our parents and grandparents prevent unwanted pregnancies back in the days before the Pill and IUD—all of twenty years ago? Some used diaphragms or rhythm, others abstained or used oral sex, but many used condoms, also known as rubbers and prophylactics.

The humble condom has prevented more unwanted pregnancies throughout history than any other contraceptive device. Condoms were the world's most popular birth control method until as recently as the mid-1960s when the Pill bumped them from the top spot to number two, where they have remained ever since. An estimated 25 million couples around the world use condoms as their primary contraceptive—4 million in the United States. In 1977, world production topped 3 billion, enough, if placed end-to-end, to circle the equator 13 times. An estimated 20 percent of American lovers use rubbers regularly, a small proportion compared to some other industrialized nations. In England and Sweden, 40 percent choose condoms, in Japan, 70 percent.

When the Pill and IUD were introduced on a mass scale in the mid-1960s, most men removed the condoms from their wallets and bade them farewell. Most felt relieved. Until then, contraception had been the *man's* responsibility in many relationships. Most men were delighted to see the responsibility shift to women.

As a result, condom sales plummeted and kept falling until 1970. About that time, the health hazards associated with the Pill and IUD began to receive wide publicity and women started to abandon them in favor of the more traditional methods—including condoms—that worked virtually as well, but without side effects. Condom sales took off in 1975 and have been increasing more than 10 percent per year, according to manufacturers.

Today, condoms have become *popular*. They are now more widely used in the United States than they were in their former heyday before the Pill and IUD. Contrary to lingering myths, condoms work, and an increasing number of men feel they have little resemblance to showering with a raincoat on. These days, American lovers use a staggering half-billion condoms a year. That works out to more than *one million a day*.

Rubber Rejection Reconsidered

It's perfectly all right to dislike condoms. Many couples prefer other contraceptives. However, from the locker room to the boardroom, condoms have been saddled with a bad reputation, particularly since the introduction of the Pill. Many men who put them down have never put one on. And some men, who tried them years ago in the back seat of the family sedan, rejected them before they developed a rapport with them. It can take as long to become comfortable with condoms—or any contraceptive—as it takes to feel comfortable with a new lover.

Condoms have several advantages no other contraceptive can offer. They are the only birth control method that prevents the spread of the "love bugs," the various sexual infections that are the most prevalent illnesses in the country after the common cold and flu. Rubbers impose no one-a-day routine like the Pill. They are virtually free of side effects. They prevent "the dribbles," the run-off of semen from the vagina that hassles some women, particularly after morning lovemaking. And they spare the couple from having to consider: "Who's going to sleep on the wet spot?"

On the other hand, condoms have several time-honored drawbacks. The traditional disadvantages to condoms are discussed below. Consider them, then decide for yourself whether you'd like to experiment with rubbers or not.

They dull sensitivity. Many men refuse to use condoms for this reason. Ironically, others use condoms specifically to reduce sensitivity as a "cure" for rapid ejaculation. But many men report little or no difference in pleasure and, when costs are weighed against benefits, consider condoms preferable to other methods.

The conventional wisdom that condoms dull sensitivity is largely a result of men's traditional belief that sexual pleasure resides solely in the penis and occurs only during intercourse. If your only sex organ is covered during the only pleasurable part of lovemaking, it would make sense to suppose that the cover reduced pleasure. This book suggests a different perspective, however: that the pleasure of lovemaking happens not only on the penis, but all over the body, and not only during intercourse, but throughout lovemaking.

Men who focus their enjoyment of sex only on what the penis feels during intercourse increase their risk of developing the sex problems discussed earlier. Men whose lovestyle is rushed, tense, silent, nonsensual, and penis-centered often develop sex problems and experience no-fun lovemaking even if they *never* use a condom.

On the other hand, men who appreciate sensual, whole-body loveplay should enjoy highly sensitive, problem-free lovemaking whether they use condoms or not.

Imagine that you're at the movies with the woman you love. Suddenly, she places her hand on the inside of your thigh and begins stroking it. The strokes become longer and reach higher until she is fondling your crotch. Many men would become highly aroused from this kind of loveplay, despite the fact that their pants, shirttails, and underwear stand between their penises and their lovers' hands. These garments are several millimeters thick, more than *10,000 times* as thick as the average rubber. How much sensation could condoms actually block?

Lovers, not rubbers, dull sensation. Couples who enjoy sensual lovemaking can make love for hours and may use a condom only if many intimate amusements happen to include intravaginal ejaculation. Far from showering with a raincoat on, lovemaking that includes a condom is more like showering while wearing a ring on one finger.

Sensitivity happens in your mind, not in your condom. However, the condom manufacturers assert that their products "deliver" sensitivity, and they promote condoms on the basis of their product's competitive sensitivity delivery. These claims verge on consumer fraud. Condoms cannot bestow sensitivity any more than one lover can bestow an orgasm on another. Orgasms come from within us with the help of a lover we trust. So does sensitivity in lovemaking. Condoms do not "deliver" sensitivity; lovers *create* it.

Youngs Drug Products, Schmid Labs, and Akwell Industries manufacture about ninety of the estimated one hundred condom brands available in the United States. Each brand promises to "deliver" more sensitivity than the next. Trojans give "greater sensitivity." Sheiks promise "a special experience in sensitivity." And Contures claim to be "totally different" for "the utmost in sensitivity." Then, there are "natural skin" condoms made from lamb's intestines. Because they sell for several times the price of latex rubber condoms, many men and some birth control counselors believe they must be "more sensitive."

In an attempt to investigate these confusing sensitivity claims, I asked each manufacturer to rank its products from most to least sensitive. In view of their advertising claims, the responses were illuminating. Spokesmen for the two companies that responded dismissed the entire sensitivity issue as subjective.

Akwell Vice President John Quinn wrote: "I doubt there is any way to measure sensitivity . . . because of variations in individuals and circumstances. Exact measurement of sensitivity is surely impossible."

Lewis Brenner, product development manager for Youngs, maker of Trojan, wrote: "Sensitivity delivery is really too individual and subjective to measure. Sexual satisfaction is cerebral."

Undaunted, I turned to Dr. Henry Haxo, a quality control engineer whose specialty for more than thirty years has been rubber products. Starting from most men's assumption that the thinner the rubber the more sensitive, Dr. Haxo measured the thicknesses of twenty-five leading brands and found the differences among American brands to be infinitesimal.

"You're talking about differences of thousandths of a millimeter, less than a hair's breadth, less than the eye can see," Dr. Haxo said. "You should see the size and complexity of the equipment we have to use to measure those differences. I doubt that any man could tell the difference between the thickest and thinnest condom with his eyes, fingers, or anything else."

These days, the condom manufacturers are introducing new brands which are described as delivering even more sensitivity than their old ultimately sensitive lines. Akwell claims its Nuda brand is "the thinnest condom made in the United States." However, the Nuda sample tested by Dr. Haxo was thicker than some other brands, notably one line of Trojans, which many men assume to be thick and old-fashioned because the brand has been around so long.

The only noteworthy differences among rubber condoms are their shapes and lubricants. Some condoms have straight sides, others are fitted—they taper behind the head to match more closely the shape of the erect penis. Some men say they prefer shaped condoms because the tighter fit makes the penis look larger and helps the condom stay on better. But this is a matter of individual taste. Condoms come either lubricated or unlubricated. Lubricants are either wet or dry. Condom manufacturers say wet lubricants are "water-soluble jellies" and dry lubricants are "silicone-based powders." However, all three major manufacturers refused to identify the ingredients of their lubricants, and the Food and Drug Administration has never pressed the issue, except to ban all mercury compounds several years ago. Today, dry-lubricated condoms far outsell wet-lubricated or unlubricated. Some couples say wet-lubricated condoms feel too cold and messy. You might experiment to decide which type you prefer.

Are high-priced skin condoms any better than rubbers? Some couples prefer them, which is fine. Skins cost more only because lambs' intestines cost more than latex rubber. Skins are no thinner and no more effective than rubbers. They must be wet-lubricated to preserve the integrity of the lamb tissue and some lovers dislike wet lubricants. The amount of lubricant used makes skins feel a bit heavier than rubbers. Skins usually come crushed instead of rolled, so they must be pulled on like a sock, which some lovers find inconvenient.

If you use condoms, decide which kind you prefer: skins or rubbers; wet, dry, or unlubricated; straight-sided or shaped. Beyond that, a condom is a condom. Do not be fooled by competitive sensitivity claims. Thicknesses are virtually identical. And with or without a condom, sensitivity in lovemaking is no more and no less than what lovers make it.

They interrupt lovemaking. Some men like "spontaneous" sex. Others say condoms are a pain to open. Some men object to their interference with oral loveplay. Others say they lose their erections while fiddling with them. Men who experience these drawbacks as serious problems might prefer to use another contraceptive, but with a little imagination, these issues can usually be resolved happily. Opening the wrapper can be incorporated into loveplay as easily as undressing one another. Oral caresses can be enjoyed before the condom goes on. And if the woman places the condom on the man while continuing to caress him, erection loss is less likely and there is less feeling of interruption. Besides, there is no reason why condom use should fall entirely on the man. Placement by the woman shares the responsibility.

They're embarrassing to buy. Many men identify with the scene in the film, *The Summer of '42*, where the young protagonist cannot work up the courage to ask the pharmacist for condoms. Nowadays similar scenes rarely happen. In the last ten years, condoms have emerged from behind the druggist's counter into the light of open display. You rarely have to ask for them anymore—they're right there on the shelf. Mail order sales now account for a significant share of the condom market, so there is no need to go to a drugstore if you'd rather not. In addition, the U.S. Supreme Court ruled in 1977 that states cannot forbid condom sales to minors.

They break. Condoms by themselves have a theoretical effectiveness of 97 percent and a use effectiveness of 90 percent. The condom-foam combination is rated 99 percent theoretically effective with a use effectiveness of 95 percent. Condoms are reasonably reliable, but they are far from indestructible. They can break. However, most breakage can be prevented by taking a few simple precautions:

—Open the wrapper carefully. It's a good idea to open the wrapper before you get into bed to prevent tearing during the excitement of loveplay.

—*Make sure the woman is fully lubricated before you insert.* Lack of lubrication is a major cause of breakage. Lubricated condoms are no substitute for lubricated erotic openings. The penis—

whether condom-covered or not—should be able to slide into the woman effortlessly. Any pushing might hurt or annoy her and increase the risk of breakage.

—Store condoms in a cool place. Heat deteriorates rubber. The *worst place* to store condoms for more than a few hours is in your wallet because body heat rots the rubber. Wallet-baked rubbers are a prime cause of many men's bad experiences with condoms. Do not store condoms in the glove compartment of a car; engine heat can also rot them. Do not buy condoms from gas station vending machines in the middle of summer for the same reason. Whenever possible, carry condoms in outer garments, for example, jacket pockets. Or ask the woman to carry them in her purse.

—Do not use Vaseline or other petroleum jellies as a lubricant if you use condoms. Petroleum jellies also rot rubber.

More Tips for Enjoyable Condom Use

—Comparison shop: prices vary considerably. Buy in bulk. Purchasing a gross at a time can save a good deal of money. You might consider buying condoms cooperatively with friends. Mail order condoms are sometimes less expensive than drugstore products.

—Buy condoms with "receptacle ends." As a rule, most have them. The nipple catches the ejaculate which reduces the risk of breakage and "backfiring" semen out the open end. If a condom does not have a receptacle end, leave a little space at the head of the penis to catch the ejaculate.

—*Do not buy colored condoms.* The Food and Drug Administration has received many complaints of "severe burns," "colored discharges," and stains "not removable with soap." Condom manufacturers insist that the dyes used in colored condoms are safe and FDA-approved. However, only one of the three major manufacturers agreed to identify its dyes; the others said the information was a "trade secret." Each of the four known dyes turned out to be prohibited by the FDA, according to an FDA official, who added that one of the four, carbon black, contains carcinogenic compounds.

—Don't fall for "textured surface" condoms. These contain tiny raised ribs or dots that purportedly "give her beautiful sensations." Like manufacturers' sensitivity claims, this notion verges on consumer fraud. Most women say they cannot feel the ribs at all. Ribbed rubbers perpetuate the notion that intercourse is what turns women on. However, most women prefer clitoral massage to infinitesimal lumps or bumps on condoms.

—Never use a condom whose wrapper has come unsealed.

—Most birth control counselors tell couples: Put it on before you put it in, because some research suggests that preejaculatory fluid may contain sperm. However, some couples like the man to "ride bareback" until he feels close to ejaculation. If you do this, it should be a mutual decision because it may increase the risk of pregnancy. Also, the man should have good ejaculatory control.

—Birth control counselors sometimes insist that condoms should never be used without foam. Foam does increase condom effectiveness, but many lovers dislike foam, which is fine. If used carefully, condoms by themselves should provide enough protection. Most lovers who use condoms—including many birth control counselors—do not use foam.

—Sometimes, in the woman-on-top position, the vaginal lips lift the condom off the penis because the penis penetrates deeper. Shaped condoms may help prevent lift-offs and slippage. Another approach is for the man to hold the condom onto the base of the penis between two fingers. In addition to securing the condom, the man's knuckles can provide direct clitoral stimulation for the woman.

—After ejaculation, it is *crucial* for one lover to hold the condom onto the penis to prevent leaving the ejaculate-filled condom inside the vagina.

—Use each condom only once.

If a Condom Breaks

Even when used carefully, a condom may occasionally break. If this happens to you, try not to panic. Remember, scientists estimate that the chance of becoming pregnant from a single unprotected intercourse is no greater than 30 percent. There are steps you can take to minimize the risk of pregnancy, and other steps you should avoid.

Keep some foam on hand, whether for use with condoms or not. Sperm travel at about three millimeters per minute. At that rate, it takes them from two to five minutes to move through the cervix into the uterus on their way to the Fallopian tubes where fertilization usually occurs. If a condom breaks, insert three or four applicators of foam as quickly as possible to kill sperm before they pass through the cervix.

Then, assess whether the woman is likely to be fertile. Nursing mothers are somewhat less likely than nonnursing women to become pregnant because nursing suppresses ovulation, the release of eggs (see "Fertility Awareness" in Chapter 11).

Some research suggests that morning-after insertion of the Copper 7 IUD can prevent pregnancy (see "IUD" in Chapter 11).

Therapeutic abortion may be the alternative of last resort (see the discussion of men's participation in abortion decisions in Chapter 11).

Two approaches are not recommended: douching and the morning-after pill. Douching may increase pregnancy risk by pushing the sperm through the cervix. The morning-after pill, which contains the carcinogen DES, is rarely given nowadays except in cases of sexual assault.

Finally, report the broken condom to the nearest FDA office. Despite condom manufacturers' claims of strict FDA scrutiny, federal officials say the condom industry is one of the *least* regulated industries under FDA jurisdiction. The intensity of FDA regulation is proportional to the number of complaints received. Tell a consumer affairs officer which brand broke, under what circumstances, and, if possible, where it ripped. The FDA is listed in the white pages of the phone book under United States Government, Department of Health and Human Services.

Some men get all prepared to give condoms a chance only to find that their *lovers* don't like them. Some women may have become pregnant while using them. Others may have seen men use them improperly. Some may have esthetic objections. Others may feel uncomfortable giving up control over contraception. Some women simply don't like them, and there's nothing wrong with that. However, a problem may arise if the man believes his lover's refusal to use condoms robs him of the chance to "prove how liberated" he is. A man can show his concern for contraception by taking an active interest in it. When birth control decisions are mutual, the method agreed upon makes no difference.

A final note: Even if condoms are not your preferred contraceptive, it's a good idea to keep some on hand in case one lover suspects he or she might be developing a reproductive infection. There is no reason to risk passing an infection to a lover (see the discussion of sexual infections in Chapter 12).

Chapter 11

WHAT MEN SHOULD KNOW ABOUT THE OTHER CONTRACEPTIVES

Americans' twenty-year infatuation with the Pill and IUD is cooling. More and more couples have decided that the risks of these methods outweigh their benefits. Pill sales declined 25 percent from 1976–1979, and drug industry claims that birth control pills are the "ultimate contraceptive" ring rather hollow these days. The age of high-technology contraceptives is giving way to an era of appropriate technology contraceptives, the new-and-improved traditional methods. To provide protection against unwanted pregnancy, appropriate technology contraceptives require the active participation of men informed about their use. This chapter outlines the advantages and disadvantages of the available methods with an emphasis on men's participation. For more detailed information, see *The Birth Control Handbook* and *Contraceptive Technology*, both listed in the Bibliography.

Nonintercourse Lovemaking

The birth control literature uniformly assumes that lovemaking involves vaginal intercourse, but there are several marvelous ways to make love that do not involve insertion of the penis into the vagina. Ejaculation into a woman's mouth, for example, is a 100 percent effective birth control method. It is always available and does not interrupt lovemaking. It does not depend on chemicals, mechanical devices or keeping track of anything, nor does it require a doctor's prescription or special medical care. It costs absolutely nothing and causes no side effects. And lovers who prefer not to have intercourse during a woman's period might find this method particularly attractive at those times.

Oral loveplay and other nonintercourse forms of lovemaking can be convenient, satisfying, effective, and hassle-free—assuming that both lovers find them enjoyable—yet these alternatives are rarely mentioned in contraceptive publications.

Why not? One reason is our legacy of the Victorian morality that reviled oral-genital loveplay as loathsome. A sexual psychology book published in 1886 blamed this "perverse impulse" on "men who have become impotent or satiated from excessive indulgence in the normal way." Oral lovemaking between consenting adults is *still illegal* in some states, and the Playboy Foundation has assisted the appeal efforts of at least one individual imprisoned for "copulation by mouth."

The first challenge to the "perversion" theory came in 1948 when the Kinsey research team reported that oral loveplay was a routine part of many people's lovemaking. Based on interviews conducted from 1938–46, Kinsey showed that 15–52 percent of married couples engaged in oral loveplay, with increasing education correlated with increased likelihood of oral sex. By the time of the Hunt-Playboy survey in 1972, the figures had jumped to 52–72 percent. In 1974, a survey of 100,000 *Redbook* magazine readers led to this conclusion about oral loveplay: "Among people under age 25 (born after 1950), it is virtually a universal part of sexual relationships. . . . Basically, almost all women are doing it and liking it. Less than 10 percent have never tried cunnilingus or fellatio, and the overwhelming majority like oral sex." (It should be noted that while 90 percent of *Redbook's* respondents liked receiving oral-clitoral loveplay, only 72 percent said they enjoyed oral-penile stimulation; 13 percent declared "no feelings" about giving oral caresses, and 15 percent said they found it unpleasant.) In sum, it would appear that today's lovers would not be shocked if oral loveplay were mentioned as a contraceptive option.

Another reason why oral lovemaking is ignored as a method of birth control is that most providers and recipients of birth control counseling have difficulty discussing lovemaking so specifically. It's much easier to discuss tangible objects such as diaphragms or IUDs. Birth control counselors are trained not to make assumptions about the loveplay preferences of couples they counsel, and lovers often have enough trouble discussing oral sex in the privacy of their own beds. The subject can be more difficult to raise in the impersonal clinic setting where professionally "arm's length" counselors sometimes view those they counsel, not as lovers, but as "partners," as though they were in business with one another, not in bed together.

Family planning owes a great deal of its public acceptance to the popularization of the Pill and IUD, the methods whose uses are least involved with the specifics of lovemaking. Sadly, many family planning clinics project a public image so asexual that a naive visitor might not realize that the discussions there have anything to do with lovemaking. This medical-asexual image is understandable given the location of many clinics in conservative communities. However, it also tends to perpetuate professional silence about oral sex, a highly effective birth control method beautifully suited to many lovers' needs.

Finally, the corporations that manufacture contraceptives have a financial interest in promoting products, not ideas. The pharmaceutical industry has not attempted to suppress information about the contraceptive application of oral ejaculation—many lovers have figured it out for themselves. However, because no business profits from oral loveplay, the potential advantages of this approach tend to get buried beneath sophisticated media campaigns which promote contraceptives that provide a return on investment.

A major concern about oral ejaculation as birth control is the safety of swallowing semen. Semen contains nothing unhealthy. Like the rest of the human body, it is mostly water. Its other components include: protein, in sperm and enzymes; fructose, the sperm-nourishing sugar found in fruit; citric acid, the substance in citrus fruit that prevents scurvy; small amounts of zinc, an essential mineral; and traces of cholesterol. Far from being harmful, semen has some nutritional value, though this should not be over-emphasized. It is also nonfattening. Doctors estimate that the average ejaculate contains no more than 25 calories, about as much as a raw carrot.

Beyond the issue of safety, however, some women might object to oral ejaculation for personal reasons. If this is an issue, lovers should discuss their feelings about it. A man should not insist that his lover swallow semen if she has objections. To insist would be boorish and aggressive and could contribute to stress in the relationship.

Fertility Awareness: Scientific Rhythm That Works

Fertility awareness, a method of charting a woman's fertility pattern, appeals to lovers who desire a "natural" birth control method as opposed to the "artificial" methods that rely on mechanical devices or chemicals. It tends to be particularly attractive to women who have had unpleasant experiences with other methods.

A major advantage of fertility awareness is that during a woman's safe time, no birth control is necessary. During fertile days, the couples can choose among: condom, diaphragm, foam, nonintercourse lovemaking, or abstinence. There are no side effects from fertility awareness, and after a couple has learned how to use this method, which takes a certain discipline, it requires only a few minutes each morning. In addition to its contraceptive application, it can also be used to pinpoint a woman's fertile days by couples who want to conceive a child.

A woman is fertile for only part of each menstrual cycle. She releases an egg, or ovulates, about two weeks before monthly periods. After ovulation, the vaginal environment changes to become more hospitable to sperm. Sperm live for less than one day in an infertile woman's vagina, but some can survive for four to five days when a woman is fertile. Most eggs live only twelve hours, but some can survive for up to two days. Allowing for a margin of error, a union of egg and sperm (fertilization) might occur during a nine-day interval about halfway between a woman's periods.

Both fertility awareness and the traditional calendar rhythm method attempt to identify a woman's fertile days each month. The key difference between the two is that to practice traditional rhythm, a woman pays attention to the calendar. To practice fertility awareness, she pays attention to the changes she observes in her own body.

Traditional rhythm assumes that women ovulate with absolute regularity during each menstrual cycle and that, consequently, women's fertile days occur in regular patterns that can be calculated on a calendar. But few women ovulate so regularly, and the menstrual cycles of those who do can shift unexpectedly if they travel, get sick, use drugs, suffer fatigue, or experience emotional stress (for example, a fear of being pregnant). Fertility awareness allows women to identify their fertile days precisely, whether their menstrual cycles are regular or not.

Fertility awareness teaches women to understand and identify their fertility cycles. The body clearly announces its fertile time each month to a woman—or man—trained to recognize the signals.

Fertility awareness has been practiced only in the last few years, mainly as a grassroots phenomenon. For this reason, few lovers know much about it. But studies to date suggest that it works as well as the other methods considered to be reliable. A five-country study of 2,000 couples in 1974 showed a use effectiveness of 98 percent among couples committed to *preventing* pregnancy, though it was less effective among couples who only wanted to *delay* pregnancy a while. More than most methods, fertility awareness works with you, not for you.

Lovers learn to use fertility awareness by reading a reference book or taking a class. Several books on the subject have been published (see Bibliography). Courses vary but the San Francisco Health Department offers one that meets for three hours one evening a week every other week for six weeks, a total of nine hours. Fertility awareness takes some time to learn, but it quickly becomes second nature. The longer a couple uses the method, the less time it takes each day.

Women who use this method identify ovulation by recording their temperatures each morning using a special thermometer calibrated in tenths of a degree, a basal body thermometer. Body temperature rises slightly, but noticeably, during ovulation. Basal body thermometers are sold at drugstores for about $5.00.

Changes in the amount and texture of cervical mucus are another indicator of fertility. The cervix, the mouth of the uterus that extends down into the back of the vagina, secretes small amounts of mucus as part of its normal functioning. Around the time of ovulation, cervical mucus becomes comparatively abundant, clear, slippery, and elastic—it stretches easily between thumb and index finger. At other times, the mucus is less abundant, thicker, stickier, and less elastic. Fertile mucus extends the life of sperm to facilitate fertilization.

The cervix itself also undergoes cyclic changes. It opens and softens around the time of ovulation, then closes and hardens when the woman is no longer fertile.

Women record their cyclic temperature, mucus, and cervical changes on a daily chart that includes other factors that can affect the menstrual cycle: overall health, stress, travel, drug use, and lovemaking. Women's charts differ and fertility awareness classes include individualized chart interpretation to introduce each couple to the woman's unique cycle. After several months of charting, a fertility pattern begins to emerge, and as a woman and her lover become comfortable with the pattern, they can begin to use the chart to calculate her fertile days.

Men are encouraged to attend fertility awareness classes with their lovers and many enjoy them. Many couples say that joint chart consultation enhances their level of intimacy. Some women experience a decrease in sexual energy during their periods and an increase around the time of ovulation. These changes can be taken into consideration in the timing of lovemaking invitations when both lovers have access to the woman's chart.

The impetus behind the development of fertility awareness came from Roman Catholics, for rhythm is the only form of birth control the Church allows. Drs. John and Evelyn Billings, an Australian husband-and-wife team, correlated the cervical mucus cycle with fertility during the 1950s, when contraceptive research in the United States focused on the Pill and IUD.

Fertility awareness is a newcomer on the contraceptive scene not only because of American fascination with technology and pills, but because pharmaceutical companies have supported most birth control research here. Such companies had an enormous financial stake in developing IUDs and the Pill, the first drug prescribed on a massive scale for a nondisease condition. Drug companies did not back fertility awareness research for the same reason that they do not promote the contraceptive application of oral sex—it allows lovers to rely on themselves, not exclusively on drug company products.

At this writing, fertility awareness is the avant-garde birth control method, but its popularity and recognition are increasing rapidly. Couples interested in this method should contact a family-planning facility for a referral to a fertility awareness class or book on the subject.

Diaphragm with Spermicidal Jelly

The diaphragm is the woman's version of the condom. It is a rubber cup that holds spermicidal jelly over the cervix. The diaphragm provides a barrier to the sperm, and the spermicide kills any sperm that approach the cervix.

The diaphragm's theoretical effectiveness is 97 percent.* Use effectiveness is rated at 83–98 percent. The use effectiveness upper limit of 98 percent, which tops the diaphragm's theoretical effectiveness, has led some birth control authorities to suggest that the method's theoretical effectiveness is actually higher than has been believed. The only side effect associated with the diaphragm is a possible allergic reaction to the spermicide, usually alleviated by changing brands.

Diaphragms must be fitted to the individual woman because vaginal sizes vary. A refitting is advised if the woman gains or loses fifteen pounds. No prescription is necessary to buy spermicide at a drugstore and a properly stored diaphragm can last several years.

Men can be involved in diaphragm use, and research confirms the common-sense view that when couples share its use the contraceptive is more effective. The man may load the diaphragm with the recommended tablespoon of jelly. He might also insert it—some women have trouble—or check to see that it's properly placed. Before attempting either of these, he should practice on the plastic models used for this purpose at most family-planning clinics.

Some men are surprised at the diaphragm's large size. It covers more than just the cervix. To stay in place, one side fits behind the cervix and the other tucks up behind the pubic bone. (See the diagram of women's pelvic anatomy in Appendix I.)

A diaphragm must be inserted before penile entry because pre-

* Effectiveness statistics that follow are from *Contraceptive Technology*, 1980–81. See Bibliography.

ejaculatory fluid may contain sperm. However, it may be inserted up to two hours before intercourse, which adds to its convenience. It must be left in for eight hours after lovemaking to allow the spermicide to kill all the sperm. Couples who make love a second time before eight hours have elapsed should insert more spermicide with a plunger applicator without removing the diaphragm.

A diaphragm need not interrupt lovemaking if it is kept handy and if both lovers are involved in its use. Like condoms, placement may be incorporated into loveplay.

The jellies tend to have a medicinal odor and may distract some men during oral-clitoral loveplay. Different brands have different aromas. Men upset by medicinal odors might prefer to provide oral stimulation before diaphragm insertion.

Some men are concerned about "eating" spermicide during oral loveplay. Unlikely. The diaphragm holds the spermicide in the back of the vagina, and even allowing for some run-off, most of it stays there. A tongue involved in oral-clitoral loveplay should not touch any spermicide because the clitoris is located outside and above the vagina.

On the other hand, the *woman* might eat spermicide if this sequence occurs: insertion of diaphragm and jelly followed by some penile-vaginal loveplay followed by the woman taking the man's penis into her mouth.

Women say spermicides have an unpleasant taste, and it's ill-advised to ingest anything designed to kill living cells. Lovers who combine diaphragm use with oral loveplay should discuss when they would like to enjoy what.

A properly fitted diaphragm should not slip out of place, even with the woman on top, nor should she feel its presence. A woman who is aware of her diaphragm should check its placement and fit. Sometimes a man may feel the diaphragm, but most men say they do not. Some lovers who do not use the diaphragm as their regular method enjoy it during the woman's period—it catches the menstrual flow and does not interfere with intercourse as tampons may.

Foam

Foam is a spermicide inserted into the vagina with an applicator. By itself, foam has a theoretical effectiveness of 97 percent and a use effectiveness measured at 79–98 percent. The foam-condom combination is rated 99 percent theoretically effective with a use effectiveness of 95 percent. The only side effect is an occasional allergic reaction, usually alleviated by changing brands. Foam is sold in drugstores without a prescription.

The man may load the applicator, insert the foam, and/or wash the applicator afterward. Foam should be incorporated into loveplay because it loses its effectiveness after a short time. Insert it no more than twenty minutes before intercourse. Couples should insert another applicator each time they make love.

Some lovers find foam messy and inconvenient; others do not. Foam raises the same issues concerning oral loveplay as does diaphragm jelly.

Intrauterine Device (IUD)

An IUD is any of several plastic or plastic-metal objects inserted semipermanently into the uterus.

After almost twenty years of observing the effects of IUDs, scientists still are not sure how they work. The theory most frequently advanced is that while in place the IUD causes a permanent irritation of the uterus that prevents implantation of a fertilized egg.

Theoretical effectiveness is 95–99 percent. Use effectiveness is 90–94 percent. Women who have delivered a child tend to enjoy greater effectiveness with fewer side effects.

IUDs can only be inserted by doctors or family planning nurse-practitioners. Women with IUDs should monitor their health carefully and consult their clinician regularly. They should learn the signs of potentially hazardous side effects and see their clinician promptly if any danger signs appear.

IUD advantages include: convenience, nonmessiness, and no interruption of lovemaking. Once an IUD is in place, the woman is relatively well protected against unwanted pregnancy. However, an important maintenance check must be performed each month. An IUD comes with a string that hangs down through the cervix into the vagina. A week after her period, the woman or her lover should check to make sure the string is still in place. If it has disappeared, if its length has changed markedly, or if the plastic part of the IUD can be felt protruding into the vagina, the woman should see her clinician *immediately*.

IUD disadvantages are its side effects, some of which may be serious—even fatal. Although some women experience no disagreeable side effects, only 60–88 percent of women who have them inserted keep them a full year. Some IUDs are expelled spontaneously; others are removed at the women's request.

Women with any of the following should not use an IUD: pelvic infection, history of recurrent pelvic infections, history of ectopic (Fallopian tube) pregnancy, certain kinds of heart disease, painful periods, abnormally heavy menstrual bleeding, abnormal Pap smear, or anemia.

Minor IUD side effects include: more painful menstrual cramps, heavier menstrual flow, and more frequent uterine infections thought to result from bacteria "climbing" up the string.

Major IUD complications include: severe uterine infections, puncture of the uterus, sterility, loss of consciousness, seizures, irregular heartbeat and heart failure.

Women with IUDs should consult their clinician right away if they develop a fever, pelvic pain or tenderness, severe cramps, or unusual vaginal bleeding. These may signal IUD-related infection. Untreated IUD-related infections can lead to hysterectomy (removal of the uterus resulting in sterility) or death.

Men whose lovers use IUDs should familiarize themselves with the possible side effects and danger signs and be prepared to react if any occur. Women whose menstrual cramps become more painful with an IUD in place might feel less open to lovemaking invitations around the time of their periods.

The Pill

Birth control pills change a woman's hormone balance to prevent the release of eggs from her ovaries.

The Pill's theoretical effectiveness is higher than 99 percent. Use effectiveness is rated 90–96 percent. Birth control pills are available by prescription only and regular clinic visits are necessary. Women should never share or borrow birth control pills.

A woman on the Pill must take one pill a day, every day. If a Pill-user forgets one pill, she may take two the next day and still be protected. If she misses two pills, she can also make them up, but she should use a back-up method of contraception in addition to the Pill until her next period. A woman who forgets to take her pill more than once a month should reconsider this method.

Advantages include: convenience, nonmessiness, and regularization of irregular periods. Disadvantages include: the necessity to take a pill every day, decreased effectiveness in interaction with some other drugs, possible need for vitamin supplements, and side effects that may be quite serious.

Drugs that decrease the Pill's effectiveness include: sedatives, particularly meprobamate (Miltown) and phenobarbital (used in about fifty drug brands); the antibiotic ampicillin; antihistamines; phenylbutazone, an antiinflammatory used in many arthritis drugs; and tranquilizers.

The Pill also affects the body's absorption of vitamins and minerals. It increases blood levels of vitamin A, iron, and copper, and decreases blood levels of the B vitamins and vitamin C. Many Americans have B vitamin deficiencies because these important substances tend to be removed from foods during processing. A woman on the Pill might consider a B vitamin supplement.

Some women report decreased vaginal lubrication with the Pill. Other lubricants may be introduced into loveplay.

Since the introduction of the Pill in the mid-1960s, its side effects have become a major concern. About 40 percent of Pill-users report some side effects. Some are considered minor, others life-threatening. Only 45–75 percent of women who begin taking birth control pills use them a full year. Reasons most frequently cited for going off the Pill are its side effects and anxiety about its side effects.

In every age group, women who smoke cigarettes have much greater risk than nonsmokers of serious circulatory system side effects. Birth control counselors advise women who smoke not to use the Pill and/or to stop smoking.

Because of the risk of serious health problems, women with any of the following should *absolutely not use* the Pill: a current case or history of breast or reproductive cancer, internal blood clotting, circulatory system disease, heart or liver disease, hepatitis, varicose veins, or epilepsy.

Women with any of the following should probably not use the Pill: a current case or history of high blood pressure, migraine headaches, diabetes, sickle-cell anemia, gall bladder disease, or abnormal vaginal bleeding.

Women about to have surgery and women with a leg in a cast should also avoid the Pill because of possible circulatory system problems.

Women are now generally advised to stop using the Pill by age thirty-five, definitely by forty. Teenaged women, whose menstrual cycles have not become firmly established, are usually advised not to use the Pill.

Women with any of the following are advised to monitor their health carefully if they take the Pill: a current case or history of kidney disease, alcoholism, depression, or asthma.

Common minor side effects include: loss of interest in lovemaking, nausea, headaches, weight gain, breast enlargement and/or tenderness, depression, fatigue, irritability, problems with contact lenses, spotting (vaginal bleeding between periods), and increased susceptibility to vaginal infections and gonorrhea.

Serious, but not life-threatening, side effects include: increased risk of high blood pressure, infertility, skin diseases, hepatitis, and gall bladder disease.

Potentially fatal side effects include: increased risk of stroke, internal blood clots, heart attack, and rupture of the liver.

The issue of the Pill's relationship to cancer remains unresolved. Estrogen, a major component of many birth control pills, has long been known to be a potent carcinogen. The human carcinogen DES is a synthetic estrogen, and estrogen given to postmenopausal women has been linked to cancer of the uterine lining. Some studies have shown unexpectedly high cancer rates in Pill-users. Other research has not shown increased cancer risk. Women with cancer or a cancer history should not use the Pill. Women with a family history of cancer should probably not use the Pill.

Men in relationships with women who use the Pill should learn the danger signals associated with its serious side effects and be prepared to react if any occur:

—Severe abdominal pain, which might signal a liver tumor, blood clot, or gall bladder problem.

—Chest pain or shortness of breath, a possible sign of a blood clot in the lung or a heart problem.

—Severe headaches, which might indicate high blood pressure or danger of stroke.

—Blurred vision or vision loss, possible signs of high blood pressure or impending stroke.

—Severe leg pain, which might indicate an internal blood clot.

Severe side effects are more common in women who have been on the Pill more than four years.

Many men encourage their lovers to take the Pill—or insist they take it—because these men believe it provides the best protection with the least hassle in bed. These advantages apply to some relationships, but not to others. Several other methods have equivalent use effectiveness ratings. In addition, evaluation of the hassle of any method should not be limited solely to its convenience in bed, but should also include its effects on lovers' overall health and their feelings about making love. Some Pill side effects that doctors call minor—loss of sexual interest, lubrication problems, nausea, headaches, depression, and irritability—may have major impact on a relationship and on a couple's ability to enjoy problem-free lovemaking.

Current Attitudes Toward Contraceptives Among Health Professionals

Ideally, health workers who provide birth control counseling should present unbiased views so people can decide for themselves which method or method combination is best for them. However, the American faith in high technology combined with extensive Pill and IUD promotion in professional journals have apparently introduced unconscious biases into some birth control counseling that may steer lovers to these methods. A recent study of 300 doctors, nurses and birth control counselors showed that *theoretical* effectiveness figures, or higher, were often cited for the Pill and IUD, while *use* effectiveness figures, or lower, were frequently cited for all the other methods. The best way to avoid possibly biased counseling is to request written information, then decide for yourself.

Abortion

Probably the only agreement between those who favor legal abortion and those who oppose it is that the best way to deal with the abortion issue is to avoid unwanted pregnancies altogether. But accidents do happen—even when both lovers are involved in birth control—and if abortion becomes the contraceptive of last resort, couples usually feel better about it, and about one another, when the emotional and financial strains are shared.

The decision whether to have an abortion ultimately rests with the woman because the pregnancy involves her body. However, many women are eager to learn how their lovers feel about the prospect of an abortion. The couple should discuss their feelings about this pregnancy at this time—and about parenthood in general—and try to reach a mutual decision. But if a difference of opinion emerges, the woman has every right to make up her own mind. Abortion decisions are stressful enough when both lovers agree on a course of action. If they disagree, it's probably a good idea to consult family, if possible, friends or a family planning counselor to help sort out the specifics of the disagreement. Disagreements over abortion decisions contribute to many breakups.

When the decision to have an abortion is mutual, the man can accompany his lover throughout the experience, except for her time in the operating room, just as a woman might share the experience of her lover's vasectomy.

Men sometimes feel ignored or poorly treated in abortion clinics because enough men "fuck 'em and forget 'em" to perpetuate a stereotype of the uncaring man. The best way to counteract this myth is to be there and show that you care.

The first step might be to attend preabortion counseling together after a woman's positive pregnancy test. Try to sort out your own feelings. It's fine to feel ambivalent about abortion even when you support a lover's decision to have one. Some men feel guilty for their role in necessitating the abortion, while at the same time, they may feel relieved to know that they are, in fact, fertile. Some men feel concerned about their lovers' safety or angry at themselves or their lovers for a lapse in contraceptive vigilance. All these feelings are normal, and couples usually benefit from discussing the range of emotions they feel.

In counseling, couples also learn which of the various abortion procedures is appropriate to their situation. They also learn whether the woman's medical history increases her risk of surgical complications. Legal abortion is one of the safest forms of surgery, but every operation entails some risk.

On the appointed day, the man can accompany his lover to the clinic. A woman tends to feel nervous beforehand and woozy afterward. In addition to being there for emotional support, the man can take his lover home and attend to her postoperative comfort. He should also familiarize himself with the warning signs of possible complications, and help his lover observe postabortion recommendations including the two-week ban on vaginal intercourse. The man might also attend the postoperative checkup with his lover and take a more active role in using preconception birth control.

Studies show that men who share a lover's abortion experience tend to develop fewer stress effects than those who absent themselves from the process. Their relationships are more likely to survive and thrive, and their lovemaking afterward is more likely to be problem-free.

Vasectomy

Sterilization has become one of the most popular contraceptives in recent years among couples who have completed their families. As of 1970, it was the birth control method used by 8 percent of American married couples. By 1975, that figure had increased to 22 percent. Either the man or woman may be sterilized.

A discussion of women's several sterilization alternatives is beyond the scope of this book. Couples interested in this should consult a doctor.

Compared to women's sterilization options, vasectomy is safe, simple, and inexpensive. Vasectomy involves cutting and sealing the two vas deferens tubes that carry sperm from the epididymis to the urethra.

Vasectomy takes about a half-hour. It is performed in a doctor's office under local anesthetic and costs about $125.

Most men say vasectomy feels less uncomfortable than having a tooth pulled. After the man has shaved his scrotum, the doctor makes two small incisions and cuts the vas tubes. He then seals them shut and sews up the incisions with thread that the body absorbs as the incisions heal. The only painful part is the pin-prick of the anesthetic injection.

Vasectomy fails in less than 1 percent of cases. In about 1 case in 1,000, the vas tubes rejoin spontaneously.

Postoperative complications resemble those following tooth extraction: soreness, swelling, discoloration, or infection. About 5 percent of men experience some complication after vasectomy. The doctor should provide a twenty-four-hour telephone number for consultation if concerns develop.

Most men feel fine after a recovery period of a day or two, during which time they should wear jockey shorts for support, take it easy, and not lift heavy objects. Vasectomies are often performed on Friday or Saturday, and most men can return to work the following Monday.

Vasectomy has no known effects on a man's sexuality. It has no effect on production or circulation of sex hormones, so a man experiences no changes in physique, body hair, or depth of voice. The only effect is the removal of sperm from the ejaculate. Vasectomized men still ejaculate normally. Sperm comprise only about 3 percent of the volume of semen. Men rarely notice any difference in seminal volume, and women rarely notice any difference in taste.

After vasectomy, the testicles continue to make sperm, but they are reabsorbed by the body like other unused cells. This is a natural process and has no harmful effects. However, about half of vasectomized men develop "sperm antibodies" which attack and destroy sperm as though they were foreign intruders in the body. Sperm antibodies have no known relationship to postvasectomy complications, but for a time, urologists believed they might preclude successful reversals, surgical procedures that reattach the vas tubes to restore fertility. This issue remains controversial, but vasectomies have been successfully reversed in men with sperm antibodies.

Vasectomized men should feel free to make love again as soon as it feels comfortable. However, they should not push themselves. Impatience with convalescence contributes to some men's sex problems.

Vasectomy *does not* result in immediate sterility. Billions of live sperm remain in the vas deferens tubes above the doctor's incisions. These must be expelled before the man becomes sterile, which takes fifteen to twenty ejaculations. The doctor should schedule a sperm count a few weeks after the operation. The man masturbates to produce a semen sample which is examined microscopically. If no sperm are present, the man is pronounced sterile. Until then, he should use contraception.

Sterilization is a serious, deeply personal decision that should *never* be made hastily, impulsively, or under duress. Men and couples who feel satisfied with their vasectomies usually mull over the idea for a good long time—such as one to five years—and are prepared for it to be permanent.

A man or couple considering vasectomy should give serious consideration to several issues most people prefer not to think about: What if your children were killed? What if your relationship ended and you wanted children in a new relationship? What if your values changed and you wanted more children with your present lover?

There is nothing wrong with a man who decides *not* to have a vasectomy. Sometimes, however, a man might feel pressured into having one. His lover might insist that it's his turn to deal with their birth control. She might face serious health problems if she becomes pregnant again. She may feel heartsick from a recent abortion, or want "proof" of his love. Although men should participate equally in birth control, no man should have a vasectomy simply because his lover wants him to. The decision to become sterile should involve careful consideration over a long period of time. Some vasectomy facilities will not perform the operation on men who have thought about it for less than one year.

Is Vasectomy Reversible?

That depends on what you mean and whom you talk to. Most vasectomy counselors insist that the operation is permanent. Meanwhile, the media regularly report improving rates of successful reversals.

Counselors stress the permanence of vasectomy because no surgeon can guarantee a successful reversal and because no man should have a vasectomy with the hope of reversing it later. However, reversals are becoming more available and success rates are improving. A "successful reversal" must be defined. One measure of success is the reappearance of sperm in semen; another is actual impregnation. Sperm reappear in semen more often than vasectomy-reversed men make their lovers pregnant. Reversal rates vary depending on the surgeon and his technique, but at this writing, sperm reappear in somewhat more than 50 percent of cases while impregnation rates are lower, about 50 percent. A new technique called microsurgery has reportedly improved reversal success rates to 70–90 percent. Most authorities believe that vasectomy will be largely—but never absolutely—reversible within the next twenty-five years.

During the foreseeable future, it will probably remain permanent for most men because reversal attempts cost up to $4,000. There is no guarantee of success, and health insurance does not pay for the operation.

SPERM BANKS

Some men turn to sperm banks as a way of preserving fertility after vasectomy. Like reversals, sperm banking is controversial and most vasectomy counselors advise against it. They tell men not to get a vasectomy if they still may want children.

Nonetheless, sperm banks are an option for men or couples who want "fatherhood insurance." Sperm samples are frozen in liquid nitrogen and stored at temperatures near absolute zero. Sperm lose up to 50 percent of their motility, or "wiggle-power," during the first six to twelve months of storage. Motility loss reduces the chance that thawed sperm will have enough energy to swim into the Fallopian tubes and fertilize an egg. The longer the sperm are stored, the greater the motility loss. Nevertheless, women have become pregnant from sperm stored for several years.

Scientists say storage does not increase the likelihood of genetic damage to offspring—defective sperm tend to suffer more motility loss than healthy ones.

There are about fifteen sperm banks in the United States. Costs vary, but in 1978, the Tyler Clinic in Los Angeles charged $140 for the first year and $40 per year after that.

Curiously, only a small proportion of men who invest in sperm storage ever withdraw their deposits.

Men who store sperm do so at their own risk. No sperm bank guarantees the viability of a depositor's sperm, and refrigeration systems have been known to fail. Like vasectomy reversals, sperm banking is a calculated risk. Men considering this option should be aware of its limits.

Don't Bet on a Pill for Men

From time to time, the news media report that a Pill for men is close to being perfected. The problem is that the long-sought Pill has been "just around the corner" for the last ten years, and still appears nowhere near ready for general use. Last year, the research director for a drug company that pioneered the Pill for women and that is heavily committed to the men's Pill said he believed it was still at least ten years away from FDA approval.

The problem with the men's Pill has always been its side effects at doses large enough to reduce sperm counts to zero. During the late 1950s, researchers administered experimental hormone-based contraceptives to both men and women. Enovid, the first birth control pill to win FDA approval, was found to reduce men's sperm counts to zero quickly and effectively. However, the estrogen-based Pill also caused a loss of sexual energy, shrinkage of the testicles, and breast enlargement. These side effects were considered unacceptable and the emphasis shifted to developing the estrogen Pill for women.*

As work on the Pill for men continued, scientists stopped giving female hormones and tried large doses of male sex hormones. These were also found to suppress sperm production, but the elevated blood levels of male sex hormones in the men who took them increased the risk of prostate cancer and also of heart disease which is the number one killer of men. Another problem was that orally ingested male sex hormones were less effective than injected hormones, which were judged to be unmarketable. Recently, an orally active testosterone has been developed, but it appears to cause liver damage.

For a while, a drug used to treat dysentery looked promising as a Pill for men. It reduced the sperm count to zero with good reversibility, but it proved to be incompatible with alcohol. Even small amounts of alcohol caused vomiting, dizziness, and blurred vision.

If a men's Pill could be developed that did not cause grossly harmful side effects, it would still face an arduous struggle for FDA approval. Since the approval of the women's Pill, the laws governing drug experimentation on humans have been tightened to the point where one researcher at work on the Pill for men lamented

---

* It is interesting to note that while loss of sexual interest was one Pill side effect considered "alarming" in men, contraceptive researchers did not consider it a drawback for women. A 1959 report on side effects of experimental birth control pills for women stated: "Another side effect was a lessening of libido. Frequency of coitus was not reduced since the male was not affected by the medication. Libido in the female is not a positive force but is best expressed as 'passive acquiescence.' In those females in whom libido is marked, prolonged [use of the Pill] does appear to dampen their ardor." Quote from Dr. Robert B. Greenblatt's discussion statement following a paper by Dr. Gregory Pincus et al.: "Effects of certain 19-NOR steroids on Reproductive Processes and Fertility," *Federation Proceedings* (December 1959): 1055–56.

that it was very difficult to locate healthy men (mostly prison inmates) willing to be guinea pigs in experimental Pill tests. In addition, the FDA requires more prerelease testing than it did when the first women's Pill won approval. (Some FDA officials say privately that under current laws, the side effects of the birth control pills now in use might preclude their release if manufacturers had to apply for original new drug licenses today.) Finally, public disenchantment with hormonal contraceptives has grown considerably in recent years, and it is unclear whether the introduction of a men's Pill would be greeted with the enthusiasm that marked the introduction of the Pill for women in the mid-1960s.

Still, the search for a men's Pill continues. The Chinese claim to have found an effective nonhormonal Pill in "gossypol," a cottonseed derivative. So far, little is known about its effects. U.S. authorities say gossypol, used here in the synthesis of rubber and vinyl, is toxic and can prove fatal if allowed to accumulate in the body. Even if gossypol turned out to be a safe, effective Pill for men, the FDA would require several years of testing before it could be released to the public.

Other Possible Contraceptives for Men

For a while, a tiny on-off valve implanted into the vas deferens looked promising. Unfortunately, valves have proved unreliable in human tests and research emphasis has shifted to refining microsurgical vasectomy reversals.

Another non-Pill possibility is ultrasound. Sperm die if exposed to temperatures slightly higher than normal body temperature. Ultrasound birth control uses high frequency sound waves to elevate testicular temperature. A man sits in a special chair, similar to a toilet, and exposes his scrotum to ultrasound once a week for ten to fifteen minutes. This reportedly cuts sperm counts to zero. Longer, more frequent treatments cause sterility and may replace surgical vasectomy. Scientists say they have obtained good results in animal tests, but the technique has yet to be tested on humans. The earliest it could be available would be the mid-1980s.

There are two possible problems with ultrasound: the possibility of genetic damage or testicular cancer. Doctors have long known that undescended testicles, those that remained in the main body after birth without dropping into the scrotum, increase the risk of testicular cancer. The reasons for increased cancer risk are unknown, but some scientists speculate that exposure to body temperature, which is higher than intrascrotal temperature, may be a factor. It remains to be seen whether testicular cancer incidence would be affected by short-term exposure to the temperatures involved in ultrasound contraception.

The trend in contraception is away from the Pill and IUD and toward the barrier methods (condom and diaphragm) and the lifestyle methods (nonintercourse lovemaking and fertility awareness).

Couples who decide to change methods should do so gradually. Haste can cause accidents and relationship stress. One way to evolve from one method to another is to continue using your current method while slowly developing comfort with a new one. Take your time. Talk about your own cost-benefit appraisals of each method. You might ask friends how they have adjusted to any recent contraceptive changes. Remember, there is no "best" method for everyone, just as there is no "best" lovestyle. The method for you is the one—or more—that you and your lover feel best about using consistently.

Chapter 12

A BRIEF GUIDE TO
SEXUAL INFECTIONS

Any genital area infection in one lover automatically becomes an issue in a sexual relationship. The discomfort and contagion may detract from the pleasure of lovemaking, or preclude it altogether. Sexual infections can be difficult to discuss because lovers often fear being considered "dirty." And in relationships presumed to be monogamous, a sexual infection can raise suspicions of unfaithfulness, threaten mutual trust, and cause resentment or breakups.

Most people find it painful to discuss the possibility that they may have passed a sexual infection to a lover, or caught one from her or him. It hurts to risk mutual trust for any reason, let alone a sexual infection that can raise other thorny issues. However, lovers who attempt to conceal a sex-related illness risk a good deal more in the long run than those who have the courage to discuss the situation right away. They risk worse resentments when their lovers finally discover the truth. They may also risk their lovers' lives. Women have *died* because their lovers were too embarrassed or unconcerned to inform them about infections that could have been cured easily if treated early. Men have a duty to inform their lovers about sexual infections because several that can cause life-threatening complications produce no discernible symptoms in women. In addition, an infection that remains untreated in one lover can keep reinfecting the other.

Some people assume that any infection of a lover's sex organs signals unfaithfulness. This may be the case, but many infections potentially passed by lovemaking can develop without sexual contact: You don't have to kiss a cold-sufferer to catch a cold. However, in cases where a sexual infection reveals a lapse of monogamy—or causes suspicions—the couple can expect an increase in stress in the relationship with an attendant increase in risk that other sex problems may develop.

In this context, it becomes important to know whether a sexual infection can develop only as a result of lovemaking, or whether it might develop without sexual intimacy. The infections discussed here are arranged by manner of transmission. They are divided into three groups: those possibly passed by lovemaking, those probably passed sexually, and those only passed that way.

Whenever possible, lovers should try to support one another's recovery from sexual infections and refrain from pressuring each other to make love again before it is advisable. In addition to the danger of "ping-ponging" the infection back and forth, pressure to make love while ill can prolong the illness.

Although sexual infections are caused by germs—viruses, bacteria, and other microorganisms—their development into full-blown illnesses is in part determined by lovers' general health and stress levels. For example, the chance of catching gonorrhea from a single intercourse with an infected lover is about 50 percent (unless a woman takes the Pill, in which case her chance of catching it is much higher). Healthy lovers who have evolved a problem-free lovestyle are less susceptible to these diseases than run-down lovers whose lovestyle frustrates them. Sex problems can contribute to sexual infections and vice versa. This is not to suggest that sex problems necessarily increase risk of sexual infection. It does mean that the factors affecting sexual pleasure are interdependent. Lovers concerned about frequent sexual infections might look beyond the confines of the germ theory of illness to the quality of their relationship and beyond that to their overall life circumstances.

A more comprehensive discussion of sexual infections can be found in The VD Handbook, distributed free at many public health and family-planning clinics. (See Bibliography.)

Infections Possibly Passed by Lovemaking

NONSPECIFIC OR NONGONOCCOCAL URETHRITIS (NSU/NGU) IN MEN

NSU is caused by any of several bacteria other than the one that causes gonorrhea. It is associated with fatigue, stress, poor diet, injury, or irritation of the urethra and low resistance as a result of other illness. Long regarded as a minor illness, NSU has received increased attention from public health authorities lately because its incidence has reached epidemic proportions (an estimated 2 million cases a year in the United States) and because recent research has linked it to other diseases: in children, pneumonia and ear infections; in men, epididymitis; and in women who pick it up during intercourse, pelvic inflammatory disease (PID), an infection of the Fallopian tubes that can cause sterility and death.

Transmission is poorly understood. Sexual transmission is possible; women usually show no symptoms. However, sexual transmission is by no means necessary. NSU can develop from any of the causes listed above that weaken the urethra's resistance to bacterial growth.

Men diagnosed as having NSU should refer their lovers for treatment to avoid "ping-ponging" the infection and because its effects in women may be quite serious.

Condoms prevent sexual transmission. It is also a good idea to avoid oral sex while infected. It is wrong to ask a woman to wrap her mouth around a penis that is discharging disease organisms. NSU also spoils the taste of the penis.

Symptoms for men include: pain or burning on urination and/or white, greenish, or yellowish pus discharge from the penis. These symptoms resemble those of gonorrhea and the two are sometimes confused.

Diagnosis is made by microscopic examination of the discharge. NSU shows no gonorrhea bacteria.

Two treatments are available. The nondrug approach involves flushing the bacteria out by drinking eight to ten glasses of water a day for a week or two. Also recommended are a balanced diet, plenty of rest, and avoidance of spicy foods and alcohol, both of which irritate the urethra.

Tetracycline is the drug used to treat NSU (penicillin is often ineffective). Tetracycline makes some people sensitive to sunlight —avoid extensive sunbathing during treatment. Also avoid milk products and antacids because they interfere with the body's absorption of the antibiotic.

YEAST VAGINITIS

Yeast infections in a woman's vagina are caused by microscopic fungi similar to those that make bread rise.

Yeast live in the healthy vagina. The reasons this organism sometimes causes infection are not understood. It may be sexually transmitted—yeast can live in the foreskin of uncircumcised men. However, it may develop without sexual contact as a result of low resistance, fatigue, stress, or diabetes, which changes the vaginal environment to stimulate yeast growth. Estrogen birth control pills also alter vaginal chemistry and allow yeast to grow more easily.

Women's symptoms include: intense itching, pain on urination, and a "cheesy" discharge that changes the taste of the vaginal-clitoral area. Diagnosis is made by symptoms and by microscopic examination of the discharge.

A man who orally caresses a lover with yeast may develop the throat infection, thrush.

Yeast is treated with vaginal suppositories of the antibiotic nystatin (Mycostatin) used nightly for about a month. Symptoms usually disappear in a few days, but treatment should continue for the full month to avoid recurrence.

TRICHOMONAS

Trichomonas is caused by a single-celled organism, the trichomonad. It may be transmitted heterosexually; men usually show no symptoms. Lesbians can pass it during close vaginal contact. Nonsexual transmission is also possible: At room temperature, trichomonads can survive several hours on moist objects, for example, towels, wash cloths, hot tubs, toilet seats, etc. Condoms prevent transmission.

Women's symptoms include: pain, often severe, and an abundant, frothy discharge with an unpleasant odor.

Diagnosis is made by symptoms and by microscopic identification of the trichomonads. Trichomonads are almost never found in infected men for unknown reasons. However, men in relationships with infected women are assumed to be capable of transmitting the infection and should be treated.

Women are treated with the drug metronidazole (Flagyl) and are instructed to use condoms during intercourse for a week. *Do not drink any alcohol for three days after taking Flagyl or you will become extremely ill.*

Lovers of infected women are also asked to take Flagyl and to use rubbers for a week. However, a nondrug treatment is available to men. The penis is less hospitable than the vagina to trichomonads. Frequent urination from drinking eight to ten glasses of water a day for two to three weeks usually flushes the infection out of men. Remember to use condoms.

Flagyl is a powerful drug. People with histories of cancer, or blood, liver, or nervous system illness should not take it, nor should pregnant or nursing women.

In the early 1970s, mice fed large doses of Flagyl for a long time showed unexpectedly high cancer rates, which led to fears that it might be carcinogenic in humans who take comparatively low doses infrequently. At this writing, Flagyl's relationship to human cancers is unknown. Some health activists have requested a ban. Other authorities say it is safe.

Another drug, Tricofuran, may also be used to treat trichomonas. It is reportedly less effective than Flagyl, but has not been associated with increased cancer rates in animals.

Urinary Tract Infections in Women (UTIs)

UTIs, also known as cystitis or bladder infections, are usually caused by the bacteria that normally inhabit the intestines and anal area. Introduction into the vagina, combined with irritation of the urethra and low resistance, cause the infection.

Women's symptoms include: burning on urination, urgent need to urinate frequently, possibly blood in urine, itching, and unpleasant odor.

Complications are rare, but potentially serious kidney infection is possible.

Diagnosis is made by symptoms and by microscopic identification of the bacteria. UTIs are treated with sulfa drugs (Gantrisin,

Gantanol). Some sulfa drugs contain a dye that turns urine bright red-orange.

Black people should be cautious about taking sulfa drugs, which kill red blood cells in 15 percent of black people and may prove fatal. Before taking sulfa, black people should be tested for "G6PD deficiency." Anyone with this enzyme deficiency should take ampicillin instead of sulfa.

UTIs need a particular internal environment to flourish. Increased urinary tract acidity kills the bacteria. Women with UTIs —or women who get them frequently—should drink cranberry juice to acidify the urinary tract.

Men rarely get urinary tract infections because men's and women's urinary systems are constructed differently. Bacteria can travel up the urethra to the bladder more easily in women than in men because women's urethras are only about two inches long, while men's are about eight inches. Also, the female urethra opens closer to the anus making bacterial contamination easier. Lovers who enjoy anal loveplay should not introduce anything into the vagina that has touched the anal area. And women should wipe themselves from front to back to keep anal bacteria away from the vagina.

Vigorous vaginal intercourse can irritate a woman's urethra and contribute to UTI development. Women inexperienced in lovemaking tend to be particularly susceptible to this infection. It was once called "honeymoon cystitis" back when most women's first intercourse happened on their honeymoons.

CRABS (PUBIC LICE)

Crabs are tiny bugs, barely visible to the naked eye, that live in pubic hair, in the scalp, or underarms. They may be transmitted sexually or from any close contact with infested individuals, clothing, towels, linens, etc. Crabs cause itching and sometimes can be seen in pubic hair.

Diagnosis is made by identification of the crabs.

The recommended treatment is Kwell, a prescription lotion or shampoo containing a powerful poisonous insecticide similar to DDT. It is applied to the body after showering, then washed off twelve to twenty-four hours later. Dress in fresh clothes after applying Kwell. Wash all potentially infested clothing, linens, towels, blankets, etc., in hot water and dry in a hot dryer. Don't forget to clean sleeping bags, beach blankets, and other occasionally used items.

People who object to covering themselves with a powerful insecticide might use Rid or Triple-X, over-the-counter products less potent and less expensive than Kwell. In 1977, the Haight-Ashbury Free Medical Clinic in San Francisco surveyed crab patients and found these products to be about as effective as Kwell.

SCABIES

Scabies are tiny mites that burrow under the skin anywhere on the body below the head, though they prefer the genitals, hands, arms, legs, and abdomen. Transmission is similar to crabs. It may or may not be sexual. Scabies cause itching, particularly at night, and little bumps on the skin. Kwell is the usual treatment.

Infections Probably Passed by Lovemaking

VENEREAL WARTS

Relatively little is known about venereal warts, small bumps on the penis, vaginal lips, in or around the anus.

Scientists assume they are caused by a virus similar to the one that causes warts on the hand.

Doctors believe venereal warts are almost always passed sexually, but they have appeared in people whose only lover shows no sign of them. Some might be immune; perhaps nonsexual transmission is possible.

Another unresolved issue is incubation period. Incubation period is the time between contact with the infection and appearance of the warts. Estimates vary from a few weeks to several months.

Warts appear to develop more often in uncircumcised men.

On the penis, they resemble warts of the hand. On the anus or vaginal lips, which are more moist, they look like little bumps with a cauliflowerlike aspect. There may be itching or odor. Anal warts may cause pain or bleeding on bowel movement and are sometimes confused with hemorrhoids.

Condoms prevent transmission.

Diagnosis is made by appearance.

The most widely used treatment is podophyllin, a chemical that burns the warts off. It is brushed on the warts by a doctor and left on for four to six hours, then *washed off thoroughly* to prevent burning healthy skin. Dichloroacetic acid also may be used to burn warts off. It acts faster than podophyllin and need not be washed off after treatment. Internal warts are usually removed surgically. Other treatments include freezing with liquid nitrogen or electrocautery with an instrument that resembles a soldering gun.

For unknown reasons, anal warts tend to recur spontaneously more often than warts located elsewhere. Several treatments are often necessary. Curing anal warts requires determination.

HERPES

Genital herpes sores are caused by the herpes simplex virus, a cousin of the virus that causes cold sores on the lips.

Transmission is usually sexual, but herpes have appeared in people whose only lover shows no sign of them. Like venereal warts, transmission of herpes is not clearly understood. Some people may be immune; nonsexual transmission may be possible.

For unknown reasons, herpes is more common in women than men.

Herpes lesions appear on the penis, on the vaginal lips, or inside the vagina as reddish, angry-looking, painful open sores that usually heal by themselves in one to three weeks. Herpes sores resemble syphilis chancres, but herpes are almost always painful, while syphilitic sores are usually painless.

Diagnosis is made by appearance and symptoms and by ruling out syphilis.

Herpes is the heartbreaker among the sex-related infections because the myth is that this infection is "incurable." Wrong. It's true that no drug has the power to destroy the herpes virus or eliminate it from the body, but the same could be said for the common cold, which is never called incurable. Having herpes is like having a cold in the genitals. Cold virus particles are present in the healthy throat, but the body prevents them from infecting throat cells unless resistance drops for any of the reasons that precipitate colds. The same is true for herpes. Many people "have" herpes—meaning that the virus is present in their bodies—but don't know it because their immune systems successfully defend against the appearance of herpes sores. Others develop sores from time to time when run down or under stress, circumstances similar to those that lead to colds. Herpes sores are not, repeat "not," incurable. They clear up by themselves after a week or two because the body cures them—just as it cures a cold. Colds recur from time to time, and each time the body cures itself of the infection. The same is true of recurrent herpes.

The problem with herpes—now estimated to affect 20 million Americans—is not so much the infection itself (annoying though the sores may be), as the social stigma attached to having what has become widely, though incorrectly, known as an incurable illness. Most people know little about herpes, and many people treat those with the infection as though they were sexual lepers. This, of course, can cause tremendous stress in those who have the infection and in their lovers. More than any other sexual infection, herpes is associated with sex problems, not because of the virus itself, but because of the stress and stigma that accompany it.

Herpes sufferers who have been misled into believing that they have an incurable illness often develop deep feelings of helplessness and hopelessness which tend to result in more frequent and more severe attacks.

Herpes prevention is similar to cold prevention. Try not to become distraught about the infection. Don't curse your fate or quarantine yourself from lovemaking. Try to stay calm about the infection and take care of yourself: eat well, get plenty of rest and exercise and try to incorporate a stress reduction program into your life to prevent herpes sores from recurring—for example, meditation, biofeedback, yoga or massage.

So what if you can't eliminate every herpes virus from your body? Many viruses and bacteria make their homes in our bodies without ruining our lives. People with herpes can adapt to this illness and enjoy problem-free lovemaking with minimal inconvenience.

Condoms are generally believed to prevent transmission of herpes when an active sore is present. Unfortunately, the infection can also be passed for the day or two *before* a developing sore becomes visible. This period is called the prodome. People with herpes should make every effort to learn the subtle signs of their prodomes. Many, for example, notice a slight tingling or itching sensation, similar to the minor physical changes that signal a cold coming on. If you make love during the prodome, the man should wear a condom.

Will there ever be a drug that can eradicate herpes virus? Maybe. At this writing, a drug that shows promise as a herpes medicine is being tested, but no drug has been licensed by the FDA for treatment of herpes.

Herpes is also associated with increased risk of cervical cancer in women. It is unclear whether herpes causes cervical cancer, but a statistical association exists between them. A woman in a relationship in which one lover has herpes should have two Pap tests a year instead of the one test usually recommended. Cervical cancer is 100 percent curable if detected early, hence the importance of frequent Pap tests.

Many home remedies have evolved to help ease the pain of the sores and hasten their healing. Recently, the American Social Health Association founded HELP to provide up-to-date information and a forum for people with herpes to share their home remedies, experiences, and perspectives on living with the infection. Those interested should send a stamped, self-addressed, business-size envelope to HELP, P.O. Box 100, Palo Alto, CA 94302.

Infections Passed Only by Lovemaking

GONORRHEA (THE CLAP)

Gonorrhea is caused by gonococci bacteria, hence the medical nickname "GC."

Gonococci can only be passed during vaginal, oral or anal intercourse. They die almost immediately on exposure to air. It is impossible to catch gonorrhea from toilet seats, towels, showers, etc.

Condoms prevent transmission.

In men, symptoms usually include: pain or burning on urination and a white, green, or yellow pus discharge from the penis. Oral gonorrhea may or may not cause a sore throat. Anal gonorrhea may or may not cause pain on bowel movement. Women with vaginal GC usually show no symptoms. A new, relatively rare strain of gonorrhea, brought to this country by soldiers returning from Southeast Asia, shows no symptoms in either men or women. Because of the epidemic proportions of this infection and the chance of catching the symptomless variety, a gonorrhea test should be part of any medical checkup.

Diagnosis is made in men by symptoms and by laboratory identification of gonococci. Women are diagnosed by an infected lover's referral, then by a lab finding of gonococci in the cervical mucus. Every possibly infected orifice should be tested.

Penicillin is the main treatment, though other antibiotics may be used. If you are allergic to penicillin, be sure to say so. Antibiotics are about 90–95 percent effective against GC, but antibiotic-resistant strains are an increasing problem. It's best to schedule a followup test a few weeks after treatment to make sure the infection has been cured.

Complications are rare in men. Although sterility is theoretically possible, it almost never occurs.

However, in women, complications are not only more frequent, but also potentially *fatal*. Untreated GC can cause pelvic inflammatory disease (PID), also known as salpingitis, a potentially life-threatening infection of the uterus and Fallopian tubes that causes high fever, vomiting, and severe abdominal pain. PID can cause sterility and death. Because women show no symptoms of gonorrhea, it is *crucial* that infected men refer all their lovers for treatment.

Babies born to women with gonorrhea are at risk for blindness. Pregnant women should be tested before they deliver.

SYPHILIS

Syphilis is caused by a bacteria-like microorganism, the Treponema pallidum.

It is passed by vaginal, oral, or anal intercourse.

Condoms *may not* prevent transmission—the germs can penetrate skin not covered by a condom.

The first symptom is a painless open sore at the site of infection. Sores of the penis tend to be more visible than those of the vagina, throat, or anus. Because women are often unaware of a syphilis sore, it is *vital* that men diagnosed for syphilis inform all their lovers. The sore heals by itself in a few weeks. Then, a nonitchy rash develops somewhere on the body. It disappears spontaneously in a few weeks. Syphilis then becomes hidden in the body for ten to twenty years, after which severe, possibly fatal complications may develop.

Diagnosis is made by a blood test called a VDRL.

Syphilis is treated with penicillin or tetracycline. Those treated are advised to abstain from intercourse for a month.

Babies born to women with syphilis are at risk for birth defects and infant death, which is why most states require syphilis tests before issuing marriage licenses.

Chapter 13

SEXUAL SELF-CARE FOR MEN: THE TESTICLES, BREASTS AND PROSTATE

Simple painless testicular and breast self-examinations that take only a few minutes a month might save your life, and self-care of the prostate by dietary means might help prevent several health problems, including prostate cancer.

Testicular Self-Examination

Testicular self-examination is easy and important, particularly in young men aged fifteen to thirty-four, because of the increasing incidence of testicular cancer. This cancer is relatively rare. It accounts for only 1 percent of all cancers in men, but it is the *most common solid tumor* in men under thirty-five, and its incidence is increasing.

A 1976 report by the National Cancer Institute showed that testicular cancer rates among whites doubled from 1950 to 1973 and tripled among blacks. The report also showed that testicular cancer is striking men earlier in life. Victims under twenty-five accounted for only 12 percent of cases during the 1950s, but that figure more than doubled to 26 percent by 1973.

Cancer is a disease of cell multiplication gone berserk. Scientists now agree that a majority of cancers are caused by exposure to environmental carcinogens. Cells that multiply quickly can develop cancer faster than slower-reproducing cells. The fastest-reproducing cells in postpuberty men are those involved in sperm production. Billions of sperm are forming all the time. Sperm-producing cells are quite delicate and because they contain a large proportion of genetic material, any harmful outside agent that does not kill them outright is likely to cause genetic damage that could produce cancer. Given exposure to carcinogens, it is reasonable to presume that testicular cancer would develop sooner—that is, in younger men—than other cancers in tissues that reproduce more slowly. Incidence data show that testicular cancer is becoming increasingly common in younger and younger men.

Men's genitals are particularly sensitive to environmental carcinogens. In fact, the first environmental carcinogen to be identified, chimney soot, isolated in 1775 by Sir Percival Pott in England, attracted medical attention because of high rates of scrotal cancer among chimney sweeps.

Men's genitals are extremely sensitive to low-level radiation produced by airborne alpha-emitters such as plutonium particles, an increasingly prevalent pollutant produced in the 1950s by above-ground nuclear weapons tests and now by the nuclear power industry. Research suggests that plutonium has an *affinity* for the testicles and tends to collect in them. Recently, a public health researcher examined cancer rates downwind from the Rocky Flats nuclear weapons production center near Denver which has released small amounts of plutonium, generally within government guidelines, for more than twenty years. Based on national testicular cancer rates, he expected to find seventeen cases in that population. He found forty cases, 140 percent higher than the national average.

An estimated 1–3 million men were exposed to DES before birth. This synthetic estrogen has been linked to vaginal cancer in some daughters of women who took it while pregnant. DES-sons have an increased risk of several genital abnormalities, and unpublished research presented to the HEW's National DES Task Force in 1978 suggests that they also have elevated testicular cancer rates.

Ten years ago, the five-year survival rate for testicular cancer victims (the proportion still alive five years after diagnosis of the disease) was very low. Most died quickly. Today, the survival rate is much higher but *only if* it is detected early. That's where frequent testicular self-examination could save your life.

The best time to examine your testicles is after a hot bath or shower when the scrotum is relaxed. Place your index and middle fingers under the testicle and your thumbs on top. Then roll each testicle between your thumbs and fingers. They should feel firm but not hard, rather like an ear lobe, with some give to them. Also, feel for the epididymis, the sperm storage tubes behind each testicle. They should feel a bit spongier.

What you're looking for and hoping *not* to find is a small hard painless lump or swelling. If you feel anything unusual, consult a urologist.

At first, it may feel strange to examine your testicles. It's normal to feel as if you don't know what you're doing. Give it time. Get to know your testicles. After a while they will become as familiar as the little idiosyncratic noises in your car.

Breast Self-Examination

Breast cancer is the most prevalent cancer in women, accounting for 26 percent of their cancers and 20 percent of women's cancer deaths. Many men know that doctors advise monthly self-examinations to check for possibly cancerous breast lumps.

However, most men are unaware that they can also develop breast cancer. The incidence in men is less than 1 percent of the incidence in women—700 cases in men in 1977 compared to 89,000 in women—but the death rate for men is *higher*—43 percent compared to 38 percent in women in 1977. Breast cancer kills a higher proportion of men because men have less breast tissue to act as a buffer between the tumor and the chest wall and because this cancer is rarely detected early in men.

The average age at diagnosis of breast cancer in men is sixty, but younger men should develop the simple habit of breast self-examination when they bathe. Move the fingertips in a circular pattern over the entire breast area. If you detect a solid, painless lump, consult a doctor.

Prostate Self-Care and "Vitamin Z"

A healthy prostate is essential to problem-free lovemaking and general well-being. Unfortunately, most men pay no attention to this important part of themselves unless it becomes infected, or until middle age when they begin to experience the symptoms of an enlarged prostate or prostate cancer.

A prostate check should be a part of any medical checkup for men thirty-five or older.

No one can guarantee freedom from prostate problems, but men can promote prostate health by incorporating a simple dietary self-care program into their lives. Prostate self-care comes down to one word—zinc.

Zinc is an essential trace element, that is, it is necessary for good health, but it accounts for less than .01 percent of body weight. Zinc is a mineral, not a vitamin, but as in vitamin deficiency, a zinc deficiency can have a major impact on a man's health and sexuality.

Of all the body's living tissues, concentrations of zinc are highest by far in sperm and in the prostate gland. Not surprisingly, zinc deficiency is associated with sperm abnormalities, sex problems, and prostate diseases, including cancer.

The American diet tends to be deficient in zinc. Food processing removes zinc from grains, frozen foods, and meats. In addition, copper plumbing introduces excess copper into the body which interferes with the assimilation of zinc.

The body cannot store much zinc, so zinc-rich foods should be a regular part of men's diets. The food richest in zinc is the oyster. For centuries, folk wisdom has described the oyster as a "virility food." Like so many legends, this one appears to be based in fact. (Unfortunately, many oysters also contain dangerously high concentrations of cadmium and other toxic heavy metals.) Eastern Europeans have long believed that nuts and seeds promoted men's sexual abilities—"Seeds for the seed." Nuts and seeds also have high concentrations of zinc. Other food sources of zinc include: whole grains, fresh peas and carrots, and milk.

The most common prostate problem in young men is inflammation of the gland, prostatitis. Symptoms include: low back pain;

pain accompanying bowel movement, during a rectal exam, and/or ejaculation; possible fever; and urine possibly clouded by pus. Prostatitis can also be caused by gonorrhea, and a VD test is a standard part of a thorough prostatitis examination. Men with recurrent prostatitis have been found to have zinc deficiencies. Prostatitis is treated with antibiotics. Zinc-rich foods are also recommended.

Noncancerous prostate enlargement, called BPH by doctors for "benign prostatic hypertrophy," causes urinary problems because, as the prostate expands, it tends to pinch the urethra which passes through it from the bladder. Symptoms include: urinary urgency (the need to go right now), slow stream, and dribbling. For any urinary difficulty, see a doctor. BPH is often treated surgically. Increased zinc intake may also help.

The older a man grows, the more likely he is to develop prostate cancer. Prostate cancer accounts for 17 percent of men's cancers and 10 percent of men's cancer deaths. Each year, 60,000 new cases are diagnosed in the United States and 20,000 men die from the disease. Incidence has increased about 20 percent in the last 25 years. Symptoms resemble those of BPH. Canadian researchers have found low levels of zinc in cancerous prostate glands removed surgically. Eastern European countries that have generally low prostate cancer rates have zinc-rich diets. Prostate cancer is treated with female sex hormones or surgery. Both treatments may cause sex problems.

Health food stores often sell zinc supplements. These should not be necessary for men who eat a balanced diet containing zinc-rich foods. However, anyone who takes a zinc supplement should be sure not to exceed the recommended dose. Although zinc is a relatively nontoxic mineral, toxic reactions are possible at high doses.

A SIMPLE GUIDE TO MEN'S AND WOMEN'S SEXUAL ANATOMY

Both men's and women's reproductive anatomies consist of two sets of tubes: the urinary tract, through which urine is excreted, and the genital tract, designed for reproduction and sexual pleasure. Together, these sets of tubes are called the genitourinary system.

Men

A man's urinary tract begins in the *kidneys,* where liquid wastes are removed from the blood and converted to urine. Urine is stored in the *bladder* and led out of the body through the *penis* along the *urethra.*

A man's genital tract begins outside the main body in the *scrotum,* the fleshy sack between a man's legs that houses his *testicles* or *testes.* Each testicle contains millions of tiny *seminiferous tubules* that produce *sperm,* a man's sex cells. Sperm production begins at puberty and continues, with few exceptions, until death. Sperm are stored in the two *epididymides.* One epididymis is located next to each testicle and consists of a collection of coiled tubes adjacent to the testicles.

From the epididymis, sperm travel up and out of the scrotum into the

Male Reproductive System

a scrotum
b testicle (one of a pair)
c epididymis (one of a pair)
d vas deferens (one of a pair)
e seminal vesicle (one of a pair)
f urinary bladder
g prostate gland
h urethra

i bulbourethral (Cowper's) gland (one of a pair)
j penis
k corpus cavernosum (one of a pair)
l corpus spongiosum
m glans
n opening of urethra

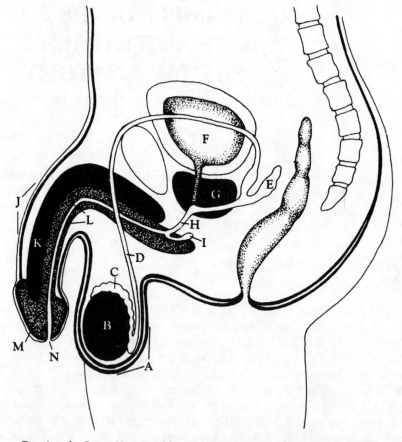

Drawings by Susan Neri. Used by permission of *Medical Self-Care* Magazine.

Female Reproductive System

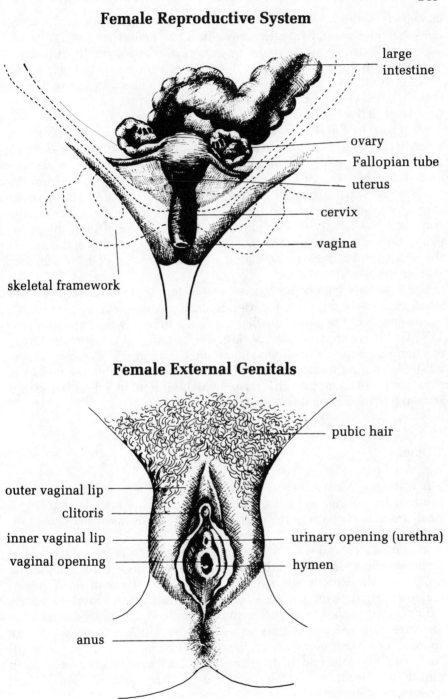

large intestine

ovary

Fallopian tube

uterus

cervix

vagina

skeletal framework

Female External Genitals

pubic hair

outer vaginal lip

clitoris

inner vaginal lip

vaginal opening

urinary opening (urethra)

hymen

anus

main body cavity along the *vas deferens*, again one per testicle. These are the tubes that are cut in vasectomy. Each vas arches around the *pubic bone*, which can be felt by pressing on the lower abdomen directly above the base of the penis, and passes the *seminal vesicles* on the way to the *prostate gland* (not prostrate—there is no "r"). The seminal vesicles secrete a thick yellowish fluid necessary for the survival of sperm, and important in the composition of *seminal fluid*, or *semen*.

The *prostate gland* is bigger than a cherry tomato but smaller than a plum. It sits toward the back of the body, above the anus. Doctors examine part of it during rectal examination. Inside the prostate, the two vas deferens tubes join and link up with the urethra on its way down from the bladder. A valve activated by erection prevents urine from passing through the erect penis, and likewise prevents semen from leaving the penis while it is flaccid. The prostate secretes *prostatic fluid*, the major component of semen, and the muscles around the prostate and between the legs contract during ejaculation to propel semen along the urethra and out the penis.

The *Cowper's glands* are located just below the prostate and secrete small amounts of fluid into the urethra during sexual arousal.

The length of the penis is called the *shaft*; the tip is the *head* or *glans*. The glans is covered by a flap of skin, the *foreskin*, which retracts during erection and exposes the glans. Sometimes the foreskin is removed surgically with a minor operation called *circumcision*. Inside the penis are three bodies of spongy *erectile tissue* which fill with blood during sexual arousal to stiffen the penis hydraulically in *erection*.

Women

A woman's urinary system is similar to a man's except the urethra is considerably shorter and ends in the *vagina*. The urethra takes up only a small amount of space in the vagina. A man cannot insert his penis into a woman's urethra.

A woman's genital tract begins with the *ovaries*, one on either side of the lower abdomen. The ovaries are almond-sized organs that release one egg per month, usually alternately but sometimes simultaneously resulting in fraternal twins if both eggs are fertilized. Eggs travel along the *Fallopian tubes* about four inches to the *uterus*, or *womb*, where the fetus develops. If a sperm fertilizes an egg, the resulting cells attach to the spongy, blood-rich uterine wall, the *endometrium*. If an egg is not fertilized, both it and the endometrium are expelled from the body each month during *menstruation*, which begins at puberty and continues until women are about fifty.

The uterus resembles an upside-down pear. Its thin neck, the cervix, extends into the vagina, the highly elastic tube where semen is deposited during vaginal intercourse and through which the full-term fetus passes during birth. The vagina is a mouthlike organ whose interior is partially covered, until first intercourse, by the hymen, a thin elastic membrane, and by two sets of lips, the inner and outer vaginal lips, flaps of skin that normally fold together over the entrance to the vagina, but open during sexual arousal.

Beneath each outer vaginal lip is a tiny Bartholin's gland, which secretes a small amount of fluid during sexual arousal.

Outside the vagina and above it lies the clitoris, the nerve-rich little organ exquisitely sensitive to sexual excitement. Above the clitoris is the Mons Veneris, the fleshy covering over the pubic bone where women's pubic hair is located.

NATIONAL DIRECTORY
OF SEX THERAPISTS

Edited by Kristi Beer

This directory lists 196 selected sex therapy services in the United States. The individuals and clinics selected met the following criteria: (1) They provide short-term sex therapy. (2) They use techniques similar to those suggested in this book. (3) They provide services to individuals and/or couples regardless of marital status or sexual preference. (4) Services are priced reasonably by sex therapy standards—about $50.00 per hour (fees subject to change). Some offer sliding scales and/or accept third-party payments.

Selections for this Directory were based on responses to a survey sent to sex therapists certified by the American Association of Sex Educators, Counselors and Therapists. AASECT publishes an annually updated National Register of Certified Sex Therapists that lists more than 750 sex therapists in the United States and Canada. The Register is available for $3.00 from AASECT, 5010 Wisconsin Ave. N.W., Washington, D.C., 20016. Telephone: (202) 686–2523.

ARIZONA

Barbara Greiff. 5211 N. 70th Place, Scottsdale, 85253. Telephone: (602) 945–4602.

Gene Gary Gruver. 6650 N. Montezuma Drive, Tucson, 85718. Telephone: (602) 299–0338.

Richard O. Gundersen. 1886 San Gabriel Drive, Yuma, 85364. Telephone: (602) 726–9229.

John W. Hudson. 2923 N. 67th Place, Scottsdale, 85251. Telephone: (602) 945–3431.

CALIFORNIA

Frances S. Alexander. 5359 N. Algarrobo, Laguna Hills, 92653. Telephone: (714) 770–4701.

Dieter Bruehl, Andrea Palella. 21385 W. Summit Road, Topanga, 90290. Telephone: (213) 455–2746.

Center for Counseling and Therapy—Carolyn Symonds. P.O. Box 1197, Santa Cruz, 95060. Telephone: (408) 426–1397.

Center for Professional Counseling—Frank T. Carroll, Shirley R. Lampert. 1100 Quail St., Suite 200, Newport Beach, 92660. Telephone: (714) 833–7810.

Ginny Connell, Phil Connell, Patty Corrigan, Frank Johnson, Priscilla Rankin, Ron Zaboski. 558 St. Charles Drive, Suite 214, Thousand Oaks, 91360. Telephone: (805) 495–8435.

Dick Dodge, Bill Shearer. 6900 Brockton Ave., Suite 2, Riverside, 92506 and 2020 Waterman Ave., Suite E, San Bernardino, 92404. Telephone: (714) 682–4444 and 886–4951.

Javad Emami. 3760 Third Ave., San Diego, 92103. Telephone: (714) 291–5034.

Family Education and Counseling Center—Steve Aizenstat, Keith Witt. 5200 Hollister Ave., Santa Barbara, 93111. Telephone: (805) 967–4557.

Beverlee H. Filloy. 3333 Watt Ave., Suite 209, Sacramento, 95821. Telephone: (916) 485–2262.

Marilyn A. Fithian, Bob Geizer, William E. Hartman, Barbie Taylor. 5199 E. Pacific Coast Hwy., Long Beach, 90804. Telephone: (213) 597–4425.

Samuel D. Gilbert. 5353 Balboa Blvd., #311, Encino, 91316. Telephone: (213) 788–1471.

Griffin Clinic. 5363 Balboa Blvd., #545, Encino, 91316. Telephone: (213) 788–5123.

Edie Greenberg, Marty Greenberg, Larry Kesner. 5045 Alzeda Drive, La Mesa, 92041. Telephone: (714) 447–9979.

Benjamin Hendrickson. 915 W. Lancaster Blvd., Lancaster, 93534. Telephone: (805) 948–1631.

Henry Sioux Johnson, Donna Spaw. 17291 Irvine Blvd., Suite 155, Tustin, 92608. Telephone: (714) 838–2130.

La Jolla Medical and Psychological Center—Rosalie Chapman, George Pratt. 6523 La Jolla Blvd., La Jolla, 92037. Telephone: (714) 454–8045.

Lamorinda Institute of Psychotherapy—Allan Furhman, Richard S. Hansen, Carol A. Whiting. One Northwood Drive, Suite 7, Orinda, 94563. Telephone: (415) 254–7800.

Ray William London. 1125 E. Seventeenth St., Suite E-211, Santa Ana, 92701. Telephone: (213) 541–4858.

Alberta Mazat. Loma Linda University, Marriage and Family Counseling Dept., Loma Linda, 92350. Telephone: (714) 824–0800. Ext. 2945.

Michael Nugent. 5075 Mt. Royal Drive, Eagle Rock, 90041. Telephone: (213) 255–9174.

Susan Rodgers. 10 La Encinal, Orinda, 94563. Telephone: (415) 254–6210.

Santa Barbara Branch of the American Institute of Family Relations. 800 Garden St., Suite I, Santa Barbara, 93101. Telephone: (805) 962–3288.

South Bay Branch of the American Institute of Family Relations. 1840 S. Elena, Redondo Beach, 90277. Telephone: (213) 375–0442.

Betty J. Calame Staten. 23717 Hawthorne, Suite 206, Torrance, 90505. Telephone: (213) 373–6359.

Mary Anne Sviland. Woodlands Hills, 91365. Telephone: (213) 348–6494.

Lee B. Teed. 470 Nautilus St., #301, La Jolla, 92037. Telephone: (714) 459–6797.

Richard P. Varnes. 4404 Riverside Drive, Burbank, 91505. Telephone: (213) 843–0711.

Los Angeles

Joseph Barry, Robert Rosenthal. 924 Westwood Blvd., Suite 535, Los Angeles, 90024. Telephone: (213) 477–6017.

Samuel Gladstone. 5460 Village Green, Los Angeles, 90016. Telephone: (213) 295–1535.

Joanne Leff. 1276 Beverly Green, Beverly Hills, 90212. Telephone: (213) 553–8893.

Ronald J. Pion. 8920 Wilshire Blvd., Suite 518, Beverly Hills, 90211.

Linda Polk, Robert Wintebourne. 1355 Westwood Blvd., #200, Los Angeles, 90024. Telephone: (213) 479–0711.

Rex Reece. 2740 Creston Drive, Los Angeles, 90068. Telephone: (213) 465–3219.

Ronald Schwartz. 141 S. Linden Drive, Beverly Hills, 90212. Telephone: (213) 278–8759.

San Francisco Bay Area

Penny Baver, Jay Mann. 1000 Welch Road, Suite 205, Palo Alto, 94304. Telephone: (415) 321–4347.

Berkeley Sex Therapy Group—Bernard Apfelbaum, Martin H. Williams. 2614 Telegraph Ave., Berkeley, 94704. Telephone: (415) 841–9119.

James H. Cox, Sarah R. Cox. 1779 Woodside Road #201, Redwood City, 94061. Telephone: (415) 365–2673.

Institute for Rational Living—Virginia Anne Church, Margaret Goldman. 2435 Ocean Ave., San Francisco, 94271; 1399 Ygnacio Valley Road, Walnut Creek, 94598 and 327 N. San Mateo Drive, San Mateo, 94401. Telephone: (415) 334–3450.

Melody Matthews. 2229 Lombard St., San Francisco, 94123. Telephone: (415) 931–6262.

Norman S. Mitroff. 1025 Fifth St., Novato, 94947. Telephone: (415) 897–7181.

National Sex Forum. 1523 Franklin, San Francisco, 94109. Telephone: (415) 928–1133.

Carol Ellison Rinkleib. 2938 McClure St., Oakland, 94609. Telephone: (415) 841–4894.

Lucy Scott. 451 Vermont, Berkeley, 94707. Telephone: (415) 525–1586.

Carol Small. P.O. Box 9404, Berkeley, 94709. Telephone: (415) 548–5477.

Saint Stroud. 108 Starview Court, Oakland, 94618. Telephone: (415) 843–4000.

University of California at San Francisco Human Sexuality Program. 350 Parnassus, Suite 300, San Francisco, 94143. Telephone: (415) 666–4623.

Ann Wolff. 1700 Second St., Napa, 94558. Telephone: (707) 252–2019.

COLORADO

Mark L. Held. 8095 E. Prentice Ave., Englewood, 80111. Telephone: (303) 773–1494.

Gretchen and W. Charles Lobitz. 360 S. Monroe St., Suite 270, Denver, 80209. Telephone: (303) 333–2922.

CONNECTICUT

George and Janet Anderheggen, Elaine Pratt. R.F.D. 1, Flat Swamp Road, Newtown, 06470. Telephone: (203) 426–3021.

Counseling Associates—Jane C. Bason, Darleen and John Wiedenheft. 40 Barker St., Hartford, 06114. Telephone: (203) 527–5523.

Reid J. Daitzman. 1425 Bedford St., Suite 1A, Stamford, 06905. Telephone: (203) 359–1779.

Family Counseling of Greater New Haven—Frank Caparulo, William F. Mecca, Irmgard Wessel. 1 State St., New Haven, 06511. Telephone: (203) 865–1125.

Marvin A. Steinberg. 26 Pendleton St., Hamden, 06518. Telephone: (203) 288–6253 or 389–9748.

DELAWARE

Benjamin F. Fileti. 583 Hemingway Drive, Hockessin, 19707. Telephone: (302) 239–5022.

FLORIDA

Associated Psychological Services—Bill Kinder. 10320 N. 56th St., Suite C, Temple Terrace, 33617. Telephone: (813) 988–2665.

Community Behavioral Services—Dawn Burgess, Harry Krop. 2614 S.W. 34th St., Gainesville, 32608. Telephone: (904) 372–6645.

James R. David. 2926 Foxcroft Drive, Tallahassee, 32308. Telephone: (904) 386–8871.

Amber Goldstein. 3421 Poinciana Ave., Coconut Grove (Miami), 33133. Telephone: (305) 445–0930 or 444–0010.

Orrin T. Hunt. 1219 Mayer Drive, Jacksonville, 32211. Telephone: (904) 744–3477.

Fred Pokrasso, Joel and Marilyn Spike, James Tracton. 223 American Savings Building, 16300 N.E. 163rd St., North Miami Beach, 33160. Telephone: (305) 947–5025.

David L. Redfering. 4575 Sailboat Lane, Pensacola, 32504. Telephone: (904) 477–4688.

JoAnn M. Saunders. 1155 Louisiana Ave., Suite 112, Winter Park, 32789. Telephone: (305) 628–0339.

Libby A. Tanner. 1600 N.W. 10th Ave., University of Miami School of Medicine, Miami, 33152. Telephone: (305) 547–6412.

GEORGIA

Johannes Causey, Jonathan Lynton, N. D. Mallary, Jr., Marianna Padgett, Robert S. Stein. 951 Edgewood Ave. N.E., Atlanta, 30307. Telephone: (404) 688–0050.

Martin Dybicz, Charles Goldman, Frances Nagata, David Rouser, Ruth Van Hoesen. 174 W. Wieuca Road, N.E., Atlanta, 30342. Telephone: (404) 255–7439.

Family Counseling Service of Athens—Carolyn Hally. P.O. Box 1564, Athens, 30606. Telephone: (404) 549–7755.

Edward J. Garcia. 1125 Fernclift Road, N.E., Atlanta, 30324. Telephone: (404) 233–6593.

HAWAII

Jack S. Annon. 1380 Lusitana St., Queen's Physicians' Office Building, Suite 909, Honolulu, 96813. Telephone: (808) 533–1711.

Carie Ramey. 47–077 Kamehameha Hwy, Kaneohe, 96744. Telephone: (808) 235–1406.

ILLINOIS

The Center for Marital and Sexual Therapy—Phyllis Levy, Bernard Levine. 1204 E. Central, Arlington Heights, 60005. Telephone: (312) 259–6076.

Blanche Freund. Human Sexuality Services, Southern Illinois University, Carbondale, 62901. Telephone: (618) 453–5101.

George S. Holden, Janice Miner-Holden. 1100 Geneva Road, #29A, St. Charles, 60174. Telephone: (312) 584–1687.

Bernard Kliska. 504 Lavinia, Joliet, 60435. Telephone: (815) 725–1800.

Rena Krizmis. 14816 Riverside Drive, Harvey, 60426. Telephone: (312) 333–5756.

Midwest Population Center. 100 E. Ohio, Suite 218, Chicago, 60611. Telephone: (312) 644–3410.

INDIANA

Alan P. Bell. 3070 Inverness Farm Road, Bloomington, 47401. Telephone: (812) 334–3890.

Diane B. Brasheak. 1010 E. 86th St., Indianapolis, 46240. Telephone: (317) 846–4693.

Robert L. Greenlee, Kathleen Rooch. 909 E. State Blvd., Fort Wayne, 46805. Telephone: (219) 482–9111.

IOWA

Herbert S. Roth, Muriel E. Roth, Nancy L. Ansevics. 8450 Hickman Road, Suite 14, Des Moines, 50322. Telephone: (515) 278–8741.

KANSAS

Jack R. Alvord. 4550 W. 109th St., Suite 135, Overland Park, 66211. Telephone: (913) 341–7020.

M. Edward Clark. Kansas University Medical Center, Kansas City, 66103. Telephone: (913) 588–6200.

Dennis M. Dailey. 403 Yorkshire Drive, Lawrence, 66044. Telephone: (913) 841–5400.

Julie Jurich. Box 141, Irwin Army Hospital, Fort Riley, 66442. Telephone: (913) 239–2966.

William B. Silverman. 3700 W. 83rd, #107, Prairie Village, 66208. Telephone: (913) 649–5515.

KENTUCKY

Arvil C. Reeb, Jr. Doctor's Park, 1517 Nicholasville Road, Lexington, 40503. Telephone: (606) 278–1315.

Theresa J. Wood. 2266 Bradford Drive, Louisville, 40218. Telephone: (502) 456–2203.

LOUISIANA

Angelo Ancona. Bayou Pines Medical Center, 812 Bayou Pines Drive, Lake Charles, 70601. Telephone: (318) 433–1031.

MARYLAND

Barry A. Bass. 600 Wyndhurst Ave., Baltimore, 21210. Telephone: (301) 377–4343.

Edward W. Cassidy, Eileen M. Waters, Robert T. Waters. 2201 Harwood Lane, Bowie, 20716. Telephone: (301) 464–0066.

Warren R. Johnson. 2010 Pelden Road, Adelphi, 20742. Telephone: (301) 445–1167.

Barry Jay Kirshner. 1906 S. Fallsmead Way, Potomac, 20854. Telephone: (301) 340–0133.

John R. May. Suite 124, 1000 Century Plaza, Columbia, 21044. Telephone: (301) 730–3130.

Sexual Behaviors Consultation Unit. The Johns Hopkins Hospital— Phipps 009, Baltimore, 21205. Telephone: (301) 955–6318.

MASSACHUSETTS

Edna Barrabee-Grace. 280 Boylston St., Chestnut Hill, 02167. Telephone: (617) 332–1184.

Rosalie Brown, Curtis P. Hinckley. 10 Sewall Ave., Brookline, 02146. Telephone: (617) 262–1862.

Arthur L. Cobb. 144A Mt. Auburn St., Cambridge, 02138. Telephone: (617) 868–0853.

Sylvia Cohen. 1 Center St., Gloucester, 01930. Telephone: (617) 283–6787.

Haskell R. Coplin. 415 S.E. St., Amherst, 01002. Telephone: (413) 253–5351.

Ronald Feintech, Margery Hartle. 9 Harvard St., Charlestown, 02129.

Hamilton School Counseling Center—Eleanor Hamilton, Gina Ogden. Sheffield, 01257. Telephone: (413) 229–2149.

Joseph Jayko. 147 Forest St., Norwell, 02061. Telephone: (617) 659–4322.

New England Institute for Marital and Sexual Counseling. 1 Granite St., Framingham, 01701. Telephone: (617) 872–0900, 875–1331.

Richard A. Pigott, Richard B. Stifler. 6 Babson Park Ave., Wellesley Hills, 02157. Telephone: (617) 237–5992, 269–7489.

MICHIGAN

Loren G. Burt. 5878 Jerome Road, Alma, 48801. Telephone: (517) 463–4027.

Reproductive Health Care Center of South Central Michigan. 4201 W. Michigan Ave., Kalamazoo, 49006. Telephone: (616) 349–8631.

Anne W. Waltersdorf, Rodney A. Zegers. 210 W. Tienken Road, Rochester, 48063. Telephone: (313) 652–0212.

MISSOURI

Rose Boyarsky, Randy Hammer, Richard Laitman, Ellen Moran, Naoia Ramzy. 4625 Lindell, Suite 315, St. Louis, 63108. Telephone: (314) 361–4227.

Community Counseling Center—E. Charles Welsh. 318 Plaza Center Bldg., 800 W. 47th St., Kansas City, 64112. Telephone: (816) 561–2600.

Alicemarie M. Miller. 8011 Clayton Road, St. Louis, 63117. Telephone: (314) 725–2275.

MONTANA

Frank W. Clark. Department of Social Work, University of Montana, Missoula, 59812. Telephone: (406) 243–5792 or 243–6550.

NEBRASKA

Elmorine R. Hites, Duane E. Spiers. 2717 S. 88th St., Omaha, 68124. Telephone: (402) 397–4880.

NEVADA

Gary P. Waters. 500 Hot Springs Road, Suite 5, Carson City, 89701. Telephone: (702) 882–4365.

NEW JERSEY

Bergen Center for Psychological Services—Eli M. S. Forman. 30 Riveredge Road, Tenafly, 07670. Telephone: (201) 569–8656.

George Bonnell. 111 Quimby St., Westfield, 07090. Telephone: (201) 232–2530.

Murray D. Gegner. 210 N. Rumson Ave., Margate, 08402. Telephone: (609) 822–6571.

James G. Iannucci. 700 N. Pearl St., Bridgeton, 08302. Telephone: (609) 455–1800.

Judy Silverberg, 58 Far Brook Drive, Short Hills, 07078. Telephone: (201) 376–9096.

Hirsch Lazaar Silverman. 123 Gregory Ave., West Orange, 07052. Telephone: (201) 731–1137.

Frank L. Singer, Greta L. Singer. 172 River Road, Red Bank, 07701. Telephone: (201) 741–8560.

Robert T. Winston. Watchung Diagnostic Center, Anderson Road, Watchung, 07060. Telephone: (201) 756–0660.

NEW MEXICO

Ruth T. Caplan, Stanley W. Caplan, Camille R. McRae, Joan Scott. 7000 Cutler N.E., La Mesa Medical Center, Suite E22, Albuquerque, 87110. Telephone: (505) 883–5214.

NEW YORK

Daniel L. Araoz. C.W. Post Center, Long Island University, Greenvale, 11548. Telephone: (516) 299–2814.

Behavioral Consultants, Sexual and Marital Therapy Division—Martha Stein. Syosset Medical Center, 175 Jericho Turnpike Syosset, Long Island, 11791. Telephone: (516) 364–1188.

Miriam Berger. 140-70 Burden Crescent, Briarwood, 11435. Telephone: (212) 657–3454.

Gail Block, Joel Block. 100 Manetto Hill Road, Plainview, 11803. Telephone: (516) 822–6809.

Daniel M. Callahan, Jean B. Callahan, Phyllis O'Flattery. 1 Fuller Road, Albany, 12203. Telephone: (518) 482–7704.

Jack J. Forest, Sherl M. Forest. 40–29 76th St., Jackson Heights, 11375. Telephone: (212) TW 9–2222.

Patricia Gagnon. 234 E. Main St., Box 326, Port Jefferson, 11777. Telephone: (516) 928–7189.

Human Sexuality Center. Long Island Hillside Medical Center, 271–11 Union Turnpike, New Hyde Park, 11040. Telephone: (212) 470–2761.

Gary F. Kelly. RD 1, Bagdad Road, Potsdam, 13676. Telephone: (315) 265–2772.

Rev. David F. Krampitz. 430 Walton Place, Westbury, 11590. Telephone: (516) 334–3499.

Arthur Lane, Selma Lane. 22 Devonshire Court, Plainview, 11803. Telephone: (516) 935–3272.

Bernice Leicher. 90 Gateway, Rockville Centre, 11570. Telephone: (516) 536–3070.

Mary-Anne Newman. 144-15 41st Ave., Flushing, 11355. Telephone: (212) 463–2870.

Sex Therapy Center. Department of Psychiatry and Behavioral Sciences, State University of New York at Stony Brook, 11790. Telephone: (516) 444–2066.

Andrew S. Sherwin, Bea R. Sherwin. 12 Pinetree Lane, Old Westbury, 11568. Telephone: (516) 626–2747.

Ruth Winkelstein. 166 Sheridan Ave., Mt. Vernon, 10552. Telephone: (914) 667–4688.

Leo Wollman. 2802 Mermaid Ave., Brooklyn, 11224. Telephone: (212) 372–4569.

NEW YORK CITY

Behavior Therapy Center of New York—Leonard A. Bachelis, director. 115 E. 87th St., Suite 8E, New York, 10028. Telephone: (212) 722–2300.

Anne H. Berkman. 345 E. 69th St., New York, 10021. Telephone: (212) 288–5982.

Carolynn Hillman. 300 W. 72nd St., New York, 10023. Telephone: (212) 580–2286.

Madeline Levy, Adalbert B. Vajay. 14 E. 60th St., New York, 10022. Telephone: (212) 751–9035.

Ronald J. Murphy. 110 E. 82nd St., New York, 10028. Telephone: (212) 288–4546.

Michael A. Perelman. 137 E. 36th St., New York, 10016. Telephone: (212) 686–8778.

Herbert J. Tannenbaum. 330 W. 56th St., New York, 10019, and 1555 E. 19th St., Brooklyn, 11230. Telephone: (212) 245–0022.

Ivan Wentworth-Rohr. 10 W. 66th St., New York, 10023. Telephone: (212) 787–6416.

NORTH CAROLINA

Crist Clinic for Women. 200 Memorial Drive, Jacksonville, 28540. Telephone: (919) 353–2115.

Barbara E. James. 240 Old Nurses' Dorm, Medical Wing C, Department of Psychiatry, University of North Carolina, Chapel Hill, 27330. Telephone: (919) 966–3377.

Richard T. Lovelace. 514 S. Stratford Road, Winston-Salem, 27103. Telephone: (919) 761–0949.

John Reckless. 5504 Chapel Hill Blvd., Durham, 27707. Telephone: (919) 489–1661.

Maynard L. Rich. 311 Idlewood Drive, Salisbury, 28144. Telephone: (704) 637–4386 or 633–2374.

Gary E. Zimmerman. 301 Le Grand St., Rockingham, 28379. Telephone: (919) 997–4444.

OHIO

Behavioral Science Center—Elizabeth R. Miller, William C. Wester, II. 2212 Victory Parkway, Cincinnati, 45206. Telephone: (513) 221–8545.

Robert W. Birch. 3230 Northwest Blvd., Columbus, 43221. Telephone: (614) 457–3979.

Sidney Levine. 3536 Westchester Road, Toledo, 43615. Telephone: (419) 841–5437.

Roger A. Woudenberg. Counseling Service, University of Cincinnati, Cincinnati, 45221. Telephone: (513) 475–2941.

OKLAHOMA

Ronald C. Passmore. 6465 S. Yale, Suite 623, Tulsa, 74136. Telephone: (918) 492–8333.

OREGON

Franklin J. Euse, Margo K. Euse. 2320 Ranch Road, Ashland, 97520. Telephone: (503) 482–5352.

Gerald D. Nathan. 530 Center St. N.E., Salem, 97301. Telephone: (503) 362–5777.

PENNSYLVANIA

Wallace E. Crider. Cedarbrook Hill Apt., Bldg. 1, Box 2, Wyncote, 19095. Telephone: (215) 576–1999.

Joanne B. Gentile, Gary Gruber. 24 E. Grant St., Lancaster, 17602. Telephone: (717) 394–9008.

Marriage Council of Philadelphia—Kenneth D. George. 4025 Chestnut, Philadelphia, 19104. Telephone: (215) EV 2–6680.

Edward Silverman. 844 Centre Ave., Reading, 19801. Telephone: (215) 374–4963.

William R. Stayton. 14 Elliott Ave., Bryn Mawr, 19010. Telephone: (215) 525–0311.

RHODE ISLAND

Richard A. Dannenfelser. Program in Human Sexuality, Box 1931, Brown University, Providence, 02912. Telephone: (401) 863–2344.

SOUTH CAROLINA

Judy C. Barnes, Yancey E. Poole, Jr. 30 Lockwood Drive, Charleston, 29401. Telephone: (803) 792–7547.

Clemson Family Practice Center—Robert D. Towell. College Ave., Clemson, 29631, and Spartanburg General Hospital, 101 E. Wood St., Spartanburg, 29303. Telephones: Clemson: (803) 654–2067, Spartanburg: (803) 573–6289.

SOUTH DAKOTA

Donna J. Dahl, Wayne A. Dahl. 2000 S. Summit, Sioux Falls, 57105. Telephone: (605) 336–0510.

Charles L. Pelton. 201 S. Lloyd, Suite 230 of Physician's Plaza, Aberdeen, 57401. Telephone: (605) 229–5990.

TENNESSEE

E. Ray Jerkins. 307 Doctor's Pavilion, 1916 Patterson St., Nashville, 37203. Telephone: (615) 327–4793.

TEXAS

Edward E. Coates. 425 Highland, Abilene, 79605. Telephone: (915) 673–5295.

Doris C. Conway. 5511 Parkcrest Drive, Suite 200–A, Parkcrest Bldg., Austin, 78731. Telephone: (512) 459–4404.

James C. Hancock. 6003 Victor St., Dallas, 75214. Telephone: (214) 824–6190.

Beverley M. Larkam. 2102 Raleigh Ave., Austin, 78703. Telephone: (512) 476–4182.

Earle R. Ramsdell. 1929 Mayflower Drive, Dallas, 75208. Telephone: (214) 946–7371.

Roz Van Meter. 3317 McKinney, Suite 103, Dallas, 75204. Telephone: (214) 521–2551.

Paul A. Walker. University of Texas Medical Branch, Dept. of Psychiatry, Galveston, 77550. Telephone: (713) 765–2361.

UTAH

Rehabilitation Sex Therapy Clinic. 50 N. Medical Drive, University of Utah Medical Center, Salt Lake City, 84132. Telephone: (801) 581–5741.

VIRGINIA

Mary Johnston Baver, Dora Dobrin, Warren Jeffrey Jones, Jr. 844 Kempsville Road, Suite 212, Norfolk, 23502. Telephone: (804) 461–1644.

Brian C. Campden-Main. 3545 Chain Bridge Road, Fairfax, 22030. Telephone: (703) 591–3831.

Commonwealth Consulting and Counseling Services—Russell Bigney, Allen B. Craven. 900 Commonwealth Place, Virginia Beach, 23462. Telephone: (804) 424–1485.

Hal W. Minor. 104 W. Franklin St., Lexington Tower #1401, Richmond, 23220. Telephone: (804) 782–1709.

WASHINGTON

Marilyn Criddle, William D. Criddle. 1214 Boylston, #201, Seattle, 98101. Telephone: (206) 323–8181.

Institute for Rational Living, N.W.—John Williams. 1214 Boylston, #201, Seattle, 98101. Telephone: (206) 323–8181.

Elspeth Wallace. 3504 N.E. 162nd St., Seattle, 98155. Telephone: (206) 363–4932.

WASHINGTON, D.C.

Ethel D. Dalmat. 3900 Watson Place, N.W., 20016. Telephone: (202) 965–0423.

June Dobbs Butts. 1055 Thomas Jefferson St., N.W., Suite 608, 20007. Telephone: (202) 337–1155.

Robert A. Harper. 4830 V. St., N.W., 20007. Telephone: (202) 337–4878.

Washington Psychological Center—Barry W. McCarthy. 2139 Wisconsin Ave., N.W., 20007. Telephone: (202) 965–5350.

WISCONSIN

Lynn J. Gauger, Rev. Robert R. Scheuermann. 130 E. Walnut, Suite 611, Green Bay, 54301. Telephone: (414) 437–8914.

Midwest Sexual Counseling Center. 505 N. Segoe Road, Madison, 53705. Telephone: (608) 231–3300.

FOR CONFIDENTIAL ANSWERS TO QUESTIONS ABOUT SEXUALITY

Three telephone hotlines provide confidential, accurate, supportive sex information to callers from all over the country:

San Francisco Sex Information: (415) 665–7300. Operates 3–9 P.M. Monday through Friday.

Los Angeles Sex Information: (213) 653–1123. Operates 3–9 P.M. Monday through Thursday.

Community Sex Information of New York: (212) 677–3320. Operates 6–8 P.M. Monday through Thursday.

TO CONTACT THE AUTHOR

Write to: Michael Castleman, 55 Sutter St., Suite 645, San Francisco, CA 94104.

Only selected correspondence can be answered. Please include a stamped, self-addressed envelope.

ACKNOWLEDGMENTS

This book could not have been written without the support, criticism and assistance of: Kristi Beer M.J., John Brockman, David (The Deke) Castleman, David Fenton, Dr. Tom Ferguson M.D., Fred Hills, Katinka Matson, Jim Ramsay, Anne Kent Rush, Joan Sanger, Dr. Anne Simons M.D. and Carol Small.

And many thanks to: Lee Ammidon, Dr. Kathy Biersack M.D., Dr. Charlie Bright Ph.D., Dan, Lou, Mim, and Steven Castleman, Tom Cherry, Dr. Don Cotton Ph.D., Dr. Rick DeNapoli D.O., Nancy Evens, Glenn Ernst, Frances Fitzgerald, Jamie Friar, Wendy Friar R.N., Keith Hefner, Gary Kell, Anne Kostick, Thea Snyder Lowry M.A., Liz Metzger M.A., Dr. Jay Mann Ph.D., Susan Neri, Dr. Bob Miller Ph.D., Doug Patt, Stan Pesick, Debbie Popkin, Harriet Power, Steve Purser M.P.H., Margaret Reiss M.S.W., Elizabeth Rintoul M.P.H., Debbie Rogow M.P.H., Dr. Maggie Rubenstein D.A., Nan Schleiger, Peter Straus, Dr. Jan Swanson R.N., Ph.D., Barbara Weinberg, Dr. Howie Winant Ph.D., Merle Wolin, Mary Yunker, and Dina Zvenko M.A.; The Ann Arbor Free People's Clinic, The Center for Investigative Reporting, The Center for Special Problems of the San Francisco Department of Public Health (SFDPH), The Haight-Ashbury Free Medical Clinic, The Men's Reproductive Health Clinic (SFDPH), Multi-Media Resource Center, The National Sex Forum, San Francisco Sex Information, The Sexual Trauma Center (SFDPH), the University of California Human Sexuality Program, and the University of California School of Journalism.

Some of the information in this book was published previously by: The Ann Arbor Sun, *Consumer Reports*, *Medical Self-Care* magazine, *Medical Self-Care: Access to Health Tools* (Summit/ Simon and Schuster, 1980), *The Nation* magazine, The National Clearinghouse for Family Planning Information, *New Roots* magazine, *New Times* magazine, Pacific News Service, and *Trax* magazine.

BIBLIOGRAPHY

Recommended books are starred.

Annon, Jack. *Behavioral Treatment of Sexual Problems*, vol. I, Brief Therapy. Honolulu, Hawaii: Enabling Systems, Inc., 1974.

* Bach, George and Peter Wyden. *The Intimate Enemy*. New York: Avon Books, 1968.

* Barbach, Lonnie Garfield. *For Yourself: The Fulfillment of Female Sexuality*. New York: Signet, 1975.

* Boston Women's Health Book Collective. *Our Bodies, Ourselves*. New York: Simon and Schuster, 1976.

Brecher, Ruth and Edward Brecher. *An Analysis of Human Sexual Response*. New York: Signet, 1966.

* Brownmiller, Susan. *Against Our Will*. New York: Bantam Books, 1976.

Burton, Sir Richard and F. F. Arbuthnot. *The Kama Sutra of Vatsyayana*. New York: Berkley Books, 1966.

Cant, Gilbert. *Male Trouble: A New Focus on the Prostate*. New York: Jove, 1976.

Chang, Jolan. *The Tao of Love and Sex: The Ancient Chinese Way to Ecstasy*. New York: E. P. Dutton & Co., 1977.

Cherniak, Donna and Allan Feingold. *The VD Handbook*. Montreal Health Press, P.O. Box 1000 Station G, Montreal, Québec, Canada, 1975.

* Comfort, Alex. *The Joy of Sex*. New York: Fireside/Simon and Schuster, 1972.

* Cooke, Chris, ed. *The Men's Survival Resource Book: On Being a Man in Today's World*. Minneapolis, Minnesota: MSRB Press, 1800 W. 76 St., 55423, 1978.

Csicsery, George. *The Sex Industry*. New York: Signet, 1973.

David, Deborah S. and Robert Bannon. *The 49% Majority*. Reading, Mass.: Addison-Wesley, 1976.

* Downing, George. *The Massage Book*. New York: Random House/Bookworks, 1972.

Dunphy, J. Englebert and Lawrence W. Way. *Current Surgical Diagnosis and Treatment*. Los Altos, Calif.: Lange Medical Publications, 1977.

* Ferguson, Tom, ed. *Medical Self-Care* Magazine. P.O. Box 717, Inverness, CA 94937.

Friday, Nancy. *Forbidden Flowers*. New York: Pocket Books, 1975.

———. *My Secret Garden*. New York: Pocket Books, 1973.

Gagnon, John H. *Human Sexualities*. Glenview, Ill.: Scott, Foresman & Co., 1977.

Ganong, W. F. *Review of Medical Physiology*. Los Altos, Calif.: Lange Medical Publications, 1975.

Garfink, Christine and Hank Pizer. *The New Birth Control Program*. New York: Bantam Books, 1979.

Gillan, Richard and Patricia Gillan. *Sex Therapy Today*. New York: Grove Press, 1976.

Gilles, Jerry. *Transcendental Sex: A Meditative Approach to Increasing Sexual Pleasure*. New York: Holt, Rinehart & Winston, 1978.

Goldberg, Herb. *The Hazards of Being Male*. New York: Nash Publishing, 1976.

* Goldstein, Michael J. and Harold S. Kant. *Pornography and Sexual Deviance*. Berkeley, Calif.: University of California Press, 1973.

Greenfield, Michael and William M. Burrus. *The Complete Reference Book on Vasectomy*. New York: Avon, 1973.

Haeberle, Erwin J. *The Sex Atlas*. New York: Continuum/Seabury Press, 1978.

Hatcher, Robert et al. *Contraceptive Technology 1980–81*. New York: Irvington Publishers, 1980.

Heidenstam, David, ed. *Man's Body: An Owner's Manual*. New York: Paddington Press, 1976.

Heiman, Julia, Leslie LoPiccolo and Joseph LoPiccolo. *Becoming Orgasmic: A Sexual Growth Program for Women*. Englewood Cliffs, N.J.: Prentice-Hall, 1976.

* Hite, Shere. *The Hite Report*. New York: Dell, 1976.

———. *Sexual Honesty*. New York: Warner Books, 1974.

Huff, Barbara B., ed. *The Physician's Desk Reference*, Oradell, N.J.: Medical Economics Co., Litton Industries, 1976.

Hunt, Morton. *Sexual Behavior in the 1970s*. New York: Dell, 1974.

Janus, Sam, Barbara Bess, and Carol Saltus. *A Sexual Profile of Men in Power*. New York: Warner Books, 1977.

Julty, Sam. *Male Sexual Performance*. New York: Grosset and Dunlap, 1975.

Kaplan, Helen Singer. *The Illustrated Manual of Sex Therapy.* New York: Quadrangle/New York Times Book Co., 1975.

* ———. *The New Sex Therapy.* New York: Brunner/Mazel/Quadrangle/ New York Times Book Co., 1974.

Kemp, Earl. *The Illustrated Presidential Report of the Commission on Obscenity and Pornography.* San Diego, Calif.: Greenleaf Classics, 1970.

Lehrman, Nat: *Masters and Johnson Explained.* Chicago, Ill.: Playboy Press, 1976.

LoPiccolo, Joseph and Leslie LoPiccolo. *Handbook of Sex Therapy.* New York: Plenum Press, 1978.

Masters, William H. and Virginia E. Johnson, with Robert J. Levin. *The Pleasure Bond.* New York: Bantam Books, 1976.

Medical Aspects of Human Sexuality Magazine. New York: Hospital Publications.

Montagu, Ashley. *Touching: The Human Significance of the Skin.* New York: Harper Colophon Books, 1978.

Montreal Health Press. *The Birth Control Handbook.* P.O. Box 1000 Station G, Montreal, Québec, Canada, 1973.

Multi-Media Resource Guide. San Francisco, Calif.: Multi-Media Resource Center, 1525 Franklin St., 94109.

Nofziger, Margaret. *A Cooperative Method of Natural Birth Control* (3rd edition). The Book Publishing Company, Summertown, Tennessee, 38483. 1979.

Pfeiffer, Carl C. *Zinc and Other Micro-Nutrients.* New Canaan, Conn.: Keats Publishing, 1978.

* Pietropinto, Anthony and Jacqueline Simenauer. *Beyond the Male Myth.* New York: Signet, 1977.

* Pleck, Joseph and Jack Sawyer. *Men and Masculinity.* Englewood Cliffs, N.J.: Prentice-Hall, 1974.

Population Reports. Dept. of Medical and Public Affairs, George Washington University School of Medicine, Washington, D.C.

Robbins, Jhan and June Robbins. *An Analysis of Human Sexual Inadequacy.* New York: Signet, 1970.

Rosenberg, Jack L. *Total Orgasm.* New York: Random House/Bookworks, 1973.

* Rush, Anne Kent. *Getting Clear.* New York: Random House/Bookworks, 1973.

* Schiengold, Lee and Nathaniel N. Wagner. *Sound Sex and the Aging Heart.* New York: Human Sciences Press, 1974.

* Seaman, Barbara and Gideon Seaman. *Women and the Crisis in Sex Hormones.* New York: Bantam Books, 1978.

Slattery, William J. *The Erotic Imagination: Sexual Fantasies of the Adult Male.* New York: Bantam Books, 1976.

Smith, Donald R. *General Urology.* Los Altos, Calif.: Lange Medical Publications, 1978.

* Tavris, Carol and Susan Sadd. *The Redbook Report on Female Sexuality.* New York: Dell, 1977.

Wade, Roger. "For Men About Abortion." R. Wade, 1705 Norwood Ave., Boulder, Colorado 80302. 1978.

Walravens, Philip. "Zinc Metabolism and Its Implications for Clinical Medicine." Western Journal of Medicine, February 1979.

"When You Don't Make It." San Francisco, Calif.: Multi-Media Resource Center, 1972.

White, John and James Fadiman. *Relax.* New York: Dell, 1976.

Woodburne, Russell T. *Essentials of Human Anatomy.* New York: Oxford University Press, 1973.

"You Can Last Longer." San Francisco, Calif.: Multi-Media Resource Center, 1972.

Zeiss, Robert A. and Antonette Zeiss. *Prolong Your Pleasure.* New York: Pocket Books, 1978.

* Zilbergeld, Bernie. *Male Sexuality.* Boston, Mass.: Little, Brown & Co., 1978.

Zorabedian, Tom. "The View From Our Side: Sex and Birth Control for Men." Emory University Family Planning Publications, Emory University, Atlanta, Georgia, 1975.

INDEX

ABOUT THE AUTHOR

MICHAEL CASTLEMAN, now Managing Editor of *Medical Self-Care* Magazine, was the founding Director of the Men's Reproductive Health Clinic in San Francisco, the nationally acclaimed first public health, birth control and sexuality clinic for men. From 1973 through 1978, he provided counseling to men in a variety of clinical settings, and has been a sex education consultant to agencies of the federal government, school systems, and universities.

His training in sex therapy includes course work offered by the Human Sexuality Program of the University of California's San Francisco Medical Center and working relationships with several Bay Area sex therapists.

A free-lance reporter for *The New York Times* and Health Editor of *New Roots* magazine, his work has also appeared in *The Nation, Consumer Reports, Mother Jones,* and elsewhere.

Castleman holds a master's degree in journalism from the University of California at Berkeley, and a bachelor's degree from the University of Michigan.

He lives in San Francisco with his wife, Anne, a family physician.